THE HUMAN TRADITION IN

MEXICO

EDITED BY
JEFFREY M. PILCHER

THE HUMAN TRADITION · AROUND THE WORLD ·

NUMBER 6

SR
BOOKS

A Scholarly Resources Inc. Imprint
Wilmington, Delaware

Scholarly Resources Inc.
104 Greenhill Avenue
Wilmington, DE 19805-1897
www.scholarly.com

Library of Congress Cataloging-in-Publication Data

The human tradition in Mexico / edited by Jeffrey M. Pilcher.
     p. cm. — (The human tradition around the world ; no. 6)
     Includes bibliographical references and index.
     ISBN 0-8420-2975-3 (alk. paper) — ISBN 0-8420-2976-1 (pbk. :
alk. paper)
     1. Mexico—History. 2. Mexico—Biography. I. Pilcher, Jeffrey M.,
1965– II. Series.

F1226 .H85 2003
920.072—dc21
[B]   2002030685

∞ The paper used in this publication meets the minimum requirements
of the American National Standard for permanence of paper for printed
library materials, Z39.48, 1984.

The Human Tradition around the World

Series Editors

WILLIAM H. BEEZLEY, Professor of History, University of Arizona
COLIN M. MACLACHLAN, John Christy Barr Distinguished
  Professor of History, Tulane University

Each volume in this series is devoted to providing minibiographies of "real people" who, with their idiosyncratic behavior, personalize the collective experience of grand themes, national myths, ethnic stereotypes, and gender relationships. In some cases, their stories reveal the irrelevance of national events, global processes, and cultural encounters for men and women engaged in everyday life. The personal dimension gives perspective to history, which of necessity is a sketch of past experience.

The authors of each volume in this historical series are determined to make the past literal. They write accounts that identify the essential character of everyday lives of individuals. In doing so, these historians allow us to share the human traditions that find expression in these lives.

Volumes in The Human Tradition around the World Series

DATE DUE FOR RETURN

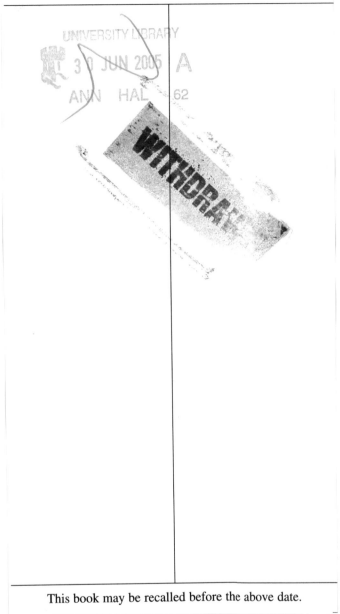
This book may be recalled before the above date.

THE HUMAN TRADITION IN
MEXICO

A mis hermanos

Jorge, Bill, Matt, Carlos, Shannon,

Victor, Tom, Daniel, James, Dina

y a los que siguen

About the Editor

Jeffrey M. Pilcher received his Ph.D. from Texas Christian University in 1993. The author of *¡Que vivan los tamales! Food and the Making of Mexican Identity* (1998), *Cantinflas and the Chaos of Mexican Modernity* (2001), and a forthcoming book on the history of the Mexico City meat supply, he is currently writing about the globalization of Mexican cuisine. He teaches at The Citadel in Charleston, South Carolina.

I believe in aristocracy, though—if that is the right word, and if a democrat may use it. Not an aristocracy of power, based upon rank and influence, but an aristocracy of the sensitive, the considerate and the plucky. Its members are to be found in all nations and classes, and all through the ages, and there is a secret understanding between them when they meet. They represent the true human tradition, the one permanent victory of our queer race over cruelty and chaos. Thousands of them perish in obscurity, a few are great names. They are sensitive for others as well as for themselves, they are considerate without being fussy, their pluck is not swankiness but the power to endure, and they can take a joke.

—E. M. Forster, *Two Cheers for Democracy* (1951)

Contents

Introduction: A Map of the System, **xiii**
Jeffrey M. Pilcher

Introduction: A Map of the System

Jeffrey M. Pilcher

*M*ost foreign tourists visiting Mexico City arrive at the Benito Juárez International Airport and then proceed directly to one of the yellow-and-white airport cabs, the *corps d'élite* of the city's variegated taxi brigade. Safe and efficient, these drivers whisk their passengers off to the many comfortable tourist hotels—assuming that traffic has not ground to a rush hour standstill on the *circuito interior* beltway. Of course, there is an alternative for intrepid backpackers, although you might not want to do this pulling multiple suitcases. After clearing customs, turn left and walk down the long hallway to the domestic terminal. Continue through the crowds of businessmen heading off for deals in Monterrey, families returning from vacations in Acapulco, and perhaps even some pilgrims coming to worship at the basilica of the Virgin of Guadalupe. Keep going out the end of the building, past the cabbies gossiping while they wait their turn for a fare, to the stylized yellow "M" marking the Mexico City metro. The subway steps lead down to another world, not the tourist Mexico, but a deep, subterranean Mexico, where cell phones do not work and ordinary people do. Riding the orange commuter trains and watching the passengers as they travel back and forth beneath the capital provides a unique perspective on the Mexican nation. In a similar fashion, this volume traverses the labyrinths of Mexican history through the lives of common people.

Studying the past "from the bottom up" seemed a revolutionary project in the 1960s, when social historians began directing attention away from the political maneuvers of the elite and toward the everyday concerns of the masses. At the time, established scholars often accused this new generation of abandoning the master narratives of the past and descending into mere antiquarianism. In retrospect, they had not turned their backs on politics but rather created new social scientific methodologies for understanding power struggles of the past. As social historians became the establishment, they, in turn, faced a new rebellion by culturally minded graduate students, who sought to understand the past through innovative linguistic analysis rather than computer-assisted head counting. Yet the call for history "from the bottom up" remains equally relevant for the present generation of cultural historians, as a reminder to connect their disembodied discourses back to the lived experience of real people.

Mexico has a particularly compelling need for a subterranean history because of the multiple layers of civilization that coexist, like subway trains passing under street traffic below office buildings. Anthropologist Guillermo Bonfil Batalla's best-selling book, *México*

Profundo, drew attention to the "deep" Mexico of Native American culture, which has been driven underground by successive waves of Spanish colonization and Western modernization.[1] The points of intersection between these civilizations, like subway stations (see map), often serve as much to accentuate differences as to connect worlds. Perhaps the most dramatic of these meeting points in Mexico City can be found at

Tlatelolco, a subway stop on the green metro line (number 3). Known as the "Plaza of Three Cultures," it juxtaposes the ruins of a pre-Hispanic city with a fortress-like Catholic cathedral and a modern office tower. The latter building, which houses the Ministry of Foreign Relations, theoretically fuses elements of Native American and Spanish civilization into a Mexican national culture, but at the same time it emphasizes the humble status of contemporary Indians.

Bonfil Batalla provided an eloquent plea for recognizing the indigenous contributions to Mexican society, yet critics have questioned his essentialist notion opposing a "deep" Indian heritage of the masses with the superficial Western fashions adopted by the elite. Mexico, in fact, comprises a far more complex mixture of ethnic and regional as well as folk and pop cultures, which congregate and intermingle daily in the metro. The image of high and low might therefore be represented as the conflicts and interactions between official projects initiated by the elite and organic movements rising up from the common people. The subway is one of the most impressive of these government projects, so it should hardly be surprising that the system map reflects an official view of history, with stations named after great leaders such as Father Miguel Hidalgo, who initiated the struggle for Independence, President Benito Juárez, who held the country together during the civil wars of the nineteenth-century Reform, and General Emiliano Zapata, who championed the campesino armies of the Revolution of 1910. Mexico's longtime ruling party portrayed itself as the heir to this trilogy of leaders, and indeed defined the national history around these three great struggles, to assure its own political monopoly for most of the twentieth century. Nevertheless, the common people reformulated this past, and indeed the spaces of the metro, to suit their own purposes. Thus, opposition party members and simple pranksters painted over political slogans and commercial advertisements in the overhead panels of subway cars, even as ambulant vendors and itinerant musicians passed through the aisles, earning a precarious living while evading the subway police.

The metro line, with its hubs and branches, also provides a geographic metaphor for the social and economic connections between Mexico's diverse regions. Residents of the capital once assured themselves of their own unique status within the nation by asserting that "outside of Mexico City, everything is Cuauhtitlán." This saying has fallen out of usage now that Cuauhtitlán is part of Mexico City, absorbed in the suburbs of the sprawling metropolis, although not yet readily accessible by mass transit. The generation of social historians made one of their greatest contributions precisely by leaving the capital and investigating the richness of Mexico's regional variation. While building on the wealth of that historiography, this volume seeks to reincorporate center and periphery into unified narratives. Even a brief ride on the metro shows the extent to which provincial Mexico has invaded the cosmopolitan capital, especially on the pink metro line (number 1), where men and women carry rustic sacks of corn and chile peppers away from the downtown La Merced market, like peasants going to any village market.

Many of the people described in this volume illustrate the intimate connections between the countryside and the capital. Juana Gutiérrez de Mendoza and Rosa Torre González came to Mexico City for political purposes, to protest against dictatorship and to lobby for female suffrage. María Félix left the provinces and became one of the biggest celebrities during the "golden age" of Mexican cinema, but a few decades later, *norteño* musician Armando Nava's dreams of stardom were drowned in the stagnation of the capital's cultural industries. Meanwhile, other people left the city for the provinces. Josefa Ordóñez, a notorious courtesan of the colonial period, was regularly sent into exile for her scandalous behavior. By contrast, Moisés de la Peña went out into the countryside on a revolutionary mission to spur regional development. At the same time, cooking teacher Josefina Velázquez de León toured the provinces to record little-known recipes that were being forgotten with the spread of modernization.

The vignettes appearing in this book focus not on the presidents, generals, industrialists, and intellectuals who traditionally are considered to "make history." Instead, these biographies depict, for the most part, ordinary people who might scarcely merit a footnote in a standard textbook of Mexican history. Yet they lived extraordinary lives, and their very uniqueness makes them worthy of attention. These people were chosen not because they represent some composite of the everyday man or woman, but because they faced challenges common to all Mexicans of their generations. They responded with creativity and purpose to the oppression of patriarchy, poverty, discrimination, and authoritarianism. Although many of their plans went astray, they exemplified E. M. Forster's "true human tradition" in their individual efforts to improve the lives of their fellow Mexicans.[2]

The mixing of high and low that is continually at work creating and transforming the Mexican nation is nowhere more evident than on the Zócalo, where sandal-clad campesinos ascend from the subway and mingle with government bureaucrats at the entrance to the National Palace. The Plaza of the Constitution, as it is more properly known, serves as a theater of state for rehearsing the authorized version of Mexican history, most notably during the celebrations on the eve of Independence, when the president appears on a balcony to exhort the crowds below. Yet this program of official nationalism has been counterbalanced by expressions of popular nationalism, whereby common people assert their civic rights, even when denied effective suffrage at the ballot box. Thus, the Zócalo has provided a space for opposition politics in which otherwise forgotten workers and indigenous groups construct shanties and stage extended protests, such as the peaceful march on Mexico City by the Zapatista rebels of Chiapas in 1997. Even the carefully scripted Independence festivities are open to contestation, as the crowds respond to official calls of "¡Viva!" with inventive obscenities. Because the celebrations invariably get out of hand, police close down the blue metro line (number 2) fifteen minutes before midnight in order to contain the crowds on this most important night of the year. Nevertheless, the colorful voices of the common people in the plaza below tell far more about the rise of the Mexican nation than the bland presidential proclamations issued from the balcony above.

Nations are often founded on a belief in a common ethnic origin, yet Mexican history is more notable for racial divisions than for harmony between the Hispanic elite and the indigenous masses; indeed, if the nation is an imagined community, as Benedict Anderson has claimed, then Mexico seems a particularly unlikely phantasm.[3] During the colonial period, the Spanish Crown went to great lengths to separate native communities from European settlers. This policy, intended at first to protect the former from exploitation, helped stifle the growth of a common identity between Creoles, those of European ancestry born in the Americas, and the indigenous people. Eighteenth-century Creole patriots such as Fray Servando Teresa de Mier therefore saw their task as grafting a European culture onto a history of Aztec kings. In his revolutionary sermon of 1794, the young priest from Monterrey proclaimed that the apostle Saint Thomas had personally evangelized the Native Americans 1,500 years before Spanish missionaries arrived, thereby overturning the religious justification for the Conquest. Fray Servando even claimed descent from the last Aztec ruler, Cuauhtémoc, thus anticipating the racial blending that a century later would provide an ethnic basis for Mexican nationalism, but inclusive views of the nation remained rare at the time of Independence.

The ideal of common citizenship can provide a counterbalance to strictly racial visions of nationalism—as in the French revolutionary slogan of "liberty, fraternity, equality"—yet for ordinary Mexicans, like the sans-culottes of Paris, the rights of citizenship were not handed down from above but rather actively demanded from below. Perhaps the strongest claim for citizenship lay in the republican tradition of military service, for the civil wars and foreign invasions of the early republic provided a constant need for soldiers. Historians often depict this as an age of praetorian generals, thereby concentrating on leaders such as Antonio

López de Santa Anna, who came to power on eleven separate occasions but never once completed a full term as president. But the campaigns of Santa Anna and other caudillos (warlords) depended on the support of countless anonymous soldiers, who were not simply the cannon fodder of charismatic leaders. The biography of Lucas Balderas, an artisan and militia commander, demonstrates that the working classes of Mexico City pursued clear political goals and used their wartime sacrifices to demand the rights of citizenship.

Nor was this popular nationalism limited to residents of the capital who could experience political debates and palace coups at first hand; instead, it extended like a vast subterranean network through the regional hubs of provincial cities and even to remote villages, where campesinos were mobilized politically by their military service to the patria. Peasants are often portrayed as being the absolute antithesis of loyal citizens, uninterested in politics beyond their own local concerns with land and water rights, but this stereotype is refuted by the story of Felipe García and his neighbors in the Zapotec community of Guelatao, Oaxaca. The men of Guelatao joined a National Guard battalion established by Governor Benito Juárez and fought throughout the midnineteenth-century civil wars, protecting the liberal regime against both Mexican conservatives and French invaders, and at the same time acquiring a sense of belonging to the national community. Afterward, they used their record of military service to exact compensation from the federal government and to defend their village against local rivals.

If Native Americans seemed peripheral to the nation, women fell off the political map entirely, despite their valuable contributions in that same republican tradition of military service. Although camp followers have been common in armies throughout history, Mexican *soldaderas* have shown particular initiative, not only in provisioning male soldiers but also in taking up arms in combat. Within the patriarchal structures of Mexican society, their services were usually ignored, particularly by caudillos who cultivated an image as fathers of the nation. Even the Zapotec veterans, in their struggle to gain recognition for their own contributions during nineteenth-century campaigns, subordinated the participation of women from Guelatao. Yet a generation later, during the Revolution of 1910, women such as Juana Gutiérrez de Mendoza and Rosa Torre González rejected the ideal of female submission and embraced the role of *soldadera*, even claiming the lofty rank of *coronelas*. Although their backgrounds and goals differed, both used women's military participation to assert political demands, including the right to vote, in postrevolutionary Mexico.

The Revolution of 1910 initiated a broad movement to reconcile the struggles of elites and masses, of Hispanic and Native American culture, and of men and women, in order to forge a unified national identity. Unlike nineteenth-century theories of scientific racism, which disdained people of mixed blood as degenerate, José Vasconcelos exalted the mestizo not only as the embodiment of Mexican national identity but also as the highest stage of human evolution, *La raza cósmica* (The cosmic race), as he titled his influential 1925 book. In his position as minister of education, Vasconcelos encouraged the mural movement led by Diego Rivera, José Clemente Orozco, and David Alfaro Siquieros in order to provide dramatic public art to disseminate this nationalist vision. Perhaps to justify racial blending, revolutionary artists often depicted Native American women in a stylized new image as *la india bonita* (pretty Indian woman), thus creating a distinctively Mexican version of the 1920s Art Deco movement.[4] Still reluctant to break with ingrained class and racial prejudice, many painters favored models with Hispanic features such as Nahui Olin, the daughter of a prominent military officer and an accomplished artist in her own right, to represent these Indians. A similarly sanitized version of Native American culture gained new respectability in even the most self-consciously Creole homes, thanks in part to the work of Josefina Velázquez de León, mid-century Mexico's foremost cooking teacher, who promoted a national cuisine embracing once-scorned indigenous foods such as tamales, pozole, and enchiladas.

Still, the revolutionaries of one generation can become the symbols of a stagnant political system for the next. The official revolutionary party, originally founded in the 1920s and later known as the PRI (Institutional Revolutionary Party), employed this nationalist ideology to monopolize politics for the rest of the century. In such circumstances, globalization offered a way for people to challenge the oppressive conformity of the national culture. Already in the 1950s, young Mexicans began listening to rock 'n' roll as an alternative to the mariachi music of their parents. Nor was this simply submission to cultural imperialism from the United States and western Europe. Bands such as the Dug Dug's, who once performed English-language covers of the Beatles and the Doors, were writing their own rock music by the 1970s in response to the particular conditions of Mexican life. Nevertheless, the band's artistic creativity was still limited by multinational record companies. As this example shows, an examination of nation-building must also consider the broader process of modernization.

The construction of modernity, like the forging of Mexican nationalism, depended equally on pressure from above and below. The importance of such perspective in the mental mapping of a modern artifact like the metro can be seen in the case of Bellas Artes, the palace of fine arts, located at the intersection of the old blue and the new green subway lines (numbers 2 and 8). Originally begun in 1904 under the dictatorship of Porfirio Díaz (1876–1911), the building was not completed until three decades later, following the Revolution of 1910. The problems with Bellas Artes, however, date all the way back to the time of Moctezuma, when Mexico City was an island metropolis surrounded by the shallow waters of Lake Texcoco. Although the canals of this American Venice have long since dried up, the soil beneath it remains as porous as any lakebed, and like the Doge's Palace, this stately marble structure is slowly, inevitably sinking. Successive attempts to prop up the building's foundations have failed, leading popular wits to conclude that one day it would be possible to enter Bellas Artes directly from the subway, without having to climb the stairs.

In the spirit of E. M. Forster's "true human tradition," Mexicans have responded with a sense of humor to the vicissitudes of life; indeed, one could venture that the joke is the most sublime art in Mexico, for the obvious gag conveys only a fraction of the full meaning. In this case, the rest of the laugh comes from the realization that in such a class-conscious society, most visitors to Bellas Artes arrive by car, parking in the nearby underground lot, and would never risk being seen emerging from the plebeian subway.

The history of the Mexico City metro system illustrates one in a long line of elite modernization projects, dating back to the eighteenth century, that have simultaneously benefited, coerced, and confounded the Mexican masses they were intended to assist. Begun in the 1960s, the metro became one of the capstones of the so-called economic miracle, a three-decade period of rapid economic growth that had started in the late 1930s. Many residents of the capital had opposed construction of the subway system, seeking to limit the uncontrolled urbanization that was blighting their neighborhoods, but such arguments were overruled by the imperative of progress: Mexico City must provide a model of modernity, drawing more backward parts of the country into the industrial world.[5] The irony was that urban growth instead helped bring the countryside into the city. Unable to construct housing fast enough to meet the demand of rural migrants, the government simply turned a blind eye to the spread of huge shantytowns that resembled in many ways the impoverished villages of the countryside. The metro system was likewise refashioned as a popular space, right down to the appearance of visions of the Virgin of Guadalupe. In this way, elite reformers and common people reached accommodations that pleased neither group but somehow expressed a Mexican version of modernity. To the credit of its builders, however, the metro survived the shock of the 1985 earthquake and continued to run safely while collapsing buildings killed thousands of people aboveground.

Mexico first experienced the forced march toward modernity, even before gaining independence, during the Bourbon reforms of the late eighteenth century. Inspired by the Enlightenment ideals of improving society through the application of Reason, the Spanish Crown sought to install a more efficient and productive administration in its American colonies. A vital component of this reform was a program of social engineering, aimed at making the Mexican people more moral and efficient. For example, members of the racially mixed underclass of Mexico City, who were considered by the Hispanic elite to be irredeemable alcoholics, were often drafted into public works projects aimed at urban renewal. The theatrical career of Josefa Ordóñez illustrates both the Bourbon campaign to instill exemplary behavior and also how these efforts were often frustrated by common people, who defined their own standards of proper social conduct.

The quest for modernization was largely abandoned in the general chaos of the early republic, when civil war devastated the economy, but once President Porfirio Díaz had restored peace in the final decades of the nineteenth century, government officials renewed their efforts to transform Mexico in the image of Europe and the United States. The port of Tampico, Tamaulipas, on the Gulf of Mexico, provided an important testing ground for the Porfirian modernization project. Governor Alejandro Prieto, a distinguished engineer, was determined to make the port a commercial hub for northeastern Mexico, thereby helping to exploit the mining, agriculture, and oil industries developing in the region. Before such a dream could be realized, however, the government had to overcome the recurring epidemics of yellow fever that plagued the entire Caribbean basin. Prieto conceived an elaborate sanitation program for the city, but faulty implementation caused water to drain from wealthy neighborhoods and flood poor barrios. Such literally top-down modernization programs, which worked against the welfare of ordinary people, provoked a tireless crusade by opposition leaders, including Juana Gutiérrez de Mendoza, and eventually their efforts were rewarded with a broad uprising against Díaz's dictatorship.

Even after the Mexican Revolution of 1910, however, the Porfirian developmental imperative remained as strong as ever. The primary change therefore came from the attempts by postrevolutionary administrations to broaden the benefits of modernization to include all Mexicans. This was particularly true during the presidency of Lázaro Cárdenas (1934–1940), who enacted sweeping social reforms including land distribution, labor legislation, and socialist education. Implementing this ambitious program, however, required the work of skilled professionals such as Moisés T. de la Peña. A graduate of the newly created National School of Economics, he carried out a series of detailed studies intended to facilitate the construction of rural infrastructure that would enable indigenous communities to raise their incomes and thereby contribute to the national economy. Nevertheless, even socially minded development campaigns met with resistance by many rural people, who distrusted the schemes of outsiders and sought instead to preserve their local traditions and autonomy.

By the 1940s the social experiments of the revolutionary era had largely ended, leaving the state and private enterprise as partners in the single-minded pursuit of economic development. Of course, businesses were not content with simply marketing their goods to an urban elite, as had been their Porfirian predecessors; instead, they hoped to transform the rural masses, who had been mobilized by the revolution, into avid consumers. The media industry took the lead in developing this national market, and the celebrity romance of radio performer Agustín Lara and cinema actress María Félix captivated audiences throughout the country in the mid-1940s. At the same time, another distinctively national industry, tequila making, also began consolidating markets throughout Mexico and abroad. After half a century of intensive capital investment and technological improvements by experts such as Gabriel Espíndola Martínez, top-quality aged tequilas compete on an international level with the finest whiskeys and brandies.

Yet for riders on the metro, tequila could provide a reminder of the limits of the elite modernization project of the so-called Mexican miracle. When the first subway lines opened in 1969, people immediately noticed that the authorities had neglected to provide rest rooms within the stations. Chava Flores, a folk musician whose songs chronicled life in the popular barrios, captured the frustration that could grow through a succession of stops on the blue line from Tacuba:

Adiós, mi linda Tacuba,	Adios, my pretty Tacuba,
ya pasamos por Cuitláhuac,	now we pass by Cuitláhuac,
ya pasamos por Popotla	now we pass by Popotla
y el Colegio Militar;	and the *Military* Academy;
ya me estoy arrepintiendo	already I regret
no haber hecho de las aguas;	not having relieved myself;
si me sigue esta nostalgia	if this nostalgia keeps following me
yo me bajo en la Normal.	I'll get off in the Normal (station).

The tune was entitled, *"Voy en el metro"* (I go in the subway).[6]

The experience of ordinary Mexicans in the face of modernization is also relevant as a mirror for reexamining the broader human tradition. Within the last few centuries, Western society has increasingly shifted the focus of life from family and community to the individual. Considerable benefits have accompanied this social transformation, including the rise of mass democracy, concern for human rights, and unprecedented opportunities for personal consumption. Yet the price of these gains has been paid, at times unknowingly, through the anomie of modern life, the dehumanization of the workplace, the breakup of families, and the vain pursuit of happiness through the whim of fashion. The study of other cultures, with different value systems, can therefore provide valuable lessons in preserving human networks at times of social transformation, a point discussed in the following section.

Another way of mapping the Mexico City metro, one that is equally relevant to Mexican history, appears in the subway timetable, or rather the lack thereof. Unlike many European mass transit systems, where the trains run strictly on time, in Mexico, the metro has no determined schedule. The orange commuter cars traverse reliably back and forth along their routes between 5 A.M. and 12:30 A.M. on weekdays, but no one train is intended to arrive at a particular stop at any given time. This resigned attitude to scheduling is often attributed to a Mexican sense of mañana (a vague "later"), although perhaps a more accurate explanation in this case would be the recurring summer rains, which inevitably cause afternoon delays by flooding. Nevertheless, the repetitive routes of identical trains reflect a peculiarly Mexican attitude toward the individual and society. Ever since the cyclical calendars of pre-Hispanic civilizations, the notion of deterministic fate has weighed heavily on Mesoamerican people. The hierarchical, Catholic society implanted by the Spanish conquistadors likewise offered little room for individualism to flourish. As Enlightenment ideas first began to seep in to the colony of New Spain during the mideighteenth century, then reached a flood with the Liberal reforms a hundred years later, the encounter between the Western ideal of an autonomous self and traditional Mexican collective identities challenged both ways of thinking.

The family became one point of contention as individuals began to dispute the restrictions of a patriarchal society while nevertheless seeking to preserve the vital social networks that kinship provided. The Mediterranean ideals of honor, based on unequal standards of female submission and masculine virility, placed a heavy burden on both women and men. The women described in this book each challenged the prevailing male domination, yet they did so in strikingly different ways. At first glance, the most extreme rebellion came from the notorious colonial actress, Josefa Ordóñez, who flaunted her unhappy marriage to an Italian musician by taking a string of lovers from within the viceregal court. She fought a running battle with the Inquisition, which insisted on enforcing standards of domestic propriety, but Ordóñez nevertheless held fast to a belief in her own honor and eventually won recognition from Church authorities. Two centuries later, another celebrated actress, María Félix, constructed a similar role as an independent woman in defiance of the self-abnegating behavior expected of women. Hounded by paparazzi rather than priests, Félix boosted her cinema career but at the cost of her marriage to the romantic crooner, Agustín Lara.

Other Mexican women subverted patriarchy in a less flamboyant fashion and with perhaps greater awareness of family connections. Journalist Juana Gutiérrez de Mendoza dedicated herself to the campaign against the Porfirian dictatorship, yet she struggled to balance that crusade with the daily task of supporting her family. At one point she was forced to choose between her goats—and the subsistence they represented for her family—and the printing press with which she pursued Díaz. By contrast, Rosa Torre González agreed more openly with nineteenth-century gender distinctions, but she never married, thus subverting these standards in practice, and she also used the supposed moral superiority of women to demand that they be given the right to vote. Josefina Velázquez de León, a pious Catholic woman who achieved personal independence through her privileged status as a widow, adopted a similar stance, using her cooking skills to create a domestic vision of the Mexican national community. This seemingly retrograde feminism, which in the past had been used to justify gender segregation in bars and even movie theaters, still gives women access to separate cars on the metro during rush hour, thereby allowing them to avoid unwanted contact with men.

The tensions arising from gender roles in Mexico can also be revealed by looking at an outsider such as Agnes Salm-Salm, a U.S. citizen by birth and a German princess by marriage who gained notoriety for her supposed sexual escapades under the empire of Maximilian and Carlota (1864–1867). Notwithstanding the attacks on her character, it was precisely her exemption from Mexican social standards that gave Salm-Salm the freedom to negotiate directly with President Juárez in an attempt to save the life of the French-imposed emperor. One could even argue that the North American princess took up the role of the Mexican *coronela*.

Men, no less than women, have been constricted by the demands of patriarchy within Mexican society. The country is often considered to be a center of machismo, that dysfunctional extreme of masculine behavior that has supposedly caused everything from political instability, through the self-aggrandizing behavior of caudillos, to broken homes because of the Don Juanism of ordinary men. Nevertheless, examples from this book belie such a stereotype. Lucas Balderas illustrated the stable family life and exemplary patriotism that was common among Mexican artisans in the nineteenth century. A century later, Agustín Lara used his romantic melodies to cultivate a new urban image as a gentleman who could appreciate the beauty in any woman. Gabriel Espíndola Martínez meanwhile used his chemist's expertise to reformulate tequila—and the mariachi myths that accompanied it—in the hopes of replacing the machismo of binge drinking with a more sensible appreciation of the spirit of the agave plant.

Of course, no study of either masculine or feminine roles can be complete in isolation, as gender roles are constructed in relation to each other. For that reason, it is useful to consider the courtship and subsequent murder-suicide of Enriqueta and Pedro in northern Mexico during the decade of revolutionary violence between 1910 and 1920. The love letters that the two exchanged show their understandings and negotiations of popular masculinity and femininity. In the ultimately deadly dance in which they engaged, both Enriqueta and Pedro were preoccupied with deception and betrayal. Each sought reassurance—she in the form of prose and presents and he in her delivering up of her virginity in exchange for a promise of marriage—yet to no avail. Ultimately, Enriqueta's insistence on her own self-determination was unacceptable to Pedro. Her death at his hands reveals the importance of masculine honor and affirms that women paid for it with their lives.

As the love letters from Chihuahua illustrate, with their emphasis on the importance of gossip and reputation, the community no less than the family formed a vital nexus for Mexican life. Indigenous pueblos such as the Zapotec Indians of Guelatao, in particular, resisted the nineteenth-century liberal ideology with its emphasis on individualism. After centuries of fighting in colonial courts to maintain the rights to their communal land against rapacious Spanish landlords, Native American communities had learned the importance of collective action. They therefore imagined the nation not as a collection of individuals, free and equal before the law—a myth in any event—but a country united through the legitimacy of traditional village government, with its cycle of officeholding and its reliance on trusted elders. This system proved so resilient in responding to local needs and in preserving cherished identities that it continues to serve as the basis for Zapatista rebels who are still holding out in Chiapas, sending out e-mail missives demanding democracy and human rights for all.

Back in Mexico City, at the end of each evening, scattered groups of people gather on metro platforms, glancing nervously at their watches while awaiting the last train of the day. A sigh of relief passes around as it pulls into the station, and once it has departed the manager begins locking up for the night. Like the metro cars circling the city, Mexican history at times seems to repeat itself; for example, the indigenous rebels of

Chiapas take up the mantle of their Zapatista predecessors in response to a modernization program reminiscent of the Porfirian dictatorship. But despite such deeply ingrained habits, change is afoot in contemporary Mexico. New metro lines extend from the city center into the sprawling popular barrios to the east; the Zapatista rebels are armed with laptop computers and the sympathies of the world; at the turn of the millennium, the PRI finally allowed a free election, ushering opposition candidate Vicente Fox into the presidency. And the metro, however crowded and inconvenient it may seem at times, will still take you where you want to go for just two pesos.

NOTES

1. Guillermo Bonfil Batalla, *México Profundo: Reclaiming a Civilization*, trans. Philip A. Dennis (Austin: University of Texas Press, 1996).

2. E. M. Forster, *Two Cheers for Democracy* (New York: Harcourt, Brace and Company, 1951), 26.

3. Benedict Anderson, *Imagined Communities: Reflections on the Origins and Spread of Nationalism*, rev. ed. (London: Verso, 1991).

4. *Art deco: Un país nacionalista, un México cosmopolita* (Mexico City: Museo Nacional de Arte, 1997); Apen Ruíz Martínez, "Nación y género en el México revolucionario. La India Bonita y Manuel Gamio," *Signos Históricos* 5 (enero–junio 2001), 55–86.

5. Diane E. Davis, *Urban Leviathan: Mexico City in the Twentieth Century* (Philadelphia: Temple University Press, 1994), 164–73.

6. Salvador Flores Rivera, *El cancionero de Chava Flores* (Mexico City: Ageleste, 2001), 359.

PART I

INDEPENDENT SPIRITS, 1750–1850

$\mathcal{M}$exicans won their independence from Spain through a decade-long struggle that wrenched apart the colonial society and left patriot leaders hopelessly divided about the course that the new nation should follow. The first stirrings of discontent arose in the late eighteenth century in response to the increasing burdens of imperial government. The Bourbon dynasty, installed in 1700 upon the death of the last Spanish Hapsburg, was determined to establish an absolute monarchy, like the France of Louis XIV. The new kings, trusting only peninsular Spaniards with bureaucratic appointments, strictly curtailed the opportunities for home rule by Creoles born in the colonies. The Bourbon reforms also sought to extract as much wealth as possible from the colonies, both by stimulating the economy and by raising taxes. New Spain indeed experienced a period of economic expansion in the eighteenth century, although more from population growth than from improved productivity. As a result, the royal coffers prospered while colonial subjects, for the most part, did not.

Bourbon absolutism extended beyond merely a concern with economic efficiency and included a strict policing of colonial morality. The society of New Spain comprised an elaborate racial hierarchy that ranked Europeans, Native Americans, and a variety of mixed-race *castas* such as mestizos and mulattoes. The lower orders of Indians and *castas* were looked down on by the elite as lazy, alcoholic, and dangerous. In an attempt to limit drinking, the Crown restricted the sale of pulque, the fermented juice of the agave, the same plant that is distilled to make tequila. The effectiveness of this temperance campaign was undermined, however, by the nobles who made fortunes growing agaves on their estates and marketing the brew. Meanwhile, the Inquisition kept a close watch on the popular theater and its scandalous performers (Chapter 1).

Except for occasional outbursts of resentment, such as the 1794 sermon of an impetuous young priest, Servando Teresa de Mier (Chapter 2), colonial subjects remained quiescent until crisis struck the Spanish empire. In 1808, Napoleon invaded the peninsula, removed the Bourbon dynasty, and imposed his brother, Joseph, as king. Unwilling to accept a foreign monarch, the Spanish people fought a prolonged guerrilla war that bled the strength of the French army. Open town councils, known as *cabildos abiertos*, organized this resistance and as the war progressed they sent representatives to the port of Cádiz. Protected from

1

the French by British naval forces, they wrote a constitution in 1812 asserting their rights to local autonomy. Delegates from the Spanish American colonies also joined the proceedings to demand equal representation, but once Napoleon was defeated in 1814, the restored Bourbon king Ferdinand VII revoked the liberal constitution and asserted his powers as an absolute monarch.

Already in 1808, many Creoles used the crisis of Napoleon's invasion as a pretext to demand an open council meeting in Mexico City as well. Peninsular Spaniards in the colony feared that this would become a vehicle for rebellion and staged a preemptive coup against Viceroy José de Iturrigaray in order to install a more reliable figure. Their concern seemed justified, for two years later, another Creole conspiracy was uncovered in the provinces. Warned of his imminent arrest, Father Miguel Hidalgo issued his "Grito de Dolores" on September 16, 1810, calling on his parishioners to rise up against the Spanish empire. The movement quickly gained followers among poor campesinos, both Indians and mestizos alike, who sacked the city of Guanajuato, then marched on the colonial capital. The peasant army paused outside of Mexico City, fearing an attack by Royalist forces, and rather than attempt an immediate assault, retreated to gather strength. A few months later, Spanish authorities defeated the rebels outside Guadalajara and captured and executed Hidalgo. His place was taken by another priest, José María Morelos, who brought much of the colony under patriot control before he, too, was executed in 1815.

Nevertheless, the insurgency dragged on until 1821, when Royalist general Agustín Iturbide made a pact with rebel commander Vicente Guerrero and declared Mexico's independence. Iturbide tried to grab power, taking the title Emperor of Mexico, but with the economy devastated by a decade of fighting, he was soon overthrown in an 1823 revolution. The new leaders proclaimed a republic, but remained divided on its form, particularly regarding the federalist question. Having just won independence from Spain, provincial leaders wished to limit the tyranny of politicians in Mexico City, but centralists feared that without a strong national government the entire country would split apart. Indeed, Central America, formerly part of the viceroyalty of New Spain, promptly seceded from Mexico, although Chiapas thereupon seceded from Guatemala and rejoined the union.

Ideological divisions compounded the instability, as three separate groups contended for power. Conservatives wished to preserve Spanish colonial institutions while radical liberals (*puros*) wanted to destroy the power of the Church and the army. Moderates, meanwhile, supported limited reforms but feared the rabble-rousing tactics of the *puros*. With politicians unable to form stable majorities, opportunistic military lead-

ers known as caudillos seized power through a succession of palace re-
volts. Foreign powers also sought to take advantage of this instability; a
Spanish invasion of 1829 failed to reclaim the colony, but two decades
later, the United States succeeded in conquering the northern half of the
Mexican republic (Chapter 3).

CHAPTER ONE

Josefa Ordóñez

The Scandalous Adventures of a Colonial Courtesan

LINDA A. CURCIO-NAGY[1]

Bellas Artes, the palace of fine arts, although gradually sinking at the intersection of two metro lines (numbers 2 and 8), nevertheless exemplifies the cultural vitality of Mexico City, with its regular staging of symphony orchestras, theatrical performances, and the national folkloric ballet. Appropriately for a city with such close connections between past and present, it is located just a few blocks from the former site of the Nuevo Coliseo theater, where Josefa Ordóñez first garnered acclaim in the eighteenth century for her performances on stage.

Doña Josefa provides a striking example of the human tradition, for as a popular actress, she gained acceptance at the highest levels of the viceregal court while nevertheless embracing what the elite considered to be the deviant morals and culture of the lower classes. According to traditional standards of honor, women had only two options in Mexican society, marriage or the convent. Ordóñez accepted the former alternative, but in no way did she submit to the domination of her husband. And although an exceptional case, her frequent appearances before Inquisition courts provide a remarkable indication of the degree to which reality could differ from the ideals of patriarchal society.

Many considered her scandalous behavior to be a natural consequence of her disreputable profession; indeed, Bourbon reformers focused on repressing immoral conduct among actors, both onstage and off, because of the example they provided for the masses. Yet Josefa always maintained a clear sense of personal honor and carefully behaved in accordance with the letter of the law, even while flouting its spirit. Ultimately, she gained recognition of her honor and piety from the authorities that had hounded her for so long.

Linda A. Curcio-Nagy received her Ph.D. from Tulane University and is associate professor of history at the University of Nevada, Reno. She is the author of Performing Power and Identity: The Great Festivals of Colonial Mexico City *(forthcoming) and coeditor of* Latin American Popular Culture: An Introduction *(2000). The connections between religion and sexuality discussed in this essay also form the subject of her current research on cases of solicitation in the confessional in seventeenth-century Mexico City.*

Josefa Ordóñez was, by many accounts, the most famous courtesan of colonial Mexico. An eighteenth-century actress, renowned for her titillating stage portrayals, she was equally scandalous outside of the theater, maintaining romantic liaisons with some of the most influential men of her day. She was also a married woman. Her lifestyle and status did not go unnoticed by state and church officials intent upon enforcing official moral standards. The struggle that ensued between Ordóñez and her detractors, played out in full view of the general public, provides a fascinating opportunity to discuss propriety, sexual mores, and the blurring of cultural norms during the eighteenth century.

In 1743, Josefa Ordóñez, at the age of fifteen, arrived in Mexico City with an acting troupe composed of her mother, father, and sister, and a group of eight musicians, one of whom was her husband, an Italian, Gregorio Panseco, some years her senior. Both she and her father, José Ordóñez, had some renown as thespians in Cádiz, and Josefa was hired as a *primera dama* (star performer) at the Nuevo Coliseo theater in the viceregal capital.[2] Not only was she an accomplished actress, but she was also something of an entrepreneur. In 1748, she became the *autor de comedias* (production manager) of the capital's playhouse, quite a feat for her day.[3] In addition, her business acumen spilled over into the illegal as she sold alcoholic beverages without a license and set up gambling houses in her residences, which were always frequented by prominent male Spaniards such as the Marquis del Valle de la Colina. Her private casinos, complete with a specially built gaming table, were places where participants routinely lost thousands of pesos. Officials ordered Ordóñez to stop these activities but she always resumed them at a later date.[4]

In addition to her economic interests, Josefa maintained relationships with several very highly placed men in government, spanning over two decades and encompassing various viceregal administrations: Fuenclara (1742–46), Revillagigedo (1746–55), Amarillas (1755–60), and Cruillas (1760–66). In the process, she became quite wealthy and notorious as a courtesan. Her amorous adventures were even celebrated in verse. During the 1760s the "Poem of the Life of Ordóñez" apparently had widespread appeal in the capital.[5]

Ordóñez's story as Mexico's most famous courtesan commenced almost immediately upon her arrival in the capital, when she began a relationship with a relative of viceroy Fuenclara. (In the documents he is referred to only by his first name, Esteban.) The nature of the relationship must have been quite serious because the viceroy had ordered her to stop seeing Don Esteban. Panseco informed the viceroy that such was not the case. This resulted in Josefa's reclusion in the Recogimiento de la Misericordia, the home for women who did not wish to live with their husbands.[6] Her stay there was quite brief and upon her release, she procured the *autor de comedias* position at the Coliseo with the financial backing of one of her lovers, Jacinto Aguirre Martínez, who offered a guarantee of 6,000 pesos and was forced to pay as much when the endeavor proved unsuccessful.[7]

Some years later, in the early 1760s, Josefa once again found herself enmeshed in scandal. At this time Josefa maintained two important lovers, namely José Gorráez (a member of a prominent family holding important viceregal positions) and Fernando Monserrat (brother of the viceroy, the Marquis of Cruillas). She and Panseco had apparently agreed to request a formal divorce (legal separation) from the ecclesiastical court. The dispute revolved around charges that she had gotten pregnant by some of her lovers (although none was specifically named) and that Panseco had severely beaten their child, for which she sought to have him arrested. Don Juan Cayetano Lezama, a longtime employee of Josefa and dressing room manager at the Coliseo, later testified that Josefa and Gregorio fought constantly, that neither one was a good spouse, and that "the charges and countercharges [between them] were so numerous and confusing that it was difficult to tell where the truth might have lain." When the dust regarding the case had settled, she sought custody of the children and alimony from him, while he sought the children and all the marital property (much of which had been acquired through her romances with distinguished gentlemen). During the divorce proceedings, they lived apart on the same street and appeared to have a more amicable relationship. That amicability turned to rancor once the ecclesiastical court notified the couple that their divorce plea had been turned down.[8]

Ordered to reunite and cohabitate with Panseco, Ordóñez, with the aid of Monserrat and Gorráez, escaped to Puebla. Apprehended there, Josefa was ordered by the bishop of Puebla to reside for eight months in the Colegio de San Joseph de Gracia, a home (*recogimiento*) for women wishing to separate from their spouses. Upon her release and return to the capital, she and Panseco were ordered to live together and Panseco was specifically directed to maintain his wife financially. They did indeed live together in the same house but maintained separate sleeping quarters. Ordóñez continued her old lifestyle, hosting games of chance for prominent men of the capital. Gorráez resumed his visits and now shared her affections with Francisco Cassaviella (secretary to the commander of the Royal Army, Juan de Villalba y Angulo).[9]

If her actions had remained more discreet, perhaps Josefa would not have made enemies of the judges of the Real Sala del Crimen (Royal

Attorney General's Office). However, she accompanied Cassaviella to seven straight days of bullfights held to honor the king. Her actions at the bullfights appear to have been the last straw for her detractors. In addition, her connection to the viceroy had been severed when Cruillas's term ended and he and his brother returned to Spain. Josefa arrived at the bullfights in a sumptuous enclosed carriage tended by liveried footmen and coachmen. Each day she wore a different fabulous gown and expensive jewels. She apparently competed with the viceroy himself for the attention of, and dedication of the bull from, the matador. Witnesses accused her of showering the bullfighters with coins in a thinly disguised attempt to flirt with the royal governor.[10]

In response, the Real Sala del Crimen began a secret investigation of Ordóñez's scandalous lifestyle with the goal of sending her into exile. In the course of the investigation, the nature of Josefa's celebrity was borne out by the many witnesses who gave testimony against her, claiming that her escapades were "public and notorious." Francisca Deza, Josefa's household servant of eight years, went so far as to state that Josefa's "adventures were so well known and the gossip [about her] such that only small children have not heard about her." Other witnesses emphasized the fact that she maintained a standard of living equal to that of elite wealthy people of quality, pointing out that she was a woman of humble background who did not know her proper place in society. They were outraged that she acted the part of great lady with her dresses and jewelry, fancy carriage, and retinue of servants and slaves and that she shamelessly paraded about, lavishing friends with expensive gifts or large sums of money. They consistently emphasized that her life-style did not correlate to her husband's salary of 800 pesos annually. In actuality, witnesses let it be known that Gorráez paid her daily expenses and lent her the carriage and servants. Monserrat and Casaviella both had given her jewels, clothing, and expensive gifts, and Monserrat had also given her slaves as gifts.[11]

The twenty-one witnesses, even her apparent enemies, did not mention her sexual activity in detail nor condemn her as a prostitute. As a matter of fact, five of the witnesses did not know Josefa personally but claimed to know of her, and had seen her only at the bullfights. None of her previous or current lovers were called to testify. The majority of the testimonies, and the most damning, came from former employees who may have used the opportunity to exact revenge against Ordóñez. Francisco Javier Moreno, the palace halberdier, implied as much when he pointed out how poorly she had treated her servants.[12] The judges of the Real Sala themselves remarked that there was insufficient evidence to condemn her as a prostitute even though they had their "suspicions." Therefore, laws regarding unlicensed gambling and the preservation of the public welfare rather than prostitution were utilized to convict Ordóñez. In addition, the judges claimed that she was in violation of the ecclesiastical court's decree. In their final deliberation, they exiled Josefa and sentenced her to another stint in a *recogimiento* in Puebla. They believed that "a tolerated crime was the beginning of another and more crimes and that the unleashing of such liberty would only produce more excesses." The judges claimed that they were concerned that her scandals would serve as a bad example to the Native Americans in the capital. In this fashion, they designated Josefa as detrimental to public morality. They gave her four days to arrange her affairs, sell her belongings, and prepare to be escorted to the Puebla *recogimiento*. They also swore her to secrecy and bluntly stated that they would not countenance pleas for leniency and attempts at appeal from any quarter, no matter how prestigious.[13]

Josefa appeared to receive the news in a relatively calm fashion and, disregarding the expressed wishes of the judges, sought to mitigate the situation. She immediately sought out her attorney, granting him all power in her stead, and requested, unsuccessfully, the right to question witnesses and present her own defense. But she was able to convince the judges to allow her more time to put her affairs in order. During the weeks that followed, she placed her most expensive jewels and dresses with close friends such as Gorráez. Casaviella and Gorráez, working together with the commander of the Royal Army, forged a plan to whisk Josefa away and hide her until the whole matter could be resolved in her favor. However, Panseco intervened and notified the Real Sala del Crimen of her impending flight, and the authorities arrested her on the morning of her supposed escape. Panseco later told witnesses that "his wife had planned to leave him with nothing, not even a mattress to sleep on." Other witnesses claimed that a horrible argument had taken place between Ordóñez and Panseco the night before her departure. Josefa demanded that their young son accompany her into exile. In contrast, Panseco wished him to remain under his care in the capital. Josefa threatened to stab Panseco to death if he tried to stop her. By denouncing her, Gregorio effectively retained custody of the six-year-old boy.[14]

In 1770, once again in Mexico City, Josefa went before the religious authorities seeking a legal separation from Panseco, an action that he countered. The actual petition was lost but in subsequent testimony she stated that she wanted a divorce because of religious incompatibility. In short, she now claimed that he was a heretic.[15] Thwarted in this endeavor by the religious judge, she took her case before the audiences of the Coliseo. What had always been blatantly public now literally became a theatrical production. This was too much for the local civil authorities who arrested and deposited her in the house for *mujeres públicas* (prostitutes). The Real Sala del Crimen rescinded the order of deposit, admonishing the courtesan to "moderate her behavior." But the archbishop claimed that Josefa "had caused much trouble in [the] capital" and that she had laughed at the Real Sala's warning and had continued her "antics." Therefore, he stated that he felt compelled "for the honor of [the institution of] marriage as well as the good opinion of the citizenry" to intervene.[16] With the aid of the viceroy, the Marques de la Croix, Josefa was once again placed in the Casa de la Misericordia. However, she caused such a scandal there that they sentenced her to Santa María de Egipciaca in Puebla for two years, with a warning that if she complained or tried anything, she would be placed in perpetual reclusion, essentially a life sentence.[17] In the meantime, the archbishop and judges of the Real Sala disputed the action. The latter believed that the former had usurped their authority. Upon her release, Josefa sought to take advantage of this situation and immediately resubmitted her petition for divorce, which the ecclesiastical judge refused to grant. The viceroy ordered the Real Sala to issue another arrest warrant for Josefa, but they refused.[18] Either Josefa had well-placed patrons on the high court or the rivalry over jurisdiction between such powerful colonial figures worked to her advantage. Unbeknownst to the royal judges and Josefa, the archbishop, in conjunction with the viceroy and the bishop of Puebla, petitioned the king. The monarch himself then interceded and decreed Josefa's exile and immediate transfer to Spain. The archbishop and the viceroy admitted in their petition that they could not manage to reunite her with her husband despite much effort. With exile, they stated that they wanted to "liberate [the] capital from the unrest that the aforementioned woman has caused." The exile mandate also extended to Panseco, who had fled and was eventually arrested.[19]

Josefa and Gregorio were escorted to Veracruz under guard because the archbishop and the viceroy believed that they were "simply too devious and it was not inconceivable to think that they would attempt to escape." According to the sergeant at arms, Josefa fell ill during the journey because the arguments between her and Panseco were so great.[20] Ordóñez and Panseco (and their now ten-year-old son) spent two years in the castle at San Juan de Ulúa and never set sail for Spain, an indication that Josefa's friends continued to lobby in her defense because initially they did indeed have enough money to pay for the passage. Nonetheless, in 1775, Panseco, on behalf of himself and his wife, wrote a letter to the archbishop requesting assistance and begging for compassion. He claimed that they had run out of money and were unable to buy medicines, especially for Josefa, who required surgery. As though to prove their destitution, he added that Josefa had been forced to sell two of her jewels in order for them to survive. The letter apparently had the desired effect, because the pair returned to the capital and Panseco even secured his old job as a musician for the cathedral choir.[21]

Although no verifying documentation exists, it is conceivable that the archbishop and the viceroy made the couple's return contingent upon the cessation of their scandalous antics and the acceptance of their definitive marital status. But instead, Ordóñez and Panseco quietly procured separate houses and in essence divorced. Josefa quickly entered into sexual relationships with other men, but they were not of the same high social standing as her previous lovers. Clearly it would have been politically unwise to antagonize the viceroy by attempting to seduce a member of his entourage. Additionally, she was famous in the capital, making her a liability to past and future wealthy lovers. Perhaps more important, she was now about forty-seven years old. But as if to remind us (and the viceroy and archbishop) of her enterprising spirit and enduring attractiveness, Josefa now turned to the Holy Office of the Inquisition to maximize her personal interests vis-à-vis her lovers.

In April of 1776, one year after returning from Veracruz, Josefa denounced her new lover Nicolás del Monte, a tenor with the cathedral choir and, at least initially, a friend of Gregorio. In the course of what appeared to be a rather volatile relationship, del Monte used allusions to Catholic doctrine to refer to sexual intercourse and to physically tease Ordóñez in public. The Inquisitors eventually realized as much. In their final report, they wrote that del Monte had not really spoken these phrases with blasphemous intent but rather "he would direct them to Josefa in order to procure some final objective dictated by their sordid passion."[22] Interestingly, none of the witnesses directly sought to contradict Josefa's denunciation of del Monte, but rather they had the effect of sowing the seeds of suspicion in the minds of the Inquisitors. Even Panseco, when asked if he felt any enmity toward del Monte, who virtually lived at Ordóñez's house, stated only that they had been friends and that they had had a falling out because of a certain actress. Never did he indicate that he was referring to his own wife.[23] (Perhaps he did not have to do so.) In the end, Josefa, after probably procuring the desired gifts and attention from del Monte, returned to the Holy Office to cast doubt on her own testimony. She essentially got del Monte off the hook.

One of the most fascinating aspects of the investigation is Josefa's presentation of herself before the Inquisitors. They were aware of her reputation and clearly elected not to address her with the title of doña. She nonetheless presented herself as an extremely pious and intelligent woman. As a matter of fact, in her descriptions of her discussions with del Monte regarding Catholic doctrine, she posited herself as something of an authority on religion. Certainly she was sophisticated in her theological retorts to del Monte. She admitted that she herself virtually drove del Monte to make blasphemous remarks because he simply could not countenance a woman calling him to task on such weighty matters.[24] Her deportment must have given quite a bit of legitimacy to her claim. Although the Inquisitors were suspicious of her denunciation, they did not render their final decision to disregard the entire affair until after she returned to discount her own testimony. In that second visit to the Holy Office, Ordóñez represented herself as a foolish and silly woman who clearly had misunderstood the entire series of discussions between herself and del Monte. She herself suggested to the Inquisitors that del Monte was trying to seduce her with his scandalous remarks. Thus, in the final exchange with the Holy Office and in an effort to save her lover from further investigation, she played upon the fact that she was a well-known courtesan.

Del Monte apparently was not discouraged by Josefa's visit to the Inquisitors. The triangle between himself, Ordóñez, and Panseco became more complicated (or volatile) because during that same year, she again sought legal separation from Panseco. Yet again, officials reissued the royal decree calling for her exile. She withdrew her petition and they did not arrest her.[25]

In 1782, with a different viceroy and different judges, Josefa reinstituted her petition for divorce. But her fame was too great. Informed of her latest attempt at divorce, the king wished to know the current status of Josefa's marriage and the viceroy, José de Gálvez, had his secretary research the pertinent history regarding her case.[26] He also appointed an official to secretly investigate the couple. This action revealed the fact that they maintained separate residences, that Panseco gave Ordóñez twenty pesos per month for support, and that their relationship was amicable. Neighbors stated that they visited regularly and that they cared for each other when ill. The investigating official ordered them to reside together and forced them to sign an affidavit stating that they would do so.[27]

Ten years later, the sixty-four-year-old Josefa denounced Panseco to the Inquisition. She described, in thirteen days of extremely detailed testimony, his sexual pronouncements about and acts performed with religious statues, paintings, relics, rosaries, and crucifixes. She claimed that Gregorio, also in his sixties, committed these acts before their granddaughter and two servant children, all of whom were about ten years old, and had encouraged especially the girls to fornicate with the statues of Christ while he did so with the statues of the Virgin Mary and the female saints. These graphically described and disturbing incidents always took place in the home when she was out, usually attending mass.[28] She admitted that she had never personally witnessed these sexual encounters with the statues and that her descriptions were based upon what the children told her; yet her denunciation was very exact and precise. This is not to discount the ability of ten-year-olds to relay events in detail, but only to state that the veracity of the case is unclear given the long, troubled history between the two. However, if we assume that her denunciation was legitimate, then Josefa herself provided clues to explain why Panseco would have engaged in such sacrilegious and obscene behavior. She stated that, over the last ten years, Panseco had repeatedly tried to initiate sexual relations with her and she thwarted him at every turn. Furthermore, when he either attempted or had sexual relations with other women, such as female servants, she immediately fired them. Panseco's attacks on the sacred items were in essence attacks on Josefa. He even stated as much: if he could not have relations with "*la vieja*" (the old woman), he would have them with her saints.[29]

In this denunciation, Josefa once again presents herself before the Holy Office as a pious woman. However, the intensity or level of her religious devotion has increased tenfold. She portrayed herself as a woman who daily attended mass. Her house was filled with religious statues, paintings, texts, and candles. Not only was this self-presentation based upon piety but on chastity as well, as she pointed out that she and Panseco did not have relations. Clearly, she relied upon an older definition of marriage based upon celibacy. Thus, she insinuated or played upon a notion of a certain saintliness. We will never know the outcome of this case or even further details because with this case, Josefa and Panseco (apparently) vanished from the colonial record.

The insight about Novohispanic society that can be gleaned from the picturesque tale of Josefa Ordóñez must include the discussion of several important factors. Let us begin with the perception of the acting profession in the capital. Actors performed street theater, puppet shows, and local and imported plays at the Coliseo, performed at religious institutions, and did private renditions at the palace for the viceroy and elite members of society. They also performed during major annual religious festivals and important civic events.[30] Although economically connected to the poorer echelons of society, they had access to power and privilege and some, like Josefa, clearly sought rich patrons and protectors, a phenomenon that greatly frustrated attempts by the Coliseo administrators to regulate productions.[31] When disputes arose, the courtesan-actresses sought the aid and intervention of their powerful lovers to resolve the issues in their favor.

Although some performers were acclaimed for their talent and skill on stage, popular perceptions of actors as individuals were quite low. Actors and actresses were considered immoral and decadent, in constant violation of larger societal norms of behavior.[32] Of particular concern to clergymen was the notion that wayward actors performed the roles of saints and the Virgin Mary before a public that clearly noted (by yelling commentary) the irony of such a situation. Such was the poor perception of dramatic performers that in 1699, Francisca Toledo, a Spanish widow, was known as the "Comedianta" (the "Actress") even though she had never been one, but she was famous for her scandalous life-style and was living in sin with one Diego Juárez, a mestizo.[33] Actors and actresses did have a reputation for living outside of the bonds of Holy Matrimony. A predisposition to immorality even followed those who had left the profession. In 1620, Juana de la Blanca, a mulatta, was shocked when a Mercedarian friar solicited her in the confessional. No action was taken against the priest; the Inquisitors pointed out that he had been an actor. Eusebio Vela, perhaps the most famous actor at the Coliseo during the early eighteenth century, was arrested in 1721 because he had the effrontery to use the title of don.[34] Thus, actors were placed and confined in an immoral space. They were inherently more lax than other citizens who comprised the popular elements of the capital's inhabitants. More important for our discussion here, actresses were occasionally courtesans or the mistresses of powerful officials and wealthy nobles in the viceregal capital.[35] However, Josefa seems to have set new standards in this regard.

The eighteenth century marked a renewed emphasis on the part of the civil authorities to mandate proper behavior and specifically to reaffirm the didactic nature of the theater. Officials believed in "the need of the people for decent diversions that will spare them from the [otherwise] pernicious things that they experience because there is no decent and appropriate diversion for young people, and the theater is such an attractive and laudable diversion and a moral school whereby they [young people] can learn about the praiseworthy [attributes] of gentlemen."[36] With this new moral imperative, new regulations were imposed upon the theater, the plays, the audience, and the actors. The Coliseo became a professional, elite-oriented theater as admission prices rose and decorum laws regarding dress and comportment in the theater were actually enforced by special judges and militiamen. Individuals were arrested for whistling, jeering, or mocking performers.[37] The viceroys began to take an active role in the business of theater production; they approved all plays and made all final decisions regarding the acting company, including setting salaries and choosing understudies.[38]

Actors had to learn their lines, attend all rehearsals, and be present and prepared at all performances. Salary contracts were legal and binding for more than one year; no opportunities existed for renegotiation until the contract expired. Salaries were based upon a percentage of receipts from audience attendance, giving actors a vested interest in the success and popularity of particular plays. The tradition of using understudies was introduced to foster competition among actors and to encourage stars to behave themselves for fear of being replaced. The administrators were to be respected and had final say regarding who would perform which roles. All this was backed up by law, and recalcitrant performers were arrested.[39]

With such an emphasis on the moral nature of theatrical productions, the personal behavior of actors outside of the theater was of great interest to authorities.[40] They expected performers to be modest, live cleanly, and be responsible. This definition did not quite fit Josefa. In her case, private actions became public and, given the spirit of the times, those actions essentially forced a confrontation with Bourbon administrators, who seemed to recognize a threat to their ability to institute moral reform. As she insisted and persisted in her desire to live as she pleased and to gain freedom from Panseco, the authorities became intransigent and were willing to involve the king himself in an effort to control Ordóñez.

Yet just as many authorities and prominent citizens came to her defense and demonstrated a degree of persistent loyalty not often seen in historical accounts. After all, Josefa's celebrity thrust her lovers into the limelight and made them the subject of gossip and popular satire. They were pitted against members of their own socioeconomic group who sought to literally run her out of town. Men such as Monserrat, Gorráez, and Cassaviella were willing to risk their personal reputations and public honor to protect the courtesan.

That notoriety made it extremely difficult for her friends to protect her and certainly made it impossible for any court to grant a petition for legal separation to such a public figure and a known adulteress. To grant her request would be to send an entirely wrong message to the capital's inhabitants. Officials would essentially have rewarded someone who they considered to be a social climber, a dishonorable woman whose husband clearly could not control her. They could not publicly and officially condone the actions of a woman who overstepped cultural boundaries regarding discretion, the proper role of married women, female sexuality, socioeconomic place, and ordered gender relations. But, like Panseco, neither could they completely control her.

That brings us to Josefa's relationship with Panseco. Without a doubt, this was a complex marriage. The honor culture shared by elite and plebeians alike assumed that men would move to control or discipline their wives, and certainly even a hint of sexual infidelity could and did lead to violent assaults and even homicide.[41] In addition to the poems about Ordóñez's life that ridiculed Panseco, Josefa's physician, Don Joseph Vicente Maldonado, recounted that one morning the Italian awoke to find *cuernos* (horns) tied to the iron bars of his window.[42] Given Panseco's position as cuckold, we could expect some violent response. However, servants in the Ordóñez household stated that Panseco lived in the same house as his wife during the height of her most scandalous relationships (over a period of some twenty years), implying that he benefited economically from her sexual activities. Many questions are left unanswered. Did her husband (or her father) make use of her apparent charms and encourage or force her to become a courtesan? Was it expected by all involved given her position as acclaimed actress? Considering this possibility, did Panseco denounce his wife to the authorities because her independence meant financial hardship for him? His wife was beautiful and charming and he seems to have felt real affection for her, but he resigned himself to having to share her with younger or wealthier men. Inquisition trial witness Francisca Deza even claimed that Josefa had developed a system in which Panseco, Cassaviella, and Gorráez each had certain hours allotted to them.[43] Panseco accepted del Monte but clearly felt animosity toward him. In addition, he supported Josefa when they lived apart and later tried to maintain sexual relations with her. Josefa and Gregorio appear to have made an awful married couple but good friends when separated.

Now let us consider Josefa. She coordinated an acting career, various businesses, several lovers simultaneously, a husband, and three children (only one of whom was Panseco's). She reveled in her own notoriety, publicly and proudly displaying the wealth procured through immoral and illegal means. Ordóñez ignored the established cultural norms regarding the actions of married women. She persisted in an attempt to create an alternative honor code (or anti-honor code) that could include a persuasive woman of independent means, relaxed sexual mores, and bold opinions. She also insisted that she could be both a courtesan and pious. Furthermore, she always referred to herself as doña and as the legitimate wife of Panseco, no doubt to the chagrin and shock of her enemies.[44]

Inquisition cases and a few of the Real Sala testimonies demonstrate that rather than expressing complete public disapproval, individuals at Josefa's level or below referred to her as doña and one even stated that she was a "a woman of truth."[45] Ann Twinam, in her monograph on illegitimacy and honor, points out that colonial society made distinctions between public and private reputation and that popular opinion was a determining factor in whether honor was accorded or not.[46] In Josefa's case, although many of the elite saw her as nothing but a prostitute, some plebeians were willing to attribute both personal virtue (a truthful woman) and (some) public respect to the courtesan by addressing her as doña. Some maintained a different standard regarding her behavior because they knew her personally. Others perhaps did so because she was something of a celebrity. Her scandalous conduct could very well have generated admiration among the more humble elements of society, the very condition feared by the judges of the Real Sala del Crimen in 1766.

The nature of gender relations in the capital may further explain how Ordóñez could manage to be an honorable woman to some and a prostitute to others. Poverty—the fact that four-fifths of the population of the city hovered just above destitution—forced many women into the streets to seek employment in taverns, shops, residences, or factories or to take in work such as sewing, embroidery, laundry, cigarette rolling, or shoe repair. One-third of the total population of the capital in 1811 was single or widowed, a disproportionate number of whom were Spanish females.[47] Employment and self-employment gave women a certain independence and access to social networks that could counter the efforts of their husbands and fathers to control or monitor their behavior. Furthermore, there is some indication that some women may have included occasional sexual activity for remuneration as part of a larger strategy of financial survival.[48]

These patterns of behavior collided with Bourbon officials' attempts to bolster the family. For example, beginning in 1740, fornicators could be arrested and forcibly married while in jail. Legal separation before the ecclesiastical court was decidedly frowned upon, but it was not unusual for couples to violate the reunification decree of the ecclesiastical court by simply effectuating their own divorces. Gabriel Haslip-Viera points out in his study of crime in the capital that the majority of female criminals arrested during this period were charged with prostitution and adultery. Charges were also levied against women who engaged in disputes with their husbands, maintained lovers, or wanted to live as libertines. Haslip-Viera also states that many of these colonial female criminals "had a strong sense of independence, and a rebelliousness that was in total contrast to the submissive ideal promoted by educated opinion and law."[49] Given this picture of the capital, Josefa was not an anomaly nor was she representative of deviant and marginalized women. She was like many women of humble background in Mexico City. The difference was that she maximized her opportunities by excelling in the very attributes that sullied the reputations of actresses.

In the final analysis and in some respects, both Josefa and the Bourbon officials succeeded. At the time when she denounced Panseco, Josefa was quite well off, living in a seven-room, finely furnished house decorated with an expensive collection of religious art. She lived with Panseco but continued to control her own life, and in an ironic twist, the sexual activity of her elderly husband. An extremely pious mature woman, Josefa appears to have upheld the religious and moral code. Perhaps she played upon the traditional notion that the greater the sinner, the greater the saint. Because of her age, her wealth, or her pious reputation, or perhaps simply because of the passage of time, the Inquisitors and their scribes accorded her the honorific title of doña, disproving the belief that honor lost can never be regained, even for a courtesan. Josefa had outlived her own celebrity.

NOTES

1. I wish to thank Mary Elizabeth Perry, Asunción Lavrín, Judith Whitenack, Mark Burkholder, Jeffrey Pilcher, John Frederick Schwaller, Alejandro Cañeque, and Roberto Beristáin for their comments, insight, and assistance regarding the many permutations of this essay. All translations are my own.

2. H. Schilling, *Teatro profano en la Nueva España. Fines del siglo XVI a mediados del XVIII* (Mexico: UNAM, 1958), 90.

3. The idea of a woman as the head of the theater was not a complete novelty in Mexico City. During the late seventeenth century, María Celis held the same position and for ten years (1731–1741), María Anna Tecla de Escota y Estensoro, the widow of famous actor and Coliseo manager Eusebio Vela, controlled the productions at the playhouse. However, she found herself embroiled in six different lawsuits and her authority was chipped away in favor of male competitors for the position. She lost the *asiento* (chairmanship) even though attendance at the theatre was on an upswing. See Archivo General de la Nación (henceforth AGN), Historia, vol. 467, exp. 9, ff.1–6v.

4. Archivo General de las Indias, Audiencia de México, Legajo 1707, "Testimonio de la averiguación secreta hecha de orden de la Real Sala sobre los escándalos y excesos de Josefa Ordóñez, cómica que fue del Coliseo de esta ciudad y mujer de Gregorio Panseco, año de 1766," f. 39. Citations from this report are henceforth referred to as "Averiguación." "Testimonio del testimonio separado correspondiente a la averiguación secreta de los escándalos y excesos de Josefa Ordóñez, mujer de Gregorio Panseco. Año 1766," ff. 1, 2, 5, 11. The separate testimonies are henceforth referred to as "Testimonio separado." The "Averiguación" provides the basic chronological information of Josefa's life before 1770 but does not list her lovers by name. In the separate and theoretically secret testimonies, the witnesses specifically named her prominent lovers. Neither the "Averiguación" nor the "Testimonio separado" folios are paginated. Consequently, I have done so utilizing modern pagination (front and back as individual and separate pages) to designate where specific information is located in the documents.

5. "Averiguación," f. 37.

6. For a detailed historical overview of the homes created for wayward or divorcing women, see Josefina Muriel, *Los recogimientos de mujeres. Respuesta a una problemática social Novohispana* (Mexico: UNAM, 1974), especially 69–70 for mention of Ordóñez's stay in the Puebla *recogimientos.*

7. "Testimonio separado," ff. 12, 15.

8. "Averiguación," ff. 8, 27–28.

9. "Averiguación," ff. 4, 9–10, 26–28, 31, 80.

10. "Averiguación," ff. 16, 19–20, 49, 70, 73–76.

11. "Averiguación," ff. 11–13, 93, 71 and "Testimonio separado," ff. 2, 5, 6, 13–14, 18.

12. "Averiguación," ff. 85–86. These witnesses included Francisco Javier Paulín, businessman; Fernando Soto Riva; Joseph Miguel Guerrero, palace door guard; Domingo Ignacio Pérez de Texada, palace halberdier; and Joaquin Reyes, palace halberdier. The former employees (or individuals from whom she regularly contracted services) included Joseph Vicente Maldonado, her personal physician; Juan Cayetano Lezama, servant and Coliseo employee; his wife, María Josefa Otón y Pasalle; María Gertrudis Raphaela Correa, household servant; Lorenzo Montalbo, attorney's assistant in the divorce case; Cecilia Hernández, the washerwoman; Antonia de la Rosa, head housekeeper; Francisca Deza, servant; and Clara Solís, servant. Another witness, Francisca Javiera de Salzedo, was actually Josefa's close friend. Other witnesses were friends or clients of Panseco.

13. "Averiguación," ff. 107, 109, 111–113.

14. "Averiguación," ff. 103, 116–117, 122–123, 136–137, 145, 152; "Testimonio separado," 19, 22–24.

15. AGN, Inquisición, vol. 1391, exp. 2, f. 16v.

16. AGN, Historia, vol. 160, exp. 1, f. 1.

17. AGN, Reales Cédulas, vol. 97, exp. 7, f. 12v.

18. AGN, Historia, vol. 160, exp. 1, f. 1–1v.

19. AGN, Correspondencia de los Virreyes, vol. 15, f. 213–213v.

20. AGN, Alcaldes Mayores, vol. 2, f. 92, 93–94.

21. AGN, Correspondencia de Diversas Autoridades, vol. 16, exp. 4, f. 13v.

22. AGN, Inquisición, vol. 1136, exp. 3, f. 463v.

23. AGN, Inquisición, vol. 1136, exp. 3, f. 468v.

24. AGN, Inquisición, vol. 1136, exp. 3, f. 465.

25. AGN, Reales Cédulas, vol. 109, exp. 76, f. 253–254.

26. AGN, Reales Cédulas, vol. 124, exp. 148, f. 284.

27. AGN, Historia, vol. 160, exp. 1, f.5–5v.

28. AGN, Inquisición, vol. 1391, exp. 2, f. 1–8.

29. AGN, Inquisición, vol. 1391, exp. 2, f. 16–19.

30. For examples, see AGN, Inquisición, vol. 595, exp. 16, ff. 225–231; *Actas del cabildo de la Ciudad de México* (Mexico: Aguilar e Hijos, 1889–1911), libro 14, 57–58, libro 9, 309; Antonio de Robles, *Diario de sucesos notables 1655–1703* (Mexico: Editorial Porrúa, 1946), vol. 3, 10, 259, 268; and, Linda A. Curcio–Nagy, *Peforming Power and Identity: The Great Festivals of Colonial Mexico City* (Albuquerque: University of New Mexico Press, forthcoming).

31. AGN, Historia, vol. 467, exp. 6, f. 28.

32. See, for example, the life of Eusebio Vela in AGN, Historia, vol. 467, exp. 6, f. 16; Walter Cohen, *Drama of a Nation: Public Theater in Renaissance England and Spain* (Ithaca: Cornell University Press, 1985); José María Diez Borque, *Sociedad y teatro en la España de Lope de Vega* (Barcelona: Antoni Bosch, 1978); and, Richard Ford, *A Hand–Book for Travellers in Spain* (Carbondale: Southern Illinois University Press, 1966; originally published in London, 1845), vol. 1, 282.

33. AGN, Inquisición, vol. 710, exp. 11, f. 70v.

34. AGN, Bienes Nacionales, vol. 810, exp. 40, f. 1; vol. 873, exp. 24; Inquisición, vol. 295, exp. 71, f. 346; and Historia, vol. 467, exp. 2, ff. 1–2.

35. This was particularly the case in Spain during the reign of Felipe III (1598–1621) and it became even more common under Felipe IV, who had a well-publicized affair with actress María Calderón. Courtesans were not new to Mexico City either. See Ana María Atondo Rodríguez, *El amor venal y la condición feminina en el México colonial* (Mexico: INAH, 1992), chap. 10.

36. AGN, Historia, vol. 467, exp. 9, f. 4v.

37. For example, one poor fellow was released from jail only after his aging and ailing grandmother beseeched the viceroy to intervene and set him free. For his story and those of many others, see AGN, Historia, vol. 478, exp. 22, ff. 1–15v, exp. 14, ff. 1–2; and, exp. 6, f. 3–3v.

38. AGN, Historia, 478, exp. 6, ff.14–17.

39. AGN, Historia, vol. 478, exp. 6, ff. 1–20v and vol. 467, exp. 6, ff. 28–29v.

40. In 1793, officials gave their definition of a "good" actor when they arrested Pedro Montoro, a *moreno*, who was erroneously suspected of being a deserter from a commercial vessel docked in Veracruz. When it became apparent to officials that they had a case of mistaken identity, they released Pedro, pointing out that he lived alone, not with a woman, and that he never missed a performance. See AGN, Historia, vol. 478, exp. 6, f.5–5v.

41. Lyman Johnson, "Dangerous Words, Provocative Gestures, and Violent Acts," in *The Faces of Honor: Sex, Shame, and Violence in Colonial Latin America*, eds. Lyman L. Johnson and Sonya Lipsett–Rivera (Albuquerque: University of New Mexico Press, 1998), 145; and Steve J. Stern, *The Secret History of Gender: Women, Men, and Power in Late Colonial Mexico* (Chapel Hill: University of North Carolina Press, 1995), 86–87.

42. "Averiguación," ff. 8–9.

43. "Testimonio separado," f. 19.

44. "Averiguación," f. 59.

45. AGN, Inquisición, vol. 1136, exp. 3, f. 471.

46. Ann Twinam, *Public Lives, Private Secrets: Gender, Honor, Sexuality, and Illegitimacy in Colonial Spanish America* (Stanford: Stanford University Press, 1999), 32, 50.

47. Silvia Marina Arrom, *The Women of Mexico City, 1790–1857* (Stanford: Stanford University Press, 1985), 140.

48. Stern, *The Secret History*, 259, 261–262.

49. Gabriel Haslip-Viera, *Crime and Punishment in Late Colonial Mexico City, 1692–1810* (Albuquerque: University of New Mexico Press, 1999), 69.

SUGGESTED READINGS

Arrom, Silvia Marina. *The Women of Mexico City, 1790–1857*. Stanford: Stanford University Press, 1985.

Cohen, Walter. *Drama of a Nation: Public Theater in Renaissance England and Spain*. Ithaca: Cornell University Press, 1985.

Curcio-Nagy, Linda A. *Performing Power and Identity: The Great Festivals of Colonial Mexico City*. Albuquerque: University of New Mexico Press, forthcoming.

Haslip-Viera, Gabriel. *Crime and Punishment in Late Colonial Mexico City, 1692–1810*. Albuquerque: University of New Mexico Press, 1999.

Johnson, Lyman L., and Sonya Lipsett-Rivera, eds. *The Faces of Honor: Sex, Shame, and Violence in Colonial Latin America*. Albuquerque: University of New Mexico Press, 1998.

Lavrín, Asunción, ed. *Sexuality and Marriage in Colonial Latin America*. Lincoln: University of Nebraska Press, 1989.

Muriel, Josefina. *Cultura feminina novohispana*. Mexico: UNAM, 1994.

Perry, Mary Elizabeth. *Gender and Disorder in Early Modern Seville*. Princeton: Princeton University Press, 1990.

Seed, Patricia. *To Love, Honor and Obey in Colonial Mexico: Conflicts over Marriage Choice, 1574–1821*. Stanford: Stanford University Press, 1988.

Stern, Steve J. *The Secret History of Gender: Women, Men, and Power in Late Colonial Mexico*. Chapel Hill: University of North Carolina Press, 1995.

Twinam, Ann. *Public Lives, Private Secrets: Gender, Honor, Sexuality and Illegitimacy in Colonial Spanish America*. Stanford: Stanford University Press, 1999.

CHAPTER TWO

Fray Servando Teresa de Mier

Anáhuac's Angry Apostle

KAREN RACINE[1]

The Mexico City metro recognizes a select pantheon of patriot leaders, including Fray Servando Teresa de Mier, whose station on the turquoise line (number 4) celebrates a long and lively career spanning the entire movement for Mexican independence. When he gave his dramatic first sermon before colonial authorities in 1794, the people of New Spain had grown weary of colonial oppression, but they were not yet prepared to form an independent nation. Bourbon absolutism had increasingly denied them the experience of home rule, while the policy of maintaining ethnically distinct societies, known as "republics" of Spaniards and Indians, hindered the development of a national identity. Independence leaders therefore faced the dual task of inflaming the desire for local autonomy into a demand for genuine sovereignty and at the same time forging a sense of common destiny among the Creole elite, the urban underclass of mixed-race castes, and the largely indigenous rural masses. Mier dedicated his life to that task, and by the time he gave his final speech at the constitutional convention of 1824, Mexico had become an independent nation.

Like his contemporary, Father Miguel Hidalgo y Costilla, who exhorted the people to rise up against Spanish oppression, thus beginning the armed struggle in 1810, Mier was a freethinker, unafraid to speak his mind. As a result, he spent much of his life in European exile, and this essay invites the reader to consider the social and intellectual connections among revolutionaries on both sides of the Atlantic. The British Enlightenment, in particular, had a formative influence on Latin America's independence generation, as many future leaders spent years in foggy London.

Karen Racine earned her Ph.D. at Tulane University with a dissertation examining the importance of exiles in Latin America's independence movement. She is the author of Francisco de Miranda: A Transatlantic Life in the Age of Revolution, 1750–1816 (2002), a biography of another colorful Spanish American patriot; and the coeditor of a collection entitled Strange Pilgrimages: Exile, Travel, and National Identity in Latin America, 1800–1990s (2000). She teaches at Valparaiso University in Indiana and has held research fellowships at the

John Carter Brown Library in Providence, Rhode Island, and at the Instituto de Investigaciones José María Luis Mora in Mexico City.

𝒜ngry times produce angry men. Fray Servando Teresa de Mier was an angry Creole patriot, a man whose own personal experience fighting for the independence of New Spain mirrored that of the greater Mexican nation. Like other ambitious Creoles of his time, Mier felt keenly the injustice of a colonial system that closed off avenues of advancement to Americans justified solely by the geographic location of their birth. He spent his entire adult life in and out of royal prisons, wandering rootlessly in exile, surviving by his wits, his charm, and the products of his plume. Having grown up on the receiving end of the Spanish colonial system, Mier angrily railed against its injustice in print and through his actions. More often than not, he himself was the immediate victim of that injustice, a personal perception that makes him thoroughly, utterly modern. As a man whose lifework was devoted to the exaltation of Americans' talents and abilities, Mier was also an apostle; his conscious creation of a new Mexican identity that restored the indigenous heritage of the land of Anáhuac to a place of respect and centrality represented the major intellectual project of that country's independence era. In the end, the independence of Mexico was caused by anger; it was carried out by angry and anxious men who, after a brief euphoric celebration of their success, redirected their anger toward each other.

José Servando Teresa de Mier Noriega y Guerra was born in Monterrey, Nuevo León, on October 18, 1765, to a prominent upper-middle-class family.[2] His mother, the lovely Antonia Francisca Guerra Iglesias y Santacruz, was the second wife of José Joaquín Mier Noriega, the interim governor of Nuevo León. Servando's childhood seems to have been busy and happy as he and his nine brothers and sisters enjoyed the substantial privileges afforded to a well-known civil servant's family. A scrawny child inclined to books, Mier entered the Dominican order at age seventeen and went on to attend the Colegio de Porta Coeli in Mexico City, where he earned a doctorate in theology just four years later. Upon graduation, the idealistic young friar immediately received an appointment as lecturer at the Dominican convent in Monterrey and returned home to the proud bosom of his family. Mier's studies and travels had changed him, however. Already before he had gone to Mexico City, the capital city and seat of civil and religious power in New Spain, Mier had been sensitive about his family's claim to a position in the colonial aristocracy; four years spent among the arrogant and exclusive peninsular Spaniards who dominated positions of authority only encouraged Mier to expand his own personal resentments to encompass those of all Mexicans. Eventually, he vengefully claimed descent from the only nobility that would have him, a Native American one. Paradoxically, Mier's anger was the type born of privilege, from the frustration that builds when one's family has played by the rules faithfully and still failed to achieve their expected recognition or rewards.

In 1794, however, angry young Mier still thought he could challenge the system from within and be rewarded for it. On the strength of a previous speech he had made in honor of the anniversary of the death of Hernán Cortés, he was asked to give the annual sermon to commemorate the day of the Virgin of Guadalupe at her shrine at Tepeyac. When the appointed day arrived, December 12, dignitaries of the viceregal court, the colonial administration, the ecclesiastical hierarchy, the fashionable elite, and members of the popular classes were present and eagerly awaiting the polished words of this bright and rising young preacher. If the audience was expecting to revisit familiar sentiments of humility and devotion to the blessed Virgin and the king of Spain, however, they were more than disappointed—they were shocked, insulted, and thrown into a state of confusion. That fateful day, Mier delivered a bold sermon that historian David Brading has characterized as nothing less than the "public declaration of the spiritual autonomy of Mexico."[3] Mier, fortified by his reason and intellect, his Creole pride, and his own healthy ego, dared to assert publicly ideas that had been floating around since the later seventeenth century, namely that there existed sufficient evidence to prove that Mexico had been evangelized by St. Thomas well before Cortés and the Spaniards arrived charged with that mission.[4] If such a claim could be substantiated, one of the major justifications for the conquest and colonization of Spanish America would be negated, thereby throwing the legitimacy of the whole project into doubt. Initially too shocked to react, the insulted Spanish authorities sat frozen to their seats by decorum and politeness; by the time Mier finished, his anger had provoked theirs. He was quickly ushered from the lectern and put in quarantine as though he manifested a contagious disease.

Two versions of Mier's Guadalupe sermon have been preserved, one put down by Archbishop Alonso Núñez de Haro when he investigated Mier's beliefs in the weeks after the Guadalupe sermon, the other recorded by Mier himself.[5] Both contain the four major points that comprised Mier's argument: first, that the cape on which the image of the Virgin of Guadalupe appeared in 1531 had actually belonged to Saint Thomas, not to the humble Indian Juan Diego; second, that the Virgin had been worshipped in Mexico for at least 1,750 years at a shrine among the Indians at Tenanyuca; third, that when these Indians apostatized, Saint Thomas hid the image of the Virgin in order to preserve it for a more propitious time in the future; and fourth, that the Guadalupe image dates from the first century of the Christian Church and had to have been painted by the Virgin herself as it was clearly, Mier observed, "superior to all human industry."[6] Mier insinuated that the Virgin Mary was the same person who had been known to the Mexica people of the Aztec nation as Tonantzín and that the recently discovered antiquities such as the Mexican calendar stone and the carving of the goddess Cuautlicue were more precious than those of Herculaneum and Pompeii.[7] If pride does indeed go before a fall, Mier's valuation of American religion and accomplishments at the expense of European pretensions to cultural superiority could not be tolerated by the equally proud Spanish authorities. Núñez de Haro charged Mier with heresy and disturbing the peace, ordered him held incommunicado, and denied him the means or right to defend himself. When his own Dominican Order refused to participate in Mier's defense, the investigation proceeded rapidly to its inevitable conclusion; three months later, Mier was found guilty, deprived of his honors and licenses, and sentenced to ten years in the Santo Domingo Convent at Cádiz. He was hustled out of the country in June 1795, complaining loudly about the "intrigue, oppression, venality, corruption and injustice" that had characterized the rigged trial.[8] Exiled from his beloved homeland, Mier became an implacable enemy of the Spanish colonial presence in Mexico and angrily extrapolated an analysis of the entire nation's oppressed condition based on his own personal circumstances.

Of course, Mier's anger was the artistic sort. He was a highly charismatic individual, one with pretensions to greatness that were only magnified by the hubris of extended exile; furthermore, being packed off to Europe was not the harshest of punishments that one could imagine, Mier's frequent and vehement protests notwithstanding. Within a year of his incarceration, Mier befriended two locals named Cornide and Filomeno who eventually helped him escape from confinement and flee to France, where he resided on and off for nearly six years. Mier's recollection of the event neatly captures his exaggerated self-image and his childlike delight at thumbing his nose at the Spanish authorities whenever he had a chance. In order to spring him from jail, he gloated that Cornide and Filomeno had "diabolically transformed me, going so far as to make a black mole on my nose and another on my lip with an infernal stone. The mother who bore me would not recognize me. Nonetheless, in view of the fact that León stated in the warrant that I was good-looking, cheerful, and affable, they exhorted me to make myself appear to be taciturn, melancholy and ugly. On spying guards, I therefore contorted my chops, looked cross-eyed and carried out to the letter the last battle cry of the Portuguese army, 'Make fierce faces at the enemy.' "[9]

Safely ensconced in revolutionary Paris in 1797, where he could make fierce faces from a comfortable distance, Mier brashly opened a correspondence with Don Juan Bautista Muñoz, the head of Madrid's Royal Academy of History; Muñoz investigated the charges in the infamous Guadalupe sermon and found that in no way did it make claims that were egregious enough to warrant censure or theological note.[10] The young exile quickly inserted himself into the sparkling social scene and associated with such luminaries as Madame Germaine de Staël, Benjamin Constant, Lucas Alamán, Francisco Antonio Zea, and Julie Recamier.[11] Mier set up a language school with Simón Rodríguez, the tutor of Simón Bolívar, and the pair collaborated on various translation projects, including a Spanish version of François-René de Chateaubriand's tale of life and romance between Europeans and North American Indians, *Atala*. Although the book appeared under Rodríguez's pseudonym Samuel Robinson, Mier claimed that he himself had undertaken the entire translation.[12]

The porous border allowed Mier to slip in and out of Spain several times, until he was recaptured and sent to finish his original sentence at Seville's notorious Los Toribios prison in September 1804. José María Rodríguez, the warden of the jail, denied his prisoner access to books or the right to physical exercise, causing Mier to complain bitterly that his temporary home was "the most barbarous of the Saracen institutions of Spain."[13] While in custody, Mier wrote an angry poem titled "Grito del Purgatorio" (Cry from Purgatory) in which he described his jailhouse experience at the hands of the Spanish as an assault on his human dignity and a degradation of his very existence. As he sat for over a year, stewing away in isolation, Mier drew links between his own personal conditions and those of his distant homeland; just as they were denying him his freedom and his franchise, the Spanish tyrants had kept all Mexicans in isolation, using the Inquisition to deny them the right to read freely and widely and employing hollow arguments to prevent them from exercising their right to equal political representation. The more he thought about it, the angrier he became, and he began to seek others like himself who wanted to do something about it.

Mier lived a peripatetic life, escaping from prison repeatedly and evading arrest by relying on the kindness of strangers. In 1808 he joined the patriot Spanish army as a military chaplain and served with General Blake against Napoleon's forces in Aragón. He was taken prisoner at Belchite on June 18 but, as he so often did, managed to wriggle out of captivity in a prisoner exchange; for his services, Blake recommended Mier to a prestigious canonry in Mexico City's cathedral, which the haughty wanderer eventually rejected because of its low pay.[14] He loitered around Spain and Portugal for another two years, eventually gravitating to the meetings of the Cortes at Cádiz in 1810, where he exhorted its members to take a hard line on the issue of American autonomy. Some delegates were amused by his antics, others were irritated, but the presence of Mier and his angry convictions managed to radicalize the proceedings. For his efforts, Mier was once again arrested and put on trial by the Inquisition in Valencia, where he spoke eloquently for five minutes about the rights of men to talk and think freely before he was forcibly removed from the podium.[15]

In early 1811 the wife of another aggrieved party, former Mexican viceroy José de Iturrigaray, who had been ousted in 1808 in retribution for his liberal sympathies, approached Mier with a proposition. She asked if Mier would be willing to write an alternate history of events that would restore her husband's good name; he would, of course, be compensated for his efforts. Mier rubbed his hands in delight and immediately started to draft the outline of the work that eventually appeared under the title *Historia de la revolución de Nueva España, antiguamente Anáhuac* (History of the revolution in New Spain, known in ancient times as Anáhuac). While still in Cádiz, he interviewed delegates from all parts of Mexico, including José Miguel Guridi Alcocer of Tlaxcala, José Ignacio Beye Cisneros of Mexico City, and Miguel Ramos Arispe of Coahuila. With their insights added to his own, Mier's *Historia* represented a quantum leap for the historical profession among Mexicans, but also a valuation of local American authority as inherently superior to European opinions when it came to their own affairs. When Cádiz was bombarded by the French, Mier said he "decided Spain was lost," packed up his papers, and fled to another safe haven in London, where a growing community of like-minded expatriate Spanish Americans was gathering.[16] He had finally found a constructive outlet for his anger.

Mier arrived in London in October 1811, around the same time as a group of young military officers from South America were passing through on their way to join the patriot forces in Buenos Aires. Meeting each evening at 9 P.M. at the Grafton Street home of Venezuelan general Francisco de Miranda, these idealistic and energetic men formed a Masonic club that was dedicated to the independence of Spanish America. In these meetings, Mier's hemispheric consciousness was raised; as he listened to José de San Martín from Buenos Aires speak with Wenceslao Villaurrutia from Guatemala in the presence of Andrés Bello from Venezuela and the Marqués del Apartado from Mexico, he realized that all their complaints were essentially the same. Fortified by the presence of his new friends and the protection offered by the English constitution, Mier began to embrace the notion of complete independence from Spain, causing a nonplussed Iturrigaray to withdraw Mier's financial support.[17] Mier did not care; his new friends would help him survive.

In London, Mier's literary production increased in inverse proportion to his funds. He was a whirlwind of activity, often seeming to get by on bile alone. Though he continued to expand his masterwork, the *Historia*, Mier simultaneously launched a vitriolic attack on the attitudes of his friend, the liberal Spanish expatriate Reverend Joseph Blanco White, which had recently appeared in the latter's influential monthly journal *El Español*. In two very public letters to the editor, written in 1811–12, Mier challenged the position taken by sympathetic liberal Spaniards like Blanco White and Gaspar Melchor de Jovellanos that Americans should be incorporated into a representative Spanish system and given greater political rights over time but remain within the empire itself. Mier angrily rejected this notion and argued instead that Americans were actually *ahead* of Europeans in political maturity, that the patriot movements did *not* represent a Jacobin insurrection but rather were legal assertions of their constitutional rights that had long been degraded and suppressed by centuries of tyrannical rule. The Americans, in other words, were acting correctly and it was the colonial authorities who were attempting to circumvent the rule of law. The violent beauty of Mier's arguments came in part from his insistence upon rigorous historical and legal arguments rather than mere republican ideology, and also in part from his own personal anger. As the apostle of an emerging nation, Mier's voice purported to include Americans of all races and classes, as he turned his wrath on a system that was built on flawed concepts of Spanish superiority.[18]

Mier's public assault on Blanco White notwithstanding, the two men were good friends in private. Blanco White used Mier as a major source for his own summary of recent events in Mexico that was passed to the British Foreign Office, and his journal *El Español* was the only publication that took notice of Mier's magisterial *Historia de la revolución de Nueva España* when it finally appeared in print in 1813.[19] Blanco White borrowed Mier's gazettes, letters, books, and papers in order to provide accurate information to his readers, and occasionally gave money to the perpetually impoverished friar.[20] Indeed, Mier often took advantage of his London friends' generosity and more secure positions. In 1812, Fermín Fastet and Company advanced £700 from the account of the Argentine legation to the Marqués del Apartado, a Mexican named Francisco de Fagoaga, so that he could pay Mier's printer's bill and bail their mutual friend out of debtor's prison.[21] Argentine representatives Manuel Moreno and Tomás Guido also bought up all the unsold copies of Mier's works and even tried to persuade the esteemed author himself to relocate to Buenos Aires. Venezuelan minister plenipotentiary Luis López Méndez offered to share his British government pension with Mier, though Mier later hinted that he had received one in his own right as "it was the custom of the English Court to offer pensions or aid to those subjects who were clearly superior in their talents."[22] Mier wrote to his friend Luis Iturribarria, "Ah, if only I had money, I would translate, annotate, and make infernal war on the *Godo* [derogatory term for a Spaniard]."[23] On February 2, 1813, Mier slipped on some treacherous ice and broke his right arm. He took full advantage of the situation to spend the rest of the cold winter in bed at several friends' homes, enjoying their forced hospitality and dictating his various manuscripts.[24]

When the *Historia* finally appeared in print toward the end of 1813, it was angrier and more brilliant than anyone could have expected. The author snickered that "if the *Cartas* [to Blanco White] were rockets, this has got to be a twenty-four-pound cannon."[25] He not only summarized the events that had taken place in Mexico in a manner favorable to the Creoles, but he also essentially codified the arguments that Spanish Americans everywhere would subsequently use to justify their drive for full independence. In fact, Simón Bolívar's famous Jamaica Letter (1815) drew heavily upon Mier's Lockean arguments. Employing the twin notions of utility and felicity to buttress his arguments of the rights and responsibilities of an administrative power toward the people, Mier clearly revealed the impact of his time in England on his ideas. According to Mier, the supreme laws of all political society were "conservation and happiness"; he quoted Filangieri's observation that "no colony which was happy under the government of its metropolis ever thought of separating itself."[26] Again, linking the personal with the public, Mier referred extensively to the experiences of his wealthy friends the Fagoagas at the hands of a capricious and vindictive Spanish colonial bureaucracy. He marveled that in England, "the King cannot make even the lowliest rustic come to his palace if the man does not wish to go, while in Constitutional Spain the King can have his Ministers seize any citizen."[27] His anger bubbled to the surface whenever he mentioned the Viceroy Venegas, variously described as a "vizier" and a "despot" whose "gothic parchments" claimed powers even grander than the Sultan of Constantinople would dare.[28] Mier was especially irritated at the lack of freedom that the system had permitted intellectuals like himself; after describing the imprisonment of José Joaquín Fernández de Lizardi, the "Mexican *Pensador* (thinker)," he asked sarcastically whether "by chance, it was lawful to think in Mexico?"[29]

Mier's patriotic anger, coupled with a sense of self-importance that had only increased in proportion to the amount of time spent in exile from his country, prompted him to resurrect the texts of Bartolomé de las Casas, formerly "Protector of the Indians" and author of several tracts that condemned the Spaniards' behavior during the conquest of America. The choice of a hero to worship is revealing. Las Casas, like Mier, was a Dominican friar who had fallen into disfavor for espousing unpopular beliefs that had championed Americans; both men had a highly polemical style and devoted their best years to the composition of angry diatribes against an unjust colonial authority. Small wonder then that Mier dusted off Las Casas's *Brevíssima relación de la destrucción de las Indias Occidentales* (Brief relation of the destruction of the West Indies) and arranged for a new edition to be printed in London with his own introduction and notes.[30] He continued his correspondence with Abbé Henri Grégoire, the Archbishop of Blois, who had befriended the young friar years before in Paris and issued his own translation of Las Casas's account as part of his own campaign against African slavery.[31]

As Mier's anger continued to boil, the end of the Napoleonic Wars in 1815 brought new possibilities for action. In London he met Francisco Javier Mina, a dashing 28-year-old Basque hero of the guerrilla wars in Spain who subsequently fell out of favor with King Ferdinand and fled to exile in London. Instantly recognizing each other as ideological and temperamental mates, Mier and Mina immediately hatched a plan to "establish the liberal system of the Constitution in Mexico" and "give liberty to all Spanish dominions."[32] In August 1815 the Whig politician Lord Holland may have held a dinner for Mina and Mier at which U.S. general Winfield Scott was also present.[33] Scott, in turn, provided introductions for the pair to John Quincy Adams, then serving as U.S. Minister Plenipotentiary to the Court of St. James's, who endeavored to procure arms and finances for their proposed expedition. Adams offered to make an exception to his rule against issuing passports for non-U.S. citizens so that Mina, Mier, and the other expeditionaries could get their emancipation project under way.[34] Mier's beleaguered friends in London were undoubtedly equally happy at the prospect of his imminent departure from their community; he continued to pester them for money they did not have, prompting the exasperated New Granadan envoy José María del Real to snap, "It is impossible for lack of funds to contribute the thirty guineas that you need for your transportation to New Orleans, *as I told you the day before I left when you spoke to me about the same subject.*"[35]

Mier, Mina, and 200 men slipped out of Liverpool's harbor on May 15, 1816. Spanish spies immediately reported the alarming turn of events to Ambassador Fernán Núñez, who in turn passed on the information to the king.[36] The expedition arrived at Norfolk, Virginia, in June 1816 to vastly inflated reports of their numbers and a warm welcome from several North American merchants. Merchant brothers Dennis and Alexander Smith in Baltimore bought and paid for a brig called the *Calypso*, which they also outfitted with arms and supplies. While Mina made a trip to Haiti to confer with Alexandre Pétion and Simón Bolívar, Mier made a trip to New Orleans to solicit the business community there for additional political and financial support.[37] The group left Galveston and made their main landing at Soto la Marina in New Spain on April 18,

1817, whereupon Mina congratulated his men for their dedication to "the liberty and independence of Mexico . . . the greatest cause that can be raised upon this Earth." He further counseled them to "respect religion, persons, and property" and to remember that "severe discipline that exists in proportion to the success of great enterprises."[38] Although royalist officials had tried to create fear in the populace by spreading rumors of the evil designs of Mina and his group, patriot bulletins tell of a warm reception wherever the troops went. While Mina seduced his listeners with grand speeches about the justice of the American cause and the coming new order of things, "Monsignor Mier" granted indulgences to those who would adhere to the noble patriot effort.[39] Those were heady days, but they did not last for long. Royal officials in Mexico put a bounty on the rebels' heads and eventually Mina was caught at the Rancho del Venadito.[40]

Mier held out until June 15, when he, too, was captured and taken into custody to face colonial justice once again. One by one, his former associates feigned no knowledge of Mier's London activities when pressed by the inquisitors.[41] Some, in a desperate effort to save themselves, made wild charges against the famous friar. Pedro Simón del Campo squealed that Mier had dressed as a bishop and performed benedictions to troops without official standing to do so, and that he was actually married to a French woman whom he sacrilegiously called "the Bishopess."[42] Juan Martinich, however, disputed these claims and said that Mier used only the legitimate title "Doctor" in reference to himself and that, although there were many women among the expeditionaries, Mier was not married and observed strict moral behavior commensurate with the canons of the Catholic Church. Mier's *Historia* was viewed by the Inquisition as being full of "false, exotic, extravagant, subversive and scandalous doctrines."[43] The authorities responded to his presence in Mexico in the same way they had after his Guadalupe sermon over twenty years earlier—by shutting him up in jail and feeding his anger. His friends in Argentina scoured the overseas papers for news of "Dr. Mier," and he became an internationally famous prisoner of conscience once again.[44]

In 1821, Juan Dávila, the governor of the jail at Veracruz, had fallen sufficiently under his charismatic prisoner's spell to agree to release him on the condition that he leave the country. Mier quickly agreed, but jumped ship on the way from Mexico to Spain and made his way to Philadelphia, where he started to turn his anger toward England's monarchy as well. If that country's leaders had failed to support Mexicans' desire for freedom, perhaps their republican neighbor to the north would be more understanding. He was lonely in Philadelphia, despite the presence of his New Granadan friend Manuel Torres, and spent much time drafting articles to counter Mexico's detractors. He wrote a *Memoria*

político-instructiva enviada desde Filadelfia en agosto 1821 (A political and
instructive memoir sent from Philadelphia in August 1821), directing
his words to "the independent chiefs of Anáhuac, called New Spain by
the Spaniards."[45] In it, Mier quoted extensively from Thomas Paine's
Common Sense and started to decry not only the ill effects of aristocracy,
but the entire cultural heritage of Spain; as a bold rhetorical move, if not
entirely accurate, he claimed that he himself was descended from
"Quatemóczin," the democratically elected emperor, or "Hueitlatoani,"
of ancient Mexico.[46] He also complained bitterly that he had lost all his
papers to the royalist Joaquín Arredondo in 1817, and was reminded of
happier times in London when he received a letter from Charlotte
Stephenson, an aging admirer whose words indicate they had shared at
least an intimate friendship if not an actual romance while he lived there.[47]

It seems Mier could not avoid entangling himself in conflicts wherever he went. In Philadelphia he found himself drawn into a battle for
control over the city's Catholic See. The Reverend Henry Conwell,
Bishop of Philadelphia, had condemned the Reverend William Hogan,
who had attempted to usurp Conwell's position through undue influence on the board of St. Mary's Church. The pope eventually sided with
Conwell, but not before a nasty and public exchange between the two
men threatened to divide Philadelphia's Catholic community indefi-
nitely.[48] Hogan, however, appealed to Mier's erudition to help substanti-
ate his claim to have a right to act outside Conwell's authority as the
United States was still considered a missionary country outside the traditional Church hierarchy. In Mier's reply to Hogan's questions, which
he wrote in Latin so as not to betray his imperfect English, he transferred his current political attitudes to the religious sphere, claiming that
the institutional Church had moved away from its original democratic
intent and had been corrupted by "the well known cruelty and despo-
tism of their bishops."[49] Oddly, despite his lifelong opposition to un-
earned titles, in his waning years Mier occasionally signed his letters as
"Señor Servando, Archbishop of Baltimore."[50] Mier took his Catholicism very seriously and was both hurt and angry when his North American brothers called him "an impostor without a conscience." He returned
to Mexico in 1822 but was soon rearrested for opposing Iturbide after he
crowned himself emperor.[51]

Mier's final important public pronouncement came, fittingly, on the
thirtieth anniversary of his Guadalupe sermon. On December 13, 1824,
he stood up on the floor of the congress and issued his famous proph-
esies about the nature of the constitution then being drafted. He voted
for Article 5, which made Mexico a federal republic, but refused to accept the part of Article 6 that included the word "sovereign" as part of
the description of the various states' juridical status.[52] He was not

opposed to the idea of federalism on principle; like so many of his generation, he genuinely feared the centrifugal forces that independence had threatened to set in motion, and so he could not accept an arrangement that would allow greater sovereignty to states than other republican models had guaranteed. In other words, it was not possible to have sovereign states within a larger sovereign state and expect the system to function smoothly.[53] After all he had sacrificed to see his beloved Anáhuac resurrected into the new nation of Mexico, Mier could not bear to watch as its politicians constructed a framework that contained the seeds of its own inevitable destruction.

Although he was nearing sixty years of age, Mier was as angry as ever. He was also getting tired. Decades spent in jails and in exile, writing and working for Mexico's independence, had made him the popular apostle of the new nation, but they had also taken their toll on his health. He wrote to his friend Andrés Bello that "after twenty-two years of being almost always in bed with sharp pains in my shoulders and right arm, back and brains, struggling against [the possibility of a] death [caused] by error of the doctors," he was deeply discouraged by the rogueries of Mexico's congressional representatives.[54] He remarked bitterly that the same men who rose to their feet to applaud him as he spoke from the heart about the need for unity and cooperation in the new Republic had failed to heed the meaning of his words. The same angry apostle who had constructed an argument that provided a constitutional justification for the independence of Mexico also predicted the bitter struggle for power that would emerge in its wake. Fray Servando Teresa de Mier Noriega y Guerra died at home in Monterrey in 1827. Four decades later, his skeleton was dug up and sold to an Italian circus owner who displayed it as part of a traveling sideshow in Argentina.

NOTES

1. The author would like to thank Yael Bitrán Goren, Iván Jaksic, John Lombardi, and Salvador Méndez Reyes for consistently useful comments and assistance in locating material for this biography.

2. Some sources, including René Jara, "The Inscription of Creole Consciousness: Fray Servando Teresa de Mier" in *1492–1991: Re/Discovering Colonial Writing*, ed. René Jara and Nicholas Spadacchini (Minneapolis: The Prisma Institute, 1989), 349 and Guillermo Leguizamón, ed., *Archivo Bonpland IV. Londres, Cuartel General de los Patriotas de la Emancipación Americana* (Buenos Aires: Imprenta y Casa Editora "Coni," 1940), xvi, give 1763 as the year of Mier's birth, but 1765 is generally accepted as the correct date.

3. David Brading, *The First America: The Spanish Monarchy, Creole Patriots, and the Liberal State, 1492–1867* (Cambridge: Cambridge University Press, 1991), 583.

4. Kathleen Ross, "A Natural History of the Old World: The *Memorias* of Fray Servando Teresa de Mier," *Revista de Estudios Hispánicos* 23, no. 3 (1989): 98n. Noted Mexican humanist Carlos Sigüenza y Góngora, Lorenzo Benaducci Boturini, and several Jesuit historians had previously made the same claim, although their audiences were far more restricted and their intent less overtly political than was Mier's sermon in 1794.

5. Both versions of the text are reprinted in Juan Hernández y Dávalos, ed., *Colección de Documentos para la Historia de la Guerra de la Independencia de México de 1808 a 1821*, vol. 3 (México: 1877–1882).

6. Artemio Benavides, "De la historia social a la historia de la sociedad: el Sermón en la Colegiata de Guadalupe de Fray Servando Teresa de Mier en 1794," *Humanitas* [Monterrey] 19 (1978): 319.

7. Jara, "The Inscription of Creole Consciousness," 364. These valuable archaeological artifacts had been unearthed in 1790 in Mexico City's Plaza de Armas.

8. José Servando Teresa de Mier Noriega y Guerra, *Memorias* (México DF: Editorial Porrúa, S.A., 1946), 1:4; John Lombardi, *The Political Ideology of Fray Servando Teresa de Mier: Propagandist for Independence* (Cuernavaca: CIDOC, 1968), 1–2.

9. *The Memoirs of Fray Servando Teresa de Mier*, trans. Helen Lane (New York: Oxford University Press, 1998), 10.

10. Jesús Silva Herzog, "Fray Servando Teresa de Mier," *Cuadernos Americanos* 154, no. 5 (set/oct 1967): 162. Mier, of course, would have felt vindicated by the pronouncement but would have bridled at the diminution of his brilliant insights that the verdict also implied. Muñoz himself had been somewhat of a Guadalupe scholar, presenting a speech entitled "El discurso histórico-crítico sobre las apariciones y el culto de Nuestro Señora de Guadalupe de México" at the Royal Academy in April 1794 in which he himself had adopted a similar position to Mier's. Jara, "The Inscription of Creole Consciousness," 368.

11. Rodolfo de León Garza, *Fray Servando: Un visionario itinerante* (Monterrey: Universidad Autónoma de Nuevo León, n.d.), 33.

12. Mier, *Memoirs*, 20–21.

13. Mier's description quoted in William Francis Lewis III, "Xavier Mina and Fray Servando Mier: Romantic Liberals of the Nineteenth Century," *New Mexico Historical Review* 44, no. 2 (April 1969): 121.

14. The incident is retold with amusing irony in David Brading, "Introducción" to Servando Teresa de Mier, *Historia de la revolución de Nueva España, antiguamente Anáhuac, o verdadera orígen y causas de ella con la relación de sus progresos hasta el presente año de 1813* (Paris: La Sorbonne, 1990), xvii.

15. Mier was tried under the pseudonym Andrés Vomeri on 21 December 1810. Lewis, "Mina and Mier," 119.

16. Mier, *Memorias*, 2:252. The best general histories of the Spanish American community in London are: Carlos Pi Sunyer, *Patriotas americanos en Londres* (Caracas: Monte Avila Editores, 1978) and María Teresa Berruezo León, *La lucha de Hispanoamérica por su independencia en Inglaterra, 1800–1830* (Madrid: Ediciones de Cultura Hispánica, 1989).

17. Lucas Alamán, *Semblanzas e idario* (México: Ediciones de la Universidad Nacional Autónoma, 1939), 4–5.

18. V.C.R. [Un Caraqueño Republicano], *Carta de un Americano al Español sobre su número XIX* (Londres: Impreso por W. Lewis, 1811), 39–41 speaks of the insult that the Cortés of Cádiz heaped upon millions of Americans when its Spanish members refused to extend rights to those of African descent in the colonies. Mier estimated that this position would disenfranchise at least eight or nine million Americans, tilting the balance of power in any representative body in the Europeans' favor.

19. Joseph Blanco White, enclosed in a letter [to Foreign Secretary Castlereagh?] (London, 31 May 1813), "A Sketch of the Disturbances in the Kingdom of Mexico since July 1808," United Kingdom, Public Record Office (PRO), Foreign Office (FO), 156; [Joseph Blanco White] *El Español* (julio de 1813), 69.

20. See, for example, the receipt Mier gave Blanco White for £26, two pennies (London, 10 abril 1812), Manchester College, Oxford, Joseph Blanco White Papers, and the letter of Blanco White to Manuel Moreno, (67 Edgware Road, 25 de mayo 1812), Archivo General de la Nación-Argentina (hereafter cited as AGN, Argentina), Sala 10 1-1-2, f.190 in which he mentions that he has lost the gazettes that Mier loaned him.

21. Fermín Fastet & Cía to Manuel Moreno, (Alderman's Walk, 18 de julio 1812), AGN-Argentina, Sala 10 1-1-2, f.134. The books were lost in a shipwreck, however, and never made it to their destination; Alamán, *Semblanzas*, 5. Mier to Tomás Guido (Londres, 12 de julio 1813) politely rejected the offer of passage to South America, AGN-Argentina, Sala 10, 1-3-5.

22. Mier, *Memorias*, 2:253. Mier states that he received official government funding for his passage to New Orleans with the Mina Expedition in 1816.

23. Mier to Iturribarria (Londres, 14 de abril 1812), Archivo Histórico Nacional, Madrid, Consejos, leg. 6310.

24. Mier in Hernández y Dávalos, *Colección de documentos*, 6:823.

25. Mier to Guido, (Londres, 9 de agosto 1813), AGN-Argentina, Sala 10, 1-3-5.

26. Mier, *Historia de la revolución*, 509, 519.

27. Mier, *Historia de la revolución*, 560.

28. Mier, *Historia de la revolución*, references scattered throughout bk. 14.

29. Mier, *Historia de la revolución*, 565–66. Fernández de Lizardi (1776–1827) was Mexico's most celebrated liberal journalist and pamphleteer. He is best known for the newspaper *El Pensador Mexicano* (1812–1814) and *El periquillo sarniento* [*The itching parrot*] (1816).

30. Bartolomé de las Casas, *Brevíssima relación de la destrucción de las Indias Occidentales* (Londres: Schulze y Dean, 1812). Mier subsequently arranged for reprinted editions in Philadelphia in 1821, and in Mexico in 1823.

31. *Apologie de Barthélemy de Las-Casas, évèque de Chiappa* (Paris: Institut National, [1801]).

32. Mier, *Memorias*, 2:253. See the description of the Mina Expedition in Estela Guadalupe Jiménez Codinach, *La Gran Bretaña y la Independencia de México, 1808–21* (México: Fondo de Cultura Económica, 1991), 264–361. Mier, *Memorias*, 2:253.

33. Lewis, "Mina and Mier," 125. Charles Winslow Elliot, *Winfield Scott: The Soldier and the Man* (New York: 1937), 206–7.

34. Adams to Mina (samedi, 20 avril 1816), Massachusetts Historical Society, Adams Papers, John Quincy Adams letterbook, reel #143; *Memoirs of John Quincy*

Adams, Comprising Portions of his Diary from 1795 to 1848, ed. Charles Francis Adams (Philadelphia: J.B. Lippincott and Co., 1874), 3:340.

35. Del Real to Mier (Cheltenham, 1 de octubre de 1815), Indiana University, Lilly Library, Latin American Manuscripts, Mexico, box 2. Emphasis added.

36. Conde de Fernán Núñez to Pedro Cevallos (Londres, 17 mayo 1816), Simancas, Estado 8.177. Cevallos' reply dated (Madrid, 17 octubre 1816), Simancas, Estado, 8.286.

37. Mina kept in close touch with his influential British patrons Lord Holland and Lord John Russell. Letters to both, dated (Puerto Príncipe, 22 de octubre 1816), Simancas, Estado 8.177.

38. "Proclama de Mina á los soldados de su expedición" (Río Bravo del Norte, 12 de abril 1817), Yale University, Stirling Library, Latin American Manuscripts 307, 1, box 11, f.181.

39. "Boletín de la División Ausiliar de la República Mexicana" [Soto la Marina]: 26 de abril 1817.

40. Archivo General de la Nación-México (hereafter cited as AGN-México), Reales Cédulas Originales, vol. 218, exp. 155, f.176, and AGN-México, Bandos, vol. 29, exp. 31, f. 82. Viceroy Juan Ruíz de Apodaca eventually added the title Conde del Venadito to the list of his others in recognition of Mina's capture.

41. AGN-México, "Catálogo de documentos para la historia de la guerra de la independencia," tomo 6, v. 4, ff. 650–750 contains these interrogation transcripts. Fr. Candido Muñoz and Fr. Iñigo de San Josef grilled Mier's fellow prisoners Lt. Col. Juan Quintero and Pedro José de la Teja (Villa Altamira, 9 de octubre 1817), in Lilly Library, Latin American Manuscripts, México, box 2.

42. "Declaración de Pedro Simón del Campo, dado por conteste por el Capitán Cevallos" (11 de agosto 1817), AGN-México, "Catálogo de documentos" tomo 6, v. 4, ff. 657–58.

43. "Calificación de la 'Historia de la Revolución de Nueva España' por el Dr. Mier," AGN-México, "Catálogo de documentos," Tomo 6, v. 4, #934.

44. [Camilo Henríquez], *El Censor* [Buenos Aires] 122, (11 de enero 1818), 6. See also "Alerta a los mexicanos" (México: Alejandro Valdés, 10 de julio 1820).

45. Mier, *Memoria político-instructiva* (Filadelfia: Juan P. Hurtel, 1821).

46. Mier, *Memoria político-instructiva*, 62.

47. Charlotte Stephenson to Mier (c. 1820–21) in Nettie Lee Benson Collection, University of Texas at Austin, Mier Papers, f. 290. Mier's reply is dated (Philadelphia, 20 de junio 1821).

48. The episode is described in John Gilmary Shea, *History of the Catholic Church in the United States* (New York: John G. Shea, 1890), 3:227–46.

49. *The Opinion of the Rt. Reverend Servandus A. Mier . . . on Certain Queries Proposed to him by the Rev. William Hogan* (Philadelphia, July 11, 1821), 7. After Conwell's camp issued their rebuttal, Hogan followed this up with *A Word Relative to an Anonymous Pamphlet Printed in Philadelphia, entitled "Remarks on the Opinion of the Rt. Rev. Servandus A. Mier"* (Philadelphia: August 17, 1821).

50. See Mier in two letters to the [Monterrey] Provincial Deputation, dated (28 de junio 1823) and (5 de julio 1823), in Lilly Library, Latin American Manuscripts, México, box 2.

51. Library of Congress, Iturbide Papers, reel 10, # 317–20.

52. "El Padre Mier en el Congreso Constituyente Mexicano," in *Ideario político*, ed. Edmundo O'Gorman (Caracas: Biblioteca Ayacucho, 1978), 236–32.

53. Nettie Lee Benson, "Servando Teresa de Mier, Federalist," *Hispanic American Historical Review* 28, no. 4 (November 1948): 515.

54. Mier to Bello (19 de noviembre 1826) reprinted in Ernesto Mejía Sánchez, "Don Andrés Bello y el Doctor Mier," *Anuario de Letras* 10 (1972): 129.

SUGGESTED READINGS

Anna, Timothy. *Forging Mexico, 1821–1835*. Lincoln: University of Nebraska Press, 1998.

_____. *The Fall of Royal Government in Mexico City*. Lincoln: University of Nebraska Press, 1978.

Arenas, Reinaldo. *Hallucinations, Being an Account of the Life and Adventures of Fray Servando Teresa de Mier*. Translated by Gordon Brotherston. New York: Harper and Row, 1971.

Benson, Nettie Lee. "Servando Teresa de Mier, Federalist." *Hispanic American Historical Review* 28, no. 4 (November 1948): 514–25.

Berruezo León, María Teresa. *La lucha de Hispanoamérica por su independencia en Inglaterra, 1800–1830*. Madrid: Ediciones de Cultura Hispánica, 1989.

Hale, Charles. *Mexican Liberalism in the Age of Mora, 1821–1853*. New Haven: Yale University Press, 1968.

Jara, René. "The Inscription of Creole Consciousness: Fray Servando Teresa de Mier." In *1492–1991: Re/Discovering Colonial Writing*, ed. René Jara and Nicholas Spadacchini. Minneapolis: The Prisma Institute, 1989.

Jiménez Codinach and Estela Guadalupe. *La Gran Bretaña y la Independencia de México, 1808–21*. México: Fondo de Cultura Económica, 1991.

Lewis, William Francis III. "Xavier Mina and Fray Servando Mier: Romantic Liberals of the Nineteenth Century." *New Mexico Historical Review* 44, no. 2 (April 1969): 119–36.

Lombardi, John. *The Political Ideology of Fray Servando Teresa de Mier*. Cuernavaca: CIDOC, 1968.

Pi Sunyer, Carlos. *Patriotas americanos en Londres*. Caracas: Monte Avila Editores, 1978.

Rodríguez O., Jaime E., ed. *Mexico in the Age of Democratic Revolutions, 1750–1850*. Boulder: Lynne Rienner, 1994.

_____. *The Origins of Mexican National Politics*. Wilmington, DE: Scholarly Resources, 1997.

Ross, Kathleen. "A Natural History of the Old World: The *Memorias* of Fray Servando Teresa de Mier." *Revista de Estudios Hispánicos* 23, no. 3 (1989): 87–99.

Silva Herzog, Jesús. "Fray Servando Teresa de Mier." *Cuadernos Americanos* 154, no. 5 (1967): 162–69.

Stevens, Donald Fithian. *Origins of Instability in Early Republican Mexico.* Durham: Duke University Press, 1991.

Valle-Arispe, Artemio de. *Fray Servando*. Buenos Aires: Espasa-Calpe, 1952.

$\mathcal{L}ucas\ \mathcal{B}alderas$

Popular Leader and Patriot

PEDRO SANTONI

 *Balderas, the cannon at the inter-section of the pink and green metro lines (numbers 1 and 3), is one of the busiest metro stops in Mexico City. Along with the crowds who pass through the station each day on their way somewhere else, there are many young people who have come to visit the Ciudadela, an old fortress that has been converted into one of the finest public libraries in Mexico. The sight of such working-class children going through his station on the way to do their homework would surely warm the heart of the crusty old war hero, Lucas Balderas.*

Historical views of the urban masses long reflected the fear and loath-ing of the elite, and nowhere more so than in nineteenth-century Mexico City. In an attempt to reassure themselves of their own pure Spanish an-cestry, Creole aristocrats commissioned series of paintings depicting the racial mixtures found among the so-called castas. *These family portraits, with titles such as "Spaniard and Indian beget mestizo," portrayed the social deviance supposedly caused by the contamination of Native Ameri-can and African blood. After Independence, the elite blamed the lower classes for Mexico's political instability and sought to restrict the franchise to property owners.*

Nevertheless, recent research by Virginia Guedea, Silvia Arrom, Ri-chard Warren, and others has substantially revised this picture of plebeian Mexico City. Their scholarship has revealed the sophistication of the work-ing classes, who informed themselves about political questions, voted regu-larly, and resorted at times to mass demonstrations to ensure that their voices were heard. This essay considers the career of one of the most impor-tant popular politicians of the early republic, a tailor named Lucas Balderas, whose service to the nation during its greatest crisis, the U.S. invasion, amply justified his claims for citizenship. Nevertheless, his biography also demonstrates the ever-present threat of political corruption, while at the same time raising the intriguing question of just who was responsible for the radicalization and fragmentation of Mexican politics, the rabble or the elite?

Pedro Santoni received his Ph.D. at El Colegio de México. A leading authority on the U.S.–Mexican War, he is the author of Mexicans at Arms: Puro Federalists and the Politics of War, 1845–1848 *(1996), and is currently writing a general history of the conflict as well as a broad study of National Guard politics in nineteenth-century Mexico. He is professor of history at California State University, San Bernardino.*

Personalist leadership has played an important role in Mexican history, as the careers of well-known individuals like General Antonio López de Santa Anna, Benito Juárez, and Porfirio Díaz attest. These and other prominent military leaders and statesmen, however, were not the sole actors in the complex political struggles that characterized nineteenth-century Mexico. The urban middle and lower middle classes, groups largely made up of small traders and artisans, also significantly influenced the country's public affairs in the years after Independence. This essay scrutinizes the endeavors of one well-known representative of the so-called popular sectors, a Mexico City tailor and National Guard colonel named Lucas Balderas. Not only did Balderas become an important political broker for the capital's urban poor between the 1820s and the war with the United States (1846–1848), but he also displayed selfless patriotism in the bloodiest engagement of that conflict—the September 8, 1847, Battle of Molino del Rey. Balderas's activities shed much light on politics and society in early republican Mexico, as well as on the means employed by Mexican leaders through the nineteenth century and beyond to construct a sense of citizenship among residents of the nation.

Historians know relatively little about Balderas's early life. Born in 1797 to a poor family in present-day San Miguel de Allende, state of Guanajuato, his parents could not provide him with a formal education. Nonetheless, Balderas learned to read and write, gained some knowledge of elementary mathematical concepts, and began working as an apprentice to a tailor. His family had moved to Mexico City by 1815, at which time Balderas found employment (probably as an unpaid apprentice) in a leading tailor shop owned by a Spaniard named Manuel Alcalde. Two years later he married an orphan, María Arauz, with whom he fathered several children, and thereafter worked diligently to learn the craft, become a master artisan, and improve his social status. In the process Balderas contracted tuberculosis and nearly died, but Alcalde's kindness helped him overcome the ravages of the disease. More importantly, Balderas's dedication had so impressed Alcalde that he cut short the apprenticeship (although no general rule existed, apprenticeships could last over eight years) and allowed his employee to rise to the position of journeyman, where he could either labor for a salary or be paid for piecework.

Besides his family and work responsibilities, Balderas spent much time polishing his military skills. In November 1815 he enrolled in the Fieles de Fernando VII, a volunteer royalist militia unit created in October 1810 by Viceroy Francisco Javier Venegas to help defend the capital against an insurgent attack. It is not clear whether Balderas joined that force at Alcalde's urging or because of his penchant for military life, which he acquired during his youth when he accompanied his father, a sergeant in the Spanish armed forces in Mexico, on various excursions. In any case, Balderas served in the Fieles de Fernando VII until the unit's disbandment in 1820. The Fieles probably broke up because the restored 1812 Cádiz Constitution, a charter that to a great extent enhanced local self-government, allowed municipal authorities to abolish militia support taxes. Their dispersal, however, did not end Balderas's avocation for martial affairs. He continued to sharpen his ability to handle weapons, and the military prowess he developed earned him a reputation as one of the best in the field. Guillermo Prieto, a keen contemporary observer and one of nineteenth-century Mexico's most prominent literary figures, referred to Balderas as an "admirable rider and swordsman."[1]

As Balderas's fortunes prospered, Mexico neared the end of its struggle for independence from Spain, which it achieved in September 1821. Following a short-lived empire (May 1822–March 1823) under Agustín de Iturbide, statesmen debated what type of government to adopt, and in 1824 the country became a federal republic. The new constitution preserved certain features reminiscent of the Spanish colonial regime—such as making Catholicism the official religion and guaranteeing special legal privileges for both the Church and the army—as it upheld progressive principles like that of popular sovereignty by granting broad suffrage rights to adult males. The 1824 constitution also awarded states even more power than states had in the United States at the time. Each state legislature, for instance, had one vote to elect the nation's president. The federal charter awakened expectations of grandeur. Mexico's first elected president, General Guadalupe Victoria (1824–1828), believed that the constitution would allow the country to "leave behind ignominy and slavery" and raise itself to the "noble rank of free, independent, and sovereign nations."[2]

Bitter partisan politics, however, were among the factors that prevented such hopes from becoming a reality. Mexico City became a cauldron of political activity in the mid-1820s as competing factions, organized around Masonic lodges, tried to gain or preserve power at the national, state, and local levels. Scottish Rite lodges, first established in 1816 by Spanish officers sent to fight the insurgents, "became the secret hub of aristocratic, centralist, and Spanish elements" after Independence.[3] *Escoceses*, as their members came to be known, sympathized with the colonial experience and wielded a great deal of clout in the Victoria administration. To offset such influence, a number of radical politicians, eager to gain greater leverage in government, established the York Rite lodge in 1825. By the end of the year these men and their accomplices (who came to be identified as *yorkinos*) had begun to mobilize the capital's urban masses in the pursuit of political power and electoral victory. To elicit popular support they demanded the expulsion of the Spaniards, who provided a visible reminder of the former colonial order, were thought to be exploiters of Mexico's wealth, and seemed a potential threat to the country's independence.

Balderas's status as a journeyman who aspired to become a master artisan probably led to his involvement in these affairs. Recent research has suggested that artisans represented the most politically active sector of Mexico City's population in the postindependence era. He joined the York Rite lodge shortly after its establishment, and he used one of the two public posts that he held at the time to further the *yorkinos'* political ascendancy. Balderas served as one of the hundred primary electors chosen for the oldest and largest of the capital's fourteen parishes (Sagrario), the city's basic electoral unit, in the August 1826 congressional elections. Parish-based voting allowed political factions to rally large numbers of people to a small group of candidates by printing reams of prefabricated ballots and recruiting election-day mobs, and Balderas almost certainly gathered supporters to help manipulate the electoral process in favor of the *yorkinos*.

With assistance from Balderas and other popular leaders, the *yorkinos* swept the 1826 elections for national and state congresses, but their success at the polls did not suffice to guarantee the victory of their candidate, General Vicente Guerrero, in the presidential elections two years later. As a result, the *yorkinos* claimed fraud and instigated a revolt to put their nominee in power. Balderas used his other post as a public official to help lay the groundwork for the uprising. At the end of 1826, while still a journeyman tailor, Balderas was elected to the Mexico City town council. The selection symbolized the *yorkinos'* growing political influence, given that during the colonial era, town council members, generally speaking, came from rich families with standing in local society. In a secret meeting of the council held in October 1827, Balderas noted that the activities of Joaquín Arenas, an eccentric friar who many believed had orchestrated a conspiracy to restore Spanish rule, confirmed Spain's unceasing efforts to reconquer Mexico. To protect the nation's sovereignty, Balderas called for the strengthening of the National Guard (also known as the civic militia), which had been established in the early 1820s as a reserve force of citizen-soldiers to preserve domestic order and security as well as to curb the army's political strength until civilian power could be consolidated. By mid-1828 other Mexico City councilmen had followed Balderas's lead and taken additional steps to fortify this military force.

The stage was thus set for Balderas and the National Guard to play a prominent role in the events that culminated with the Parián Riot of 1828. When the rebellion to install Guerrero as president began on November 30 of that year, Balderas and a group of artillerymen under his command (he had held the rank of captain in the militia since mid-June 1827) took control of the Acordada jail. They demanded prompt implementation of stricter expulsion laws against the Spaniards than those issued in May and December 1827. Then, on December 4, a crowd of approximately 5,000 pillaged shops and stores in the Parián building in Mexico City's central square (the Zócalo). According to an anonymous account, the rioters' behavior upset Balderas. Believing that their actions discredited the *yorkinos*, he turned his troops against them and moved to reestablish order in the capital. Government authorities rewarded Balderas's comportment with two quick promotions in early January 1829, first to lieutenant colonel and then to colonel of the capital's militia artillery corps.

The Parián Riot proved to be a defining event in the history of early republican Mexico. Although restricted to a relatively small amount of time (between two to three hours and twelve at most) and place (the Parián, the National Palace, and some portals surrounding the Zócalo), the disturbance left a deep imprint on Mexican elites. General José María Tornel, then governor of the Federal District, recalled that "throughout that disgraceful day and all of the night . . . [insolent plebes] stole without intermission and committed abominable crimes, including murders in cold blood to dispute both valuable articles and trinkets that passed from the hands of one thief to another."[4] While Tornel's account undoubtedly exaggerated some facts, the report vividly illustrates how the chaos unleashed by the Parián Riot dampened the democratic idealism of the nascent republic. The well-to-do viewed the upheaval as the "inevitable culmination of the political enfranchisement of the urban poor" and came to fear that mass mobilization would lead to class warfare.[5]

Moderate and conservative politicians resolved after the Parián Riot to reclaim the political realm, and their opportunity came following Guerrero's ouster in December 1829 in a coup led by General Anastasio Bustamante. The new administration assumed that Mexicans hungered for peace and stability, and to achieve these goals the regime sought to make the political arena more hierarchical and to remove the mob as a political force. Not only did the Bustamante government begin to implement constitutional reforms that curbed the power of the states, but it also sought to end "noisy mass electioneering" by restricting suffrage to more clearly defined property-owning citizens.[6] The regime also harassed *yorkino* leaders, formed a spy network to monitor rival political activities, and orchestrated Guerrero's capture and execution in February 1831.

The harsh tactics of General Bustamante's administration helped create an opposition movement that assumed political and military forms, and Balderas soon joined its ranks. His populist inclinations and martial experience—which included having served in the 1829 campaign to repel the Spanish expedition under General Isidro Barradas that had landed in northeastern Mexico—made him a valuable ally, as did the fact that he had prospered professionally after the 1827 expulsion laws had forced Alcalde to leave the country. At that time, through unspecified arrangements with creditors, Balderas became the owner of his mentor's tailor shop. Under his supervision the store specialized in the manufacture of military apparel, a shift that broadened Balderas's set of influential acquaintances and cemented his place as a prominent member of the capital's political circles.

Balderas first collaborated with one of the Bustamante regime's most outspoken foes, an Ecuadorian named Vicente Rocafuerte. This man openly challenged the government through the publication of numerous pamphlets, the best known of which was a three-part tirade against the ministers (particularly Lucas Alamán), and through writings in a major daily newspaper, *El Fénix de la Libertad*. To ridicule Rocafuerte, a staunch advocate of religious tolerance, pro-government papers such as *El Toro* portrayed him as the high priest of a heretical Protestant cult who had convinced his disciples—one of whom they claimed was Balderas—to destroy the nation. In addition, Balderas participated in the armed efforts against General Bustamante's government. Late in April 1832 he organized a popular agitation in Toluca, a vital city due to its status as the capital of Mexico state, in favor of General Santa Anna, who headed the military forces that sought to topple the Bustamante administration. Although the historical record provides few details about that uprising, subsequent rebellions prospered. By late December, General Bustamante had lost control of the states and agreed to go into exile.

Balderas then renewed his labors as a champion of the capital's popular sectors. That December he and other Mexico City activists requested annulment of the 1830 municipal council elections. The vote had taken place in accordance with legislation issued by the Bustamante government in July 1830 that changed the basic electoral unit in the capital from the parish to smaller neighborhood units called *manzanas* in order to restrict access to the ballot box. Balderas and his fellow protesters contended that the election had been a sham because it had brought to office persons "who did not merit the confidence of the people."[7] In

June 1833, Vice President Valentín Gómez Farías (who had taken office that April but was in charge of the government because of President Santa Anna's alleged ill health) granted the petitioners' request. He dissolved the sitting municipal council and reinstated the 1829 members, who then moved to fan the flames of anti-Spanish fervor.

Such zeal, as well as Balderas's efforts in fueling it, became even more evident on June 23, 1833, when the Santa Anna–Gómez Farías administration issued the so-called *Ley del caso*. The measure ordered the expulsion for six years of fifty-one individuals considered enemies of the regime, all Spanish clergymen, as well as any other person "in the same circumstances" (thus the decree's name). Three days later Balderas capitalized on his close relationship with Manuel Reyes Veramendi, a virulent hispanophobe and *yorkino* activist with whom he had served on the Mexico City town council in the late 1820s, to push for strict enforcement of the *Ley del caso*. Available information does not reveal what public post, if any, Veramendi held at the time, but Balderas urged his comrade to stand strong on the expulsion issue because individual exceptions would discredit the government.

Nevertheless, the influence Balderas exerted in public affairs through these activities paled in comparison to that which he exercised with the citizen militias of the Federal District. In their efforts to eradicate all colonial vestiges from Mexico, Gómez Farías and a number of radical (*puro*) congressmen attempted to limit the influence of the regular army and build support for civilian government by expanding the civic militia. Thus, on April 16, 1833, the national legislature issued a law that called for the formation of popular militias in the Mexican capital. Balderas, in acknowledgment of his endeavors against General Bustamante, received a crucial appointment as inspector general of those forces, which consisted of three infantry battalions, one artillery brigade, and one squadron. The decree also assigned Balderas a yearly salary of 300 pesos for office expenses and bestowed him with limited patronage powers. Balderas, in his capacity as inspector general, could nominate individuals to fill slots as colonels and officers in the militia units.

It is likely that Balderas utilized the post of inspector general to mobilize the urban poor, given both his record of accomplishment as a *yorkino* activist and that the National Guard also constituted "a means of social advancement and of creating a clientele for aspiring individuals of modest social origin."[8] But even if Balderas did not use his patronage powers to rally the populace to the *puro* cause, the way in which the capital's militia units came to be organized revived old fears about the dangers of popular mobilization. British consul Richard Packenham maintained in mid-June 1833 that these regiments were "composed of the very dregs of the people, without discipline and subordination, and ready to take advantage of any opportunity to plunder and commit excesses."[9] The conservative Mexican priest Francisco de Paula de Arrangoiz y Berzábel, who had a career as a politician in various administrations and became an ardent advocate of General Santa Anna, echoed Packenham's sentiments. He characterized the militiamen as the "sweepings of the jail" and the "lowest portion of society."[10] The establishment of popular militias in the capital, coupled with the legislation drawn up by congressmen in late November 1833 that reduced the size of the regular army and entrusted the maintenance of internal peace to the civic militia, generated a significant amount of tension. The growing number of clashes that took place in the Federal District at that time between regular army troops and militiamen provided evidence of the rising strain.

The makeup of Mexico City's National Guard battalions and their conduct led the *puros*' enemies to censure Balderas's performance as inspector general, and such criticisms tested his patience. Early in April 1834, Balderas expressed a desire to take action against his leading detractor (an individual Balderas referred to only by his last name, Zelaeta), but he also noted that he would restrain himself in order not to discredit the government. Nonetheless, the constant disparagement disturbed Balderas and in mid-May he tried to quit his post. He allegedly wanted to devote more attention to his family, which he had neglected during the past year. The government did not accept Balderas's resignation at first, but two weeks later a newspaper entitled *Los Gracos* published an article that bitterly attacked him and renewed his conviction to walk out. After defending himself by writing to the editors of *El Fénix de la Libertad* and asking that the authors of such a scandalous essay identify themselves so that he could respond to the charges, Balderas again submitted his resignation as inspector general. The government accepted it late in June.

Despite such vilification, Balderas did not remain a private citizen dedicated to his tailor shop and his family. Late in 1835 a minority of legislators dismantled the federal republic, and Mexico experimented with various forms of centralized rule during the next eleven years in a failed attempt to consolidate a long-lasting, peaceful, and stable government. A sense of profound disillusionment began to permeate the political atmosphere, particularly among supporters of federalism, and Balderas became a leading conspirator. In the spring of 1840 he joined a cabal in Mexico City to overthrow General Anastasio Bustamante, who had assumed the presidency for a second time in 1837. The government uncovered the scheme and ordered the arrest of all plotters, leading to one of four incarcerations that Balderas endured throughout his political career. Four years later Balderas mobilized his supporters into a militia battalion and joined the *moderados* during the December 6, 1844, rebellion. The movement, which one eyewitness described as the "paragon of popular revolution," toppled Santa Anna, who had held the reins of power since early October 1841.[11]

Historians do not know the reasons that led Balderas to abandon his radical past and support the *moderados*, who feared the lower classes and believed that enrollment in the National Guard should be limited to property-owning citizens. The change in allegiances notwithstanding, some elites continued to perceive Balderas as a potential rabble-rouser. Opposition to the *moderado* regime that took power after the fall of Santa Anna had increased significantly by July 1845, in part because it disbanded the militias that had helped it in December 1844 and also due to its refusal to reinstate the federal constitution of 1824. The growing discontent gave rise to the rumor that Balderas, together with disgruntled *moderado* statesman Manuel Gómez Pedraza, planned to stage a popular mutiny in the Mexican capital and proclaim the restoration of federalism. Such allegations highlighted the continuing fears that the well-to-do had toward the urban poor, an attitude that contributed to the rebellion launched by General Mariano Paredes y Arrillaga in mid-December 1845. General Paredes blamed the *moderado* government for the numerous maladies that afflicted Mexico, including a failure to exert sufficient control over the populace. Balderas again assembled his militia battalion to defend the *moderados*, but he and his troops could do little to stop the takeover. Administration officials realized that resistance would be useless and ordered militia forces to disperse.

Balderas did not remain out of the limelight for long following General Paredes' coup d'état. By early 1846 the specter of war with the United States loomed over Mexico, and when hostilities broke out between both countries late that May, journalists and other thinkers of the day urged the Paredes administration to organize a National Guard that would assist the national defense effort. General Paredes and his associates did not heed these calls, as they feared that enemies of the regime would use the militia to stage its overthrow just as the *moderados* had done in December 1844 against Santa Anna. Such caution proved to be of little use. The *puros* overthrew General Paredes in early August 1846, and one month later they issued a decree reestablishing the National Guard. It seemed that Mexico would be able to set up properly organized militia units to provide armed support in the war against the United States.

Unfortunately for the national defense effort, the new militia failed to fulfill these lofty goals. As in the past, militia reorganization alarmed both *moderados* and conservatives, especially those who feared the political and military mobilization of the lower classes. Consequently, Mexico City's well-to-do raised their own National Guard units, which for the most part attracted individuals of high-ranking social positions and members of the classes exempted from service in the National Guard. They came to be known as the *polko* battalions after the polka, which had become the most popular dance of elite society. One *polko* unit, the Mina battalion (the moniker honored one of the heroes of the movement for Mexican independence, Francisco Javier Mina), did not fit this profile. The artisans who comprised the majority of the regiment's recruits had unanimously elected Balderas as their colonel early in October, and he put political loyalties ahead of class solidarity in casting his lot and that of the battalion with the *moderados*. Leaders of this faction then moved to bolster the public image of Mina's troops by accentuating their commonalities with the elite. To offset any perceptions of those recruits as rabble, the editors of the *moderado* newspaper *Don Simplicio* characterized them as "people with common sense" and as "honest citizens with a dependable livelihood."[12]

Balderas and his unit joined the other militia regiments backed by the *moderados* in battling the *puro*-controlled National Guard battalions during the February 1847 uprising commonly known as the "rebellion of the *polkos*." The mutiny highlighted not only the ever-present threat of social dissolution but also the inability of Mexican elites to set aside their differences even when confronted with a foreign invasion. Orchestrated by *moderado* and clerical leaders, the revolt erupted in response to the *puro* government's January 1847 decision to mortgage or sell ecclesiastical property in order to finance the war against the United States. The ensuing struggle between *puro* and *polko* militia units in the capital prevented the Mexican government not only from assisting the eastern port of Veracruz, which was under attack by General Winfield Scott and the U.S. expeditionary army and surrendered on March 29, but also from strengthening the city of Puebla and the fortifications near the coast.

Although the decision to fight a civil war in Mexico City instead of marching to Veracruz to protect the nation's territorial integrity stigmatized the *polko* battalions and their leaders, these units began to reassemble on the afternoon of August 9, 1847, shortly after clanging church bells announced that General Scott and the U.S. army were approaching the capital. In his capacity as general-in-chief of the Federal District, Santa Anna ordered the militiamen, some 10,000 strong, to proceed to El Peñón, a fortified 450-foot hill that guarded the eastern approach to Mexico City. Military tactics prevented the National Guard from challenging the U.S. army at this stronghold, but Mexico's citizen-soldiers fought bravely in subsequent battles for the capital. Balderas and the Mina battalion covered themselves with glory during the Battle of Molino del Rey.

The stage for this encounter was set in the aftermath of the U.S. victories over Mexican defenders at the August 20, 1847, Battles of

Contreras and Churubusco. General Scott had the opportunity to march into the capital following the triumphs, but his army was exhausted. Scott also decided not to move into Mexico City due to hints that Mexican statesmen desired peace; instead he offered them a short truce to allow serious negotiations to proceed. Talks between U.S. and Mexican representatives did not prosper, however, and on September 6, Scott ended the armistice. The U.S. commander then met with his subordinates to discuss what steps should be taken to capture Mexico City. Acting on the assumption that General Santa Anna was collecting church bells and having them cast into cannon at a building complex known as the Molino del Rey, located some two miles southwest of the capital and 1,000 yards west of Chapultepec Castle, Scott decided to launch an attack on that compound early on the morning of September 8.

The Mexican forces that defended the Molino del Rey included the brigade of General Antonio León, made up of an estimated 350 guardsmen each from the Unión, Querétaro, Libertad, and Mina National Guard battalions. Deployed in the stone mill buildings that made up the left side of the Mexican line, the militiamen twice helped repel attacking U.S. columns. Balderas demonstrated exemplary audacity, selflessness, and patriotism during the course of the battle. Although he suffered from arthritis, he brushed aside his family's request that he remain at home because his ailments would not allow him to withstand the rigor of military life, and he joined his unit when it assembled in August. Then, shortly after hostilities commenced at Molino del Rey, Balderas, mounted on a steed, suffered a leg wound that bled profusely. Nonetheless, he remained on his horse and led a charge to retake artillery pieces captured by U.S. forces. A cannonball struck Balderas as he advanced, but his combativeness did not desert him. Brandishing his sword, Balderas continued to fight on one knee until four of his men took him from the battlefield to a nearby hut. There, as he expired in the arms of his son, Balderas inquired about the status of the battle. His poignant last words were said to have been: "My poor country!"[13]

Despite Balderas's heroics, Mexican resistance concluded shortly after the Battle of Molino del Rey. U.S. forces maintained their pressure in that engagement and eventually drove the courageous Mexican defenders out of their positions and toward Chapultepec Castle. General Scott's troops stormed that stronghold on September 13 and pressed on into the capital, which surrendered on the following day. Scattered resistance by Mexican guerrilla forces continued throughout the next few months but did not reverse the tide of events. A succession of *moderado* leaders, demoralized by defeat and convinced that the most prudent course of action was to end hostilities, embarked on peace negotiations with the United States and eventually agreed to the Treaty of Guadalupe Hidalgo.

The heart of the accord, signed on February 2, 1848, ceded California and New Mexico to the United States, and confirmed the U.S. claim to Texas along the Rio Grande River in exchange for a payment of $15 million. When Mexico's congress ratified the treaty three months later, the war with the United States finally came to a close.

Peace with the United States, however, did not bring immediate unity to Mexico. The shock of military disaster scarred Mexican society and thinkers of the day feared that national existence was in jeopardy. The United States could take over at any moment, ethnic conflict threatened the country as well, and the acrimony set off by the war had heightened antagonisms between opposing political blocs. In addition, the specter of class warfare and social anarchy that hovered over Mexico City due to the "rebellion of the *polkos*" and the three-day popular mutiny that followed the U.S. army's entrance into the capital, in which members of the underclass attacked the U.S. troops with stones, bottles, and other loose objects, compounded the uneasiness. To reconstruct a politically and socially divided nation, heal the wounds of war, and solidify its own authority, the *moderado* regime, headed by General José Joaquín Herrera, decided to hold public celebrations in Mexico City late in the summer of 1848 and for some time beyond to commemorate the 1847 heroics of the *polko* battalions. Herrera and his cohorts sought to turn those militia units and their defunct leaders into patriotic icons and symbols of nationwide solidarity.

Balderas was ideally suited for this position. His demise had deeply touched his contemporaries, many of whom believed he possessed the most genuine public spirit, and government officials and public-spirited citizens conferred upon him a prominent place in the pantheon of Mexican heroes. As the first anniversary of the Battle of Molino del Rey drew near, newspapers in Mexico City reminded their readers of the fallen hero's bravery by publishing at least six poems that commemorated that encounter and lamented Balderas's passing. In addition, public officials held a solemn memorial service in his honor on September 13, and speakers at observances such as the September 16 anniversary of the cry that in 1810 had ignited the movement for independence, Father Miguel Hidalgo y Costilla's "Grito de Dolores," took care to eulogize Balderas. The main orator on that occasion was José María Iglesias, chief editor of the *moderado* mouthpiece *El Siglo XIX*. As he praised the sacrifices made by national guardsmen in the defense of Mexico City, Iglesias remarked that Mexicans could take heart that "several feats of valor and patriotism prove[d] that we did not lack illustrious men who preferred death rather than vilification." The death of Balderas, among others, was "nothing to be ashamed of when compared to the most illustrious defenders of other nations." His name and those of the other martyrs were "already consigned to history: their memory will not perish as long as Mexico survives, and on every anniversary [of Independence] they will partake of the homage rendered to other erstwhile heroes."[14]

Balderas did not fade from the public memory during the 1850s and 1860s. Mexican statesmen of distinct political persuasions, such as Santa Anna and *moderado* enthusiast General Ignacio Comonfort, endeavored to enhance and legitimize their power by celebrating the achievements of the national guardsmen who had died defending Mexico City in 1847. Both men memorialized Balderas in a variety of ways. Santa Anna posthumously promoted him to artillery colonel in the regular army, while Comonfort not only named a new Mexico City-based National Guard regiment after him but also built a monument to commemorate the combatants of the Battle of Molino del Rey in which he interred Balderas's ashes. In addition, the Reform legislation of the mid-1850s that mortgaged and nationalized Church wealth allowed residents of the capital to further recall Balderas. These laws helped change Mexico City's layout from one dominated by religious buildings into a modern, secular landscape. Governmental authorities broke up several churches and convents to build sixteen new streets, and named one of the boulevards that opened in 1868 in honor of Balderas. This avenue remains one of Mexico City's most prominent.

By the late 1800s, however, the high profile given in public ceremony to militiamen like Balderas had dwindled significantly. The transformation of the National Guard following the war with the United States into an institution that personified democratic and popular aspirations, particularly in the mountainous regions of the states of Puebla and Morelos, contributed to its reduced stature. Such a military force did not fit with the nation-building project of Reform leaders and Porfirio Díaz, who moved to distance popular elements from the reemerging Mexican state. Not only did they repress the National Guard but Díaz and his supporters also replaced it as an institution emblematic of Mexican patriotism and nationhood, substituting other symbols more to their liking. The most famous of the new images were the *Niños Héroes*, the six cadets from the national military academy (Colegio Militar) who in September 1847 helped to defend Chapultepec Castle against the U.S. forces and supposedly chose to die rather than surrender to their adversaries. Legend has it that one of the plebes, Juan Escutia, wrapped the Mexican flag around his body and jumped over the battlements to his death.

Balderas, nonetheless, has not entirely faded from the Mexican collective memory. One of the stops on line 3 of Mexico City's subway system, which traverses the capital from the National University (UNAM) in the south to Indios Verdes in the north, is named in Balderas's honor; an artillery cannon pictorially represents the station. In addition, public officials in Balderas's hometown of San Miguel de Allende continue to remember their native son. Every September 8 local political and cultural leaders sponsor a commemorative service at the city's main plaza that pays homage to this heroic Mexican. Finally, an unexpected set of circumstances allowed Balderas to receive another elaborate tribute in the closing decades of the twentieth century. Early in February 1985 the heavy machinery used by a construction crew charged with building a subway line near the presidential residence in Los Pinos broke the base of the monument that commemorated the Battle of Molino del Rey. The mishap, however, uncovered twelve urns that contained the mortal residues of various Mexican soldiers. Personnel from the National Institute of Anthropology and History rushed to the site, where they labored for several months to preserve the memorial and identify the remains of the fallen troops, which included Balderas. Their efforts culminated with a stirring ceremony held that September 8, when cadets from the Colegio Militar transported the urns to the monument's new location near Rosario Castellanos Park, located at the junction of the Periférico and the Paseo de los Compositores.

To this day Balderas's name resonates in Mexican patriotic discourse mainly because of the heroism he displayed defending Mexico's territorial integrity at the Battle of Molino del Rey. His manifold political endeavors and their significance, however, are also deserving of public and scholarly recognition. Indeed, Balderas's activities as a *yorkino* activist, member of the capital's municipal government, conspirator, and militia officer speak loudly of the strategic role in nineteenth-century Mexico of the urban masses and their leaders. Poor residents of Mexico City and the individuals who mobilized them were not mere pawns that elites manipulated at will and used "as a battering ram in the political struggle."[15] Rather, popular chiefs like Balderas served as middlemen who linked the general populace with the well-to-do, and in doing so allowed the former to become active participants in the process of creating a Mexican nation.

NOTES

1. Guillermo Prieto, *Memorias de mis tiempos* (Mexico City: Editorial Porrúa, 1985), 253.

2. "Discurso que pronunció el presidente del supremo poder ejecutivo, general don Guadalupe Victoria, después de haber jurado en el salon del soberano Congreso la constitución federal," Mexico City, October 4, 1824, in *El Aguila Mexicana*, October 6, 1824.

3. Timothy Anna, *Forging Mexico, 1821–1835* (Lincoln: University of Nebraska Press, 1998), 168.

4. José María Tornel y Mendivil, *Breve reseña histórica de los acontecimientos más notables de la nación mexicana, desde el año de 1821 hasta nuestros días* (Mexico City: Imprenta de Cumplido, 1852), 393–94, 403, quoted by Silvia Arrom, "Popular Politics in Mexico City: The Parián Riot, 1828," *Hispanic American Historical Review*, 68:2 (May 1988), 245.

5. Richard A. Warren, *Vagrants and Citizens: Politics and the Masses in Mexico City from Colony to Republic* (Wilmington, DE: Scholarly Resources, 2001), 91.

6. Stanley C. Green, *The Mexican Republic: The First Decade, 1823–1832* (Pittsburgh: University of Pittsburgh Press, 1987), 191.

7. Archivo General de la Nación, Ayuntamiento, December 30, 1832, vol. 16, 121 ff., quoted by Richard A. Warren, "Election and Popular Political Participation in Mexico, 1808–1836," in *Liberals, Politics, and Power: State Formation in Nineteenth-Century Latin America*, eds. Vincent C. Peloso and Barbara A. Tenembaum (Athens: University of Georgia Press, 1996), 46.

8. Anna, *Forging Mexico*, 125.

9. Richard Packenham to Lord Palmerston, June 11, 1833, Great Britain, Public Record Office, Archives of the Foreign Office, Mexico (F.O. 50), vol. 79, 241–46, quoted by Donald Fithian Stevens, *Origins of Instability in Early Republican Mexico* (Durham: Duke University Press, 1991), 34.

10. Francisco de Paula de Arrangoiz y Berzábel, *Méjico desde 1808 hasta 1867*, 4 vols. (Madrid: Imprenta a cargo de Estrada, 1871–1872), 2:217, quoted by Frederick J. Shaw, "Poverty and Politics in Mexico City: 1824–1854" (Ph.D. diss., University of Florida, 1975), 329.

11. Prieto, *Memorias*, 236.

12. *Don Simplicio*, October 17, 1846.

13. María Elena Salas Cuesta, coord., *Molino del Rey: historia de un monumento* (Mexico City: Consejo Nacional para la Cultura y las Artes, 1997), 226.

14. José María Iglesias, "Discurso pronunciado el 16 de septiembre de 1848, por el ciudadano Lic. José María Iglesias, en el aniversario de la proclamación de la independencia nacional," in *El Monitor Republicano*, September 17, 1848.

15. Torcuato S. Di Tella, *National Popular Politics in Early Independent Mexico, 1820–1847* (Albuquerque: University of New Mexico Press, 1996), 247.

SUGGESTED READINGS

In addition to the works cited in the Notes, which shed light on Balderas's life as well as on the participation of the urban poor in early nineteenth-century politics, additional insight into the political, social, and economic conditions that characterized early republican Mexico can be found in Will Fowler, *Mexico in the Age of Proposals, 1821–1853* (Westport: Greenwood Press, 1998); Michael P. Costeloe, *La primera república federal de México (1824–1835)*, trans. Manuel Fernández Gasallo (Mexico City: Fondo de Cultura Económica, 1975); and *The Central Republic in Mexico, 1835–1846: Hombres de Bien in the Age of Santa Anna* (New York: Cambridge University Press, 1993). For an insightful assessment of the anti-Spanish rancor, see Harold Dana Sims, *The Expulsion of Mexico's Spaniards, 1821–1836* (Pittsburgh: University of Pittsburgh Press, 1990).

The role of the National Guard during the early nineteenth century has been analyzed by Fernando Escalante Gonzalbo, *Ciudadanos imaginarios: Memorial de los afanes y desventuras de la virtud y apología del vicio triunfante en la república mexicana: Tratado de moral pública* (Mexico City: El Colegio de México, 1992), 197–206; Juan Ortiz Escamilla, "Las fuerzas militares y el proyecto de estado en México, 1767–1835," in *Cincuenta años de historia en México*, coords. Alicia Hernández Chávez and Manuel Miño Grijalva, 2 vols. (Mexico City: El Colegio de México, 1991), 2: 272–79; Pedro Santoni, "A Fear of the People: The Civic Militia of Mexico in 1845," *Hispanic American Historical Review*, 68:2 (May 1988), 269–88; and "The Failure of Mobilization: The Civic Militia of Mexico in 1846," *Mexican Studies/Estudios Mexicanos* 12:2 (Summer 1996), 169–94.

Accounts of Mexican politics during the war with the United States include Michael P. Costeloe, "The Mexican Church and the Rebellion of the *Polkos*," *Hispanic American Historical Review*, 46:2 (May 1966), 170–78; Pedro Santoni, *Mexicans at Arms: Puro Federalists and the Politics of War, 1845–1848* (Fort Worth: Texas Christian University Press, 1996); and Miguel Soto, *La conspiración monárquica en México, 1845–1846* (Mexico City: EOSA, 1988). For an in-depth analysis of the strategic shortcomings of and operational blunders committed by General Antonio López de Santa Anna and other Mexican generals during that conflict, see William A. DePalo Jr., *The Mexican National Army, 1822–1852* (College Station, TX: Texas A&M University Press, 1997).

The material on Balderas's activities during the Battle of Molino del Rey and his posthumous exaltation was largely drawn from Pedro Santoni's research on the rituals that were intended to posthumously honor the *polko* National Guard battalions and their fallen commanders. Particularly valuable in this regard are the articles, poems, and editorials published in three Mexico City newspapers—*El Siglo XIX*, *El Monitor Republicano*, and *El Eco del Comercio*—as well as the writings of two of the period's most prolific commentators, Guillermo Prieto and Carlos María Bustamante.

PART II

HEIRS OF THE REFORMA, 1850–1910

The Liberal Reform sought to establish a stable government on the principles of democratic capitalism, thereby freeing Mexico from the palace coups of the early republic and creating the conditions for material progress. Conservative opponents, led by army officers and Catholic priests, resisted this program in a decade-long civil war that culminated with a French invasion and the imposition of the Austrian archduke Maximilian as emperor of Mexico. Liberal forces under President Benito Juárez defeated the foreign invaders and their Mexican allies, but the government ultimately sacrificed its democratic ideals in an illusory quest for capitalist progress.

The Reform movement began in 1854 as an uprising by provincial leaders against the dictatorship of Santa Anna. Once in power, the liberals set about codifying a secular society in the Constitution of 1857, which established the principle of individual equality before the law and revoked the special privileges of the military and the clergy. Another important liberal provision, the Lerdo Law, drafted by Finance Minister Miguel Lerdo de Tejada, prohibited ecclesiastical and civil institutions from owning property. By selling off Church holdings as well as the communal lands of Indian villages, the law sought to create a market-oriented society based on private property. But because campesinos had neither cash nor credit to purchase the land at auction, the benefits fell primarily to the wealthy. Indigenous communities fought for decades against this attempt to disentail their land, using legal experience accumulated during the colonial period in resisting the encroachment of Spanish and mestizo landowners. Despite the apparent common cause between communal landholders and the Church, however, countless Native American villages mobilized to defend the liberal government during the civil wars that followed.

A military coup against the liberal government in 1858 launched the first stage of the fighting, the War of the Reform. Benito Juárez established a provisional capital in the port city of Veracruz, and although conservative generals dominated the battlefield in the first year of the war, liberal recruits eventually turned the tide, marching triumphantly into Mexico City on New Year's Day in 1861. The peace lasted scarcely a year, for conservative exiles appealed to the French ruler Napoleon III, who hoped to take advantage of the Civil War in the United States to build an empire in the Americas. Mexican troops repelled the initial invasion at the Battle of Puebla on May 5, 1862, a victory celebrated as the Cinco de Mayo, but with significant reinforcements, the French occupied Mexico City the following year. Maximilian and Carlota arrived in 1864 with promises from Napoleon of the unconditional support of French troops. Nevertheless, fierce resistance by Mexican guerrilla forces prevented Maximilian from consolidating his hold on the countryside, and a combination of U.S. diplomatic pressure and the fear of Prussian aggression forced Napoleon to renege on his promises. When French troops evacuated the country, liberal forces quickly dispatched the remaining Mexican conservative forces and extinguished the Second Empire (Chapter 4).

Benito Juárez had held the nation together during the mid-century civil wars, but unity within the liberal ranks had already begun to fray, even before his death in 1872. At least three rival interpretations of liberalism contended for influence under the lengthy presidential administration of Porfirio Díaz. A hero of the Battle of Puebla, Díaz first came to power through the Revolution of Tuxtepec in 1876, calling for "effective suffrage and no re-election." But after stepping down briefly from 1880 to 1884, he held on as dictator until 1911. While flaunting liberal democracy, the government gave increasing emphasis to capitalist development. Administrators adopted the positivist slogan of "order and progress," stifling domestic opposition in order to provide a safe and profitable environment for foreign investment (Chapter 6). Exports boomed from mines as well as from plantations dedicated to monoculture, such as the henequen fiber grown in the Yucatán peninsula. Workers shared little of the benefits from this economic growth, however, for the Porfirian dictatorship repressed trade unions while campesinos labored in slavelike conditions on many plantations.

Meanwhile, a version of folk liberalism took root in the countryside among soldiers who had served in the wars of the Reform and the French Intervention. Having defended Mexico against foreign invasion, these peasants had acquired a sense of national identity and a belief in local democracy. Yet they rejected the individualism inherent within European liberalism and imagined the nation as a union of ethnic communities. They also used their records of service to protect communal land from encroachment under the Lerdo Law. As a result, the Porfirian government faced the difficult task of maintaining peace in the countryside by relying on caciques (regional bosses) who had served with Díaz in the liberal army but who also supported the rights of local communities (Chapter 5).

A third strand of liberalism emerged at the turn of the century in response to the broken promises of the Porfiriato. Liberal newspaper editors such as Filomeno Mata of the *Diario del Hogar* and Daniel Cabrera of the satirical *El Hijo del Ahuizote* were jailed regularly for articles criti-cal of Díaz's perpetual reelection and of political repression. About 1900, Camilo Arriaga began organizing opposition clubs to protest the regime's rapprochement with the Catholic Church, forsaking liberal sacrifices during the wars of the Reform. The plight of Porfirian campesinos and industrial workers attracted the attention of Ricardo and Enrique Flores Magón, publishers of *Regeneración*, who abandoned their calls for liberal reformism and became anarchists committed to social revolution. Nev-ertheless, even the Flores Magón brothers betrayed a reactionary streak when confronted with feminist radicals (Chapter 7).

A final trend of the late nineteenth century was the rise of northern Mexico as a dynamic and increasingly independent region. The desolate lands of *la frontera* had once been settled only lightly by Hispanics, but the pacification of nomadic Indians and the arrival of railroads suddenly made it possible to exploit mineral and agricultural wealth. Nuevo Laredo, Ciudad Juárez, and Nogales boomed with cross-border commerce, while Monterrey and Torreón became thriving industrial centers. With this dynamism came increasing social tensions; a strike at the Cananea cop-per mine in Sonora was crushed in 1906 by a combined force of Mexican rural police and Arizona Rangers. But just four years later, Francisco I. Madero, a wealthy landowner from the border state of Coahuila, began the revolution that toppled Díaz and transformed Mexico.

CHAPTER FOUR

Agnes Salm-Salm

An American Princess in Maximilian's Mexico

DAVID COFFEY AND EUGENIA ROLDÁN VERA

Perhaps the best way to experience the nineteenth-century splendor of Mexico City's historic center is to start on the blue line at Metro Allende, among buildings that would seem appropriate in the Paris of Napoleon III. You do not even need to stroll about the neighborhood, for just a few steps from the subway exit is the Café Tacuba, one of the oldest restaurants in the city. Sitting inside on a quiet afternoon and sipping the potent café con leche *transports you back a hundred years to another venerable dining spot. La Concordia, located just a block south on Plateros Street (now Francisco Madero), had been* the place for sophisticated Continental cuisine since the days of Mexico's Second Empire. Visitors even claimed that the restaurant was haunted by "memories of Austrian and French officers stalking down through its mirrored rooms."[1]*

Between the glamour of European culture and the intrigue of a doomed royal court, the final days of Maximilian's empire continue to this day to captivate the Mexican imagination. Once Napoleon III had withdrawn his troops, the noble but misguided Hapsburg had little hope of defeating the liberal armies under Benito Juárez; indeed, the emperor seemed to welcome his own execution. Nevertheless, a handful of loyal supporters used every expedient to try to save Maximilian's life, even after his final capture and court-martial. Agnes Salm-Salm, the wife of a German prince, took the lead in this effort, alternately trying to arrange an escape, charm liberal commanders, and even plead with President Juárez. Maximilian's fate was decided by politics, not personal appeals, but the legend of Princess Salm-Salm remains a vital part of this intriguing episode in Mexican history.

David Coffey holds a doctorate from Texas Christian University and teaches U.S. and Latin American history at the University of Tennessee at Martin. He is the author of Soldier Princess: The Life and Legend of Agnes Salm-Salm in North America, 1861–1867 *(2002) and* John Bell Hood and the Struggle for Atlanta *(1998). Eugenia Roldán Vera, a graduate of the National Autonomous University of Mexico, received her Ph.D. from the University of Cambridge and is a fellow at Humboldt*

Universität, Berlin. She is the author of a forthcoming book on trade between Britain and Spanish America in the early independence era.

When ambitious French ruler Napoleon III created an empire in Mexico, or, as it was, an empire within his own empire, he initiated a sad experiment that brought more bloodshed to the already saturated young nation and ended only in the sacrificial execution of Mexico's emperor, Maximilian. The "Mexican Adventure" featured a colorful cast of characters, from Mexican monarchists and Continental dignitaries to elite Austrian hussars, French legionnaires, and soldiers of fortune from around the world. Of all the would-be courtiers, hired swords, and low opportunists to flock to Maximilian's Mexico, one of the most compelling and, indeed, unlikely players in the unfolding tragedy was a mysterious young woman from Vermont, who carried the equally unlikely name of Princess Agnes Salm-Salm. No one played a more active or more controversial role in the events of Maximilian's final days, and perhaps no one did more to try to save the ill-starred emperor's life than did Agnes Salm-Salm. Her truly heroic effort, obscured (or enhanced) by tales of sexual intrigue and over-the-top theatrics, became one of the most celebrated features of the period.

Just how Agnes Salm-Salm came to be in Mexico at such a pivotal moment in history was a rather remarkable story in itself. She appeared at Washington, DC, shortly after the onset of the Civil War. According to her memoir, she had spent many years in Cuba, but she gave no further details about her early life. In fact, little of her personal history—even the date and place of birth—was known with certainty. Most likely, Agnes Elisabeth Winona LeClerq Joy was born at Swanton, Vermont, on Christmas Day 1844. Her name alone spawned wild speculation about her past. Rumor had it that as a youth she performed in a circus as an equestrienne, something she later denied. However she spent her formative years hardly mattered, because in 1862 she reinvented herself. That year Agnes met and married the man who changed her life—Prince Felix zu Salm-Salm, the perpetually indebted brother of the reigning prince of a small German state, who served as a volunteer officer in the Union army.

Agnes's Civil War exploits made her something of a celebrity, even if much of what passed into history was little better than myth. In later years she would be lionized as a warrior princess, fighting beside her husband and caring for the sick and wounded on the battlefield. It was widely reported that she received a captain's commission and, in an outrageous stretch of the imagination, that she commanded troops during General William T. Sherman's March to the Sea. Although she may have garnered an honorary captaincy, the rest was pure fiction. She did have some adventures, such as witnessing the New York Draft Riots, but she spent most of the war promoting her husband's interests and cultivating influential friends, which prompted much sexual innuendo. Indeed, Agnes often acted as if the war was staged for her personal amusement. In perhaps her greatest wartime triumph, she managed to wrangle a brevet promotion to brigadier general of U.S. Volunteers for her husband, who, while brave and even talented, hardly rated such recognition.[2]

With the war over and prospects of glory diminished, the Salm-Salms looked for a new opportunity. Felix had once served in the Austrian army and held high regard for the young Archduke Maximilian, who now ruled the French-sponsored Empire of Mexico. It appeared to be an ideal match. So, with a handful of lofty recommendations, the mercenary prince sailed for Veracruz. Headstrong Agnes would join him there.

But the adventurous couple had made a foolish, potentially deadly decision. In March 1866, Mexico was a most dangerous place, especially for European royalty. The conditions that allowed the empire to take root no longer existed. Rising anti-imperialist sentiment, bolstered by the resurgence of republican military forces and the noble persistence of President Benito Juárez, had loosened the imperialist grip on Mexico while mounting tensions between France and Prussia siphoned off French support for Maximilian's government; and the United States, free of its own Civil War, had stationed 50,000 battle-tested soldiers in Texas to emphasize its displeasure with Napoleon's egregious violation of the Monroe Doctrine. Maximilian's days were numbered, and the Salm-Salms should have recognized it. So, at a time when most Europeans looked desperately for ways out of Mexico, the Salm-Salms wanted in.[3]

In Mexico, Felix Salm-Salm found nothing of the warm welcome he expected, and his German pedigree only impeded his search for a position in the imperial government. Inconveniently, Prussia and Austria were on the verge of war (a bloody seven-week war that ended with the decisive Prussian victory at Sadowa). But in Mexico, Old World animosities could be set aside; Maximilian needed all the friends he could get. The Prussian minister to Mexico, Baron Anton von Magnus finally arranged an audience for Felix with Maximilian, who welcomed Salm's support. On July 1, 1866, the prince received an appointment as colonel in the Imperial Army. With a position secured, he summoned Princess Agnes, who arrived with her terrier Jimmy in August.[4]

Agnes, too, found her introduction to Mexico inauspicious, if not disturbing. Of Veracruz, she wrote, "you feel a shuddering creep over your whole body, for you are entering an atmosphere reminding you of the catacombs, coming from the surrounding swamps from which a tropical sun distills poisons." She found the colonial cities of Orizaba and

Puebla more appealing; and Mexico offered a wealth of new experiences—tortillas and pulque—and a mixture of exotic scenery. But Agnes had no interest in Mexico and no understanding of its people or its history, into which she now launched herself.[5]

Upon their arrival at Mexico City the couple was recruited for a diplomatic mission to Washington, where presumably they might use their influence to secure U.S. recognition of the empire. According to Agnes, Baron von Magnus approached her with the idea, "as I was well acquainted not only with President [Andrew] Johnson and most of the influential persons in the United States, but also with the best ways and means in which to work upon them." Despite Agnes's lofty opinion of her status among Washington's power elite, which was considerably over-estimated, the plan died. The United States solidly supported the Juárez regime. And, in reality, nothing could save the empire.[6]

France, in fact, had already given up on its Mexican adventure. Under orders from Marshal Achille Bazaine, the troops essential for the empire's survival had been retreating from frontier garrisons for months. And in late May 1866, Napoleon, bowing to U.S. pressure and concerns over Prussian intentions in Europe, announced the complete withdrawal of all French soldiers by the fall of 1867. This betrayal deprived Maximilian of his main source of support and left him in an untenable situation. His own liberal tendencies had alienated conservative supporters, yet as a foreign usurper, no matter how enlightened, he had no hope of gaining the support of Mexican liberals. Additionally, his few Mexican generals had failed to provide him with an imperial army strong enough to control the country once the foreign contingents departed. Finally, pressured by his conservative sponsors, Maximilian had reluctantly instituted heavy-handed measures, namely the infamous Black Decree, to counter pro-republican guerrilla activity. The Black Decree, which caused the executions of dozens of suspected republican sympathizers, cost him any hope of additional support and assured his own death sentence should the republicans regain power.

Maximilian's first impulse had been to abdicate, but the ambitious Empress Carlota appealed to his Hapsburg honor. He decided to hold out in Mexico while Carlota attempted to rally support in Europe. Her mission failed and soon so, too, did her mind. Swept into seclusion by her father, King Leopold II of Belgium, Carlota never saw Mexico or her husband again. Word of Carlota's collapse reached Maximilian in October 1866. Again he contemplated abdication, but he had nowhere to go—he had yielded his hereditary rights and his family had largely forsaken him. All that remained for him was his crumbling empire. He reviewed his remaining options and soon, buoyed by promises from his Mexican generals of the necessary funds and soldiers, announced that he would place himself at the head of an all-Mexican army and fight for a people and a country he still believed wanted him.

In the meantime, the Salm-Salms reviewed their options as well, and they also resolved to stay in Mexico. "An idle life was utterly disgusting to me," wrote Felix, "and I heartily desired to see active service in the field." Agnes added, "The life we were leading was pleasant enough, but my Hotspur Felix panted for war." He applied for and received permission to join Maximilian's Belgian contingent as a volunteer. In November he took the field, and Agnes and Jimmy went along, but it was to be a short-lived experience.[7] While campaigning north of Mexico City, the Belgian battalion received notice that it was to return to the capital and disband. Most foreign commands had been ordered to leave the country. The Salm-Salms should have availed themselves of this honorable exit, but they chose instead to stay.[8]

At Buena Vista, a popular stop on the road to Veracruz, Agnes caught the attention of nineteen-year-old American Sara Yorke (later Stevenson), who recalled that "we saw at some distance, against a background formed by the Belgian camp, Princess Salm-Salm, in her gray-and-silver uniform, sitting her horse like a female centaur." Miss Yorke, unlike most female observers of the day, offered a positive impression of Agnes, noting that the princess "shared the fatigues and dangers of camp life in war time—like a *Soldadera*, contemptuously said her proud sisters in society; for this mode of existence naturally drew upon her the criticism of the more conventional of her sex in the Mexican colony."[9]

The Salm-Salms learned of Maximilian's plan to fight for the empire and, in what amounted to a death wish, they cast their lot with him. The military situation had only gotten worse. When Maximilian refused to abdicate, the French accelerated their departure. In November 1866, Oaxaca fell to the republicans, followed soon by Guanajauto and San Luis Potosí, leaving only Mexico City, Puebla, Veracruz, and Querétaro in imperialist posession. The empire now controlled only a tiny fraction of Mexico. In this desperate atmosphere, Felix gained an audience with Maximilian. He received permission to raise a cavalry regiment from the various departing foreign contingents, but nothing came of this. He and Agnes moved on to Mexico City, still anxious to get into the action.[10]

On February 5, 1867, they watched from their hotel balcony as the last of the French troops marched out of the capital. Happy to be leaving Mexico, French soldiers chanted "Berlin," a reference to the looming showdown with Prussia. "I did not regard their talk," wrote Salm, "but I only wished to be in Berlin to meet them there." The French departure created great uncertainty and left the empire fully exposed, but most Mexicans on both sides of this freshly redefined civil war were happy to see them go.[11]

Imperialist commands from across the nation began to concentrate for a face-off with the republican forces at the colonial city of Querétaro. Since foreign troops had been ordered out of Mexico and granted safe passage, Juárez considered those remaining filibusters, subject to the death penalty. This should have added a final inducement for the Salm-Salms to get out while they could, but apparently the thought never crossed their minds. By the most generous reckoning, the Salm-Salms' decision to stay was reckless. At this point, Felix had not developed a strong personal relationship with Maximilian and Agnes had yet even to meet the emperor. Salm may have sensed an opportunity for glory in Mexico, but that did not explain Agnes's motivation; she had little to gain as things stood.[12]

As imperial Mexico braced for a final stand, Felix Salm-Salm remained unemployed. When he learned that Maximilian planned to take the field, he tried to secure permission to accompany the emperor. He learned that no foreigners would be permitted to go, which was utter fiction; the Imperial Army included hundreds of Europeans, mostly Austrians and former legionnaires. "It seemed to me against nature that I should not accompany the Emperor on his expedition," Salm wrote, "and I was very unhappy." But at the last minute he secured a position and prepared to follow Maximilian to Querétaro.[13]

Felix deemed the situation too dangerous to bring Agnes along. She did not take the news well: "I of course expected to go with Salm as usual, but for once he refused in a most determined manner and remained deaf to all my entreaties. Now it was my turn to become mad. I cried and screamed so as to be heard two blocks off; and Jimmy, who felt for his mistress, howled and barked; but Salm stole away and took a street where he could not hear me and I not see him. I believe I hated him at that moment, and felt very unhappy, for I knew he would come to grief, having never any luck without me. He stood firm: Agnes would remain in the comfortable residence of friends. But she had no intention of missing the show."[14]

At Querétaro, Maximilian and his small army soon found themselves surrounded, outnumbered, and outgunned by the republican forces of Division General Mariano Escobedo. The imperialists, with Maximilian in the heat of the fighting, performed well, and Felix Salm-Salm emerged as a capable leader. His relationship with the emperor blossomed as well; he quickly became Maximilian's most trusted subordinate and de facto chief of staff, eventually receiving the rank of brigade general. But hoped-for reinforcements and funds never arrived, and time was running out, not only at Querétaro but also for the empire itself.[15]

Back in Mexico City an anxious Agnes witnessed the empire's collapse firsthand while trying to gather information from Querétaro. "For many weeks we heard nothing from Queretaro but vague reports, and of a very contradictory unreliable kind," she recalled. She learned, though, that republican forces of talented young Division General Porfirio Díaz had taken Puebla. On April 12, Agnes watched as the republicans moved into the suburbs of Mexico City, beginning a siege of the capital. "During the following night," she recalled, "I dreamt that I saw my husband dying." Agnes resolved to "try what I could do to save the Emperor and my husband."[16]

Over the next several days Agnes, without any authority, passed between the lines, trying to broker a deal for the surrender of Mexico City in exchange for the safe passage of Maximilian and the other foreigners from the country. An amiable General Díaz agreed to see her but would not negotiate, nor could he discuss Maximilian and Querétaro, although he did provide passage to see General Escobedo. On April 27, Agnes, her maid, and Jimmy the terrier left Mexico City in a bright yellow carriage bound for Querétaro.[17] Agnes could not have known of the dire situation at Querétaro. A last-ditch attempt to break out had failed, and Maximilian refused to abandon his army, yielding any realistic chance for escape.

During the first week of May, Agnes arrived at Escobedo's headquarters, where she encountered a young captain who addressed her "as an old acquaintance from the United States, though," she noted, "I did not remember his face." This officer who had served in the Union army, she later learned, "boasted that 'he knew me intimately.' " Such was her reputation. General Escobedo, on the other hand, received her courteously. "I told him I heard that my husband was wounded, and requested his permission to go into the city." The general could not grant such permission, but would provide a letter of introduction to President Juárez, who had moved his headquarters to San Luis Potosí. Escobedo offered that he knew of her husband as "an extremely brave officer," and promised to treat Salm well should he be captured. With that, Agnes headed to San Luis Potosí.[18]

After a grueling three-day journey, she arrived at the temporary capital and called on President Juárez, incredibly with her dog Jimmy, who made himself at home in the president's office. Juárez listened patiently but refused to grant her request to visit Felix and Maximilian until he knew the situation at Querétaro. He suggested that she remain in San Luis Potosí, as Querétaro would likely fall soon.[19]

It was sound advice. On the night of May 14, one of Maximilian's most trusted officers led republican troops into Querétaro. After a brief fight, Maximilian, Salm, and the surviving Imperial Army surrendered. The emperor and his officers now awaited their fate, which most everyone assumed would be death.[20]

Agnes received the news at San Luis Potosí and, unable to secure a pass from Juárez, headed immediately to Querétaro without his blessing. On May 20 she saw Escobedo, who detailed Colonel Ricardo Villanueva from his staff to escort the princess to the Convent of San Teresita, where she found her husband: "He was not shaved, wore a collar several days old, and looked altogether as if he had emerged from a dustbin, though not worse than the rest of his comrades. To see him again under these circumstances affected me very much, and I wept and almost fainted when he held me in his arms." Salm soon introduced his wife to Maximilian. "I shall never forget this first interview with the Emperor," she wrote. "I found him in a miserable bare room, in bed, looking very sick and pale. He received me with the utmost kindness, kissed my hand, and pressed it in his, and told me how glad he was that I had come."[21]

Agnes engaged herself as negotiator for the prisoners and, in fact, her efforts in this area bore some fruit, which only added to her growing legend. A *New York Herald* correspondent reported: "The wife of Prince Salm-Salm, an American lady—*née* Agnes Le Clerq—closely related to President Johnson, made her way alone to San Luis Potosí to intercede with President Juarez for her husband's life as well as that of the Emperor Maximilian. This lady has sped so far in her brave mission that yesterday, on her arrival here from San Luis, herself, the Emperor and Prince Salm-Salm had a long interview with General Escobedo, and I have reason to believe that terms have been arranged by which the lives of most of the foreigners will be spared." As it turned out, the story proved mostly correct, although Agnes's role in the deliberations may have been overestimated. The lives of Maximilian and his generals remained in jeopardy. In the meantime, Agnes worked to improve the prisoners' living conditions.[22]

On May 24, Salm learned that Maximilian's trial had been set and the emperor would be isolated from the other prisoners. For now, only Maximilian and division generals Tomás Mejía and Miguel Miramón would stand trial. Agnes, who was free to come and go, offered to return to President Juárez and persuade him to postpone the trial until an adequate defense could be arranged. With a note from the emperor and a pass from Escobedo, she again dashed to San Luis Potosí.[23]

While Agnes worked on Juárez, Salm formulated plans for an escape, communicating via secret messages. But Maximilian made things difficult. He would not escape without Mejía and Miramón; he needed a disguise, since he refused to shave his elaborate beard (for fear of exposing an embarrassingly weak chin); and he provided a list of personal items that might be difficult to acquire: "two serapes, two revolvers, and a sabre. Not to forget bread or biscuit, red wine, and chocolate. A riding-whip is also necessary." As they had from the start, the players in this imperial tragedy proceeded without the slightest grasp of reality.[24]

Agnes made the trip to San Luis Potosí in less than two days and with very little sleep. Juárez agreed to see her on the morning of May 28, and she persuaded the reluctant president to grant a delay. She telegraphed the news to Querétaro and without hesitation headed there herself. She described her return: "I was worn with fatigue; my boots torn to pieces, and my feet sore; my hair in disorder, and my face and hands unwashed; I must indeed have looked like a scarecrow, but I was very happy and a little proud too."[25]

Over the next few days lawyers arrived from Mexico City to prepare Maximilian's defense, but the Salm-Salms, well aware that Maximilian's Black Decree virtually mandated his death, continued to pursue alternative approaches. Escape plans moved ahead—officers were bribed, horses and supplies had been arranged—all was set for a June 2 escape. But Maximilian would not embarrass his lawyers; he canceled the escape. According to Agnes, "The Emperor, to whom the idea of escape had been always repugnant, was glad to find a pretext or reason to postpone it." This did nothing to dissuade his friends.[26]

His visitation privileges restored, Salm spent much time with Maximilian, as did Agnes. As the trial neared its conclusion, and a guilty verdict and likely execution loomed obvious, Agnes mounted one last escape attempt, with assistance from Colonel Villanueva, with whom she had been most friendly since her arrival at Querétaro. Still, nothing could happen without the cooperation of Colonel Miguel Palacios. The plan relied on bribery, but with no money available Agnes had Maximilian sign two promissory notes for 100,000 pesos each to be honored by his brother, the emperor of Austria. It would be up to Agnes to convert Palacios.[27]

On June 13, Agnes visited Maximilian for what turned out to be the final time. Leaving the emperor at 8:00 P.M. she asked Colonel Palacios to escort her home, which he agreed to do. She invited the nervous colonel into her rooms. Palacios admitted his sympathy for Maximilian's plight, at which point Agnes revealed the scheme. The colonel, who feared for his family, rejected the bribe, defying the prevailing stereotype among imperialists that any Mexican could be bribed. "Well, Colonel," she said, "you are not well-disposed. Reflect about it, and remember your word of honour and your oath."[28]

This scene served as fodder for fantasy for years to come as, through rumor and folklore, it became a sexual seduction, which perhaps more than anything else established Agnes's historical persona. According to one account, when the colonel refused the check, Agnes asked, "Isn't the sum enough?" She then began to undress. "Well, Colonel, here am I!"

she reportedly exclaimed. The astonished Palacios threatened to jump through the window before Agnes relented. In a more general interpretation, the reliable Sara Yorke Stevenson wrote that "Princess Salm-Salm cleverly used every means in a woman's power" to save Maximilian. While Agnes may well have used sex to advance her agenda, in this instance at least she apparently did not. At some point Colonel Villanueva arrived, and Dr. Samuel Basch, Maximilian's personal physician, wrote that "a few minutes before ten o'clock I reached the princess's house, where I found both colonels." As Agnes clearly expected Basch, she most likely would not have engaged in sexual activity with either of her guests.[29]

The plan fell apart. Palacios went directly to General Escobedo and exposed the foreign conspirators. An exasperated Escobedo unceremoniously sent Agnes and Jimmy under guard to San Luis Potosí. On June 16 the court-martial rendered the death sentence to Maximilian, Mejía, and Miramón. Felix grimly awaited his own verdict, but Agnes had no intention of giving up the fight.[30]

At San Luis Potosí, Agnes lobbied Juárez relentlessly, securing the president's promise that her husband's life would be spared but failing to gain another delay. She remained determined to save Maximilian. She had impressive company, too. Appeals came from around the world, including those of U.S. Secretary of State William Seward, Italian patriot Giuseppe Garibaldi, and French novelist Victor Hugo. Even Generals Escobedo and Díaz believed that Maximilian should be spared. But Juárez and Mexico had paid heavily for past leniency; Maximilian would now pay for centuries of abuses.[31]

On the eve of the execution, Agnes made her final play. She went before Juárez one last time. "I pleaded for the life of the Emperor," she recalled, but the president refused to delay the inevitable. In another famous scene, described by Agnes, she fell to her knees and begged for Maximilian's life, to which Juárez replied: "I am grieved, madame, to see you thus on your knees before me; but if all the kings and queens of Europe were in your place I could not spare that life. It is not I who take it, it is the people and the law; and if I should not do its will the people would take it and mine also." It was over. On June 19, 1867, Maximilian, Mejía, and Miramón went before a Mexican firing squad on Querétaro's Cerro de las Campanas.[32]

Weeks later Agnes secured her husband's release. The two found their way to Europe and their next adventure—the Franco-Prussian War. In 1870 gallant Felix Salm-Salm was killed charging the French lines at Gravelotte-St. Privat. Agnes won praise for her fine work in German field hospitals and at the same time continued to cultivate her legend. She died at Karlsruhe, Germany, on December 21, 1912.

In Mexico, Agnes fought heroically to save Maximilian's life while all of Europe failed him. Uncouth, ill mannered, and often outlandish, Agnes Salm-Salm used her title, beauty, foreign status, and unconventional assertiveness to gain access to the highest ranks of the liberal army and the Mexican government. Although her feminine wiles and emotional supplications did not prevail in the end, she did add a colorful dimension to the otherwise dismal last days of the Mexican Empire.

NOTES

1. *Mexican Herald*, January 19, 1908.

2. Agnes Salm-Salm's memoir, *Ten Years of My Life*, 2 vols. (London: Richard Bentley and Son, 1876), recounts her experiences during the Civil War, in Maximilian's Mexico, and during the Franco-Prussian War. All references to this source are to volume one unless otherwise noted. For a discussion of Agnes Salm-Salm's mysterious past and her exploits during the Civil War, see David Coffey, *Soldier Princess: The Life and Legend of Agnes Salm-Salm in North America, 1861–1867* (College Station: Texas A&M University Press, 2002).

3. For the general history of the French Intervention and the Mexican Empire, numerous sources are available. For the European perspective, see Count Egon Corti, *Maximilian and Charlotte of Mexico*, 2 vols. (New York: Alfred A. Knopf, 1928); more popular accounts are in Joan Haslip, *Maximilian and His Empress Carlota* (New York: Holt, Rinehart, and Winston, 1971) and Bertita Harding, *Phantom Crown: The Story of Maximilian and Carlota of Mexico* (New York: Halcyon House, 1934).

4. Agnes Salm-Salm, *Ten Years of My Life*, 176–78. Jimmy was a gift from publishing scion James G. Bennett Jr.

5. Ibid., 181–94.

6. Ibid., 240–41; Felix Salm-Salm, *My Diary in Mexico*, 2 vols. (London: Richard Bentley and Son, 1868), 4–5. All references to this source are to volume one unless otherwise noted.

7. Felix Salm-Salm, *My Diary in Mexico*, 5; Agnes Salm-Salm, *Ten Years of My Life*, 242–43.

8. Felix Salm-Salm, *My Diary in Mexico*, 5–11.

9. Sara Yorke Stevenson, *Maximilian in Mexico: A Woman's Reminiscences of the French Intervention, 1862–1867* (New York: The Century Co., 1899), 231, 259.

10. Felix Salm-Salm, *My Diary in Mexico*, 14–15.

11. Ibid., 18.

12. Agnes Salm-Salm, *Ten Years of My Life*, 242–43.

13. Ibid., 255; Felix Salm-Salm, *My Diary in Mexico*, 20–22.

14. Agnes Salm-Salm, *Ten Years of My Life*, 255–56.

15. See Felix Salm-Salm, *My Diary in Mexico*; Salm-Salm's account of the events surrounding Maximilian's march to Querétaro and the subsequent siege is considered one of the most authoritative available. See also Samuel Basch, *Memories of Mexico: A History of the Last Ten Months of the Empire*, trans. Hugh McAden Oechler

(San Antonio: Trinity University Press, 1973). Basch, Maximilian's personal physician, offers another excellent eyewitness account.

16. Agnes Salm-Salm, *Ten Years of My Life*, 257–62.

17. Ibid., 263–80; Porfirio Díaz, *Archivo del General Porfirio Díaz: memorias y documentos*, ed. Alberto Maria Carreño, 29 vols., (Mexico, D.F.: Editorial "Elede," 1947–1960), vol. 3, 46–49.

18. Agnes Salm-Salm, *Ten Years of my Life*, 281–84.

19. Ibid., 284–86. Most Juárez biographers give Agnes little attention, and in regard to her dealings with the president refer to her version of events. Good studies of Juárez include Charles Allen Smart, *Viva Juárez: A Biography* (Philadelphia: J. B. Lippincott, 1963) and Brian Hamnett, *Juárez* (London: The Longman Group, 1994).

20. For events surrounding the betrayal and capture of Maximilian, see Felix Salm-Salm, *My Diary in Mexico*, 187–218; Basch, *Memories of Mexico*, 175–84; José Luis Blasio, *Maximilian, Emperor of Mexico: Memoirs of His Private Secretary*, trans. and ed. Robert Hammond Murray, with a foreword by Carleton Beals (New Haven: Yale University Press, 1934).

21. Agnes Salm-Salm, *Ten Years of My Life*, 286–99; Daniel Moreno, ed., *El Sitio de Querétaro: segun protagonistas y testigos (Sóstenes Rocha, Alberto Hans, Samuel Basch, Princesa Salm-Salm, Mariano Escobedo)* (Mexico, D.F.: Editorial Porrua, 1982), 179–81.

22. *New York Herald*, June 11, 1867. This is the only reference found that claimed Agnes to be a relative of President Johnson. Unlike other erroneous details, this one did not survive as part of her legend.

23. Agnes Salm-Salm, *Ten Years of My Life*, 293–96.

24. Felix Salm-Salm, *My Diary in Mexico*, 231–39.

25. Agnes Salm-Salm, *Ten Years of My Life*, 296–302.

26. Ibid., 301–2; Basch, *Memories of Mexico*, 200.

27. Agnes Salm-Salm, *Ten Years of My Life*, 318–23; Basch, *Memories of Mexico*, 211–12.

28. Basch, *Memories of Mexico*, 211–12; Agnes Salm-Salm, *Ten Years of My Life*, 321–326.

29. Corti, *Maximilian and Charlotte*, vol. 2, 812; Harding, *Phantom Crown*, 316–17; Stevenson, *Maximilian in Mexico*, 294; Richard O'Connor, *The Cactus Throne: The Tragedy of Maximilian and Carlota* (New York: G. P. Putnam's Sons, 1971), 324; Coffey, *Soldier Princess*, 76, 111 n.34. The story seems to have been advanced by Count Corti, who gives the source as an Austrian officer (who was not at Querétaro), whose own account, taken from the Vienna National Archives, was admittedly based on hearsay. Harding's version is careless but states, "Agnes Salm shook her golden mane and began to undress. . . . Her white nudity lent a bizarre note to this night that was not made for love." O'Connor takes the most artistic liberty: "[S]he offered herself—her supple equestrienne's body. . . . One glimpse of her splendidly curved torso, under the dim lamp-light . . . was enough for the colonel." Neither Harding nor O'Connor provide sources for their passages.

30. Agnes Salm-Salm, *Ten Years of My Life*, vol. 2, 3–7; Basch, *Memories of Mexico*, 212; *New York Herald*, July 11, 1867.

31. Smart, *Viva Juárez*, 380.

32. Ibid.; Agnes Salm-Salm, *Ten Years of My Life*, vol. 2, 14–16.

SUGGESTED READINGS

Although Princess Agnes Salm-Salm has been characterized in novels, plays, and some popular (and very flawed) biographical treatments, the dearth of information available on her life before 1862 and after 1872 makes a full biography of this remarkable woman impossible until new sources become available. Any study of her must begin with her own memoir, *Ten Years of My Life* (2 vols. London: Richard Bentley & Son, 1876). This is an awkwardly written, gossipy, self-serving work that covers her experiences during the American Civil War, in Maximilian's Mexico, and in the Franco-Prussian War, and must be taken for what it is—one person's largely uninformed impression of events. Still, it is essential reading for anyone interested in the last days of the empire. Far more reliable and much more valuable as it pertains to events in Mexico is her husband Prince Felix Salm-Salm's *My Diary in Mexico* (2 vols. London: Richard Bentley, 1868), which is generally regarded as an important contribution to the understanding of Maximilian's final days as emperor of Mexico. A recent scholarly treatment of Agnes Salm-Salm's adventures in Mexico is David Coffey, *Soldier Princess: The Life and Legend of Agnes Salm-Salm in North America, 1861–1867* (College Station: Texas A&M University Press, 2002).

The classic work on the Mexican Empire is Count Egon Corti's *Maximilian and Charlotte of Mexico*, 2 vols. (New York: Alfred A. Knopf, 1928). More popular accounts include Bertita Harding's *Phantom Crown: The Story of Maximilian and Carlota of Mexico* (New York: Halcyon House, 1934) and Joan Haslip's *The Crown of Mexico: Maximilian and His Empress Carlota* (New York: Holt, Rinehart, and Winston, 1971).

The numerous useful firsthand accounts from Maximilian's Mexico include those of Maximilian's secretary José Luis Blasio, *Maximilian, Emperor of Mexico: Memoirs of His Private Secretary*, translated and edited by Robert Hammond Murray, with a foreword by Carleton Beals (New Haven, CT: Yale University Press, 1934) and his personal physician Samuel Basch, *Memories of Mexico: A History of the Last Ten Months of the Empire*, translated by Hugh McAden Oechler (San Antonio: Trinity University Press, 1973). These generally support Felix Salm-Salm's version of events and add important observations. Also of value are the memoirs of Countess Paula Kollonitz, *The Court of Mexico*, translated by J. E. Ollivant (London, 1868), and Sara Yorke Stevenson, *Maximilian in Mexico: A Woman's Reminiscences of the French Intervention* (New York: The Century Company, 1899).

For the leading Mexican figures see the classic work of Carleton Beals, *Porfirio Díaz: Dictator of Mexico* (Philadelphia: J. B. Lippincott, 1932) and Brian Hamnett's more recent *Juárez* (London: The Longman

Group, 1994). The conflict between Mexico's French-backed emperor and its legitimate leader is the focus of Jasper Ridley's accessible *Maximilian and Juárez* (New York: Ticknor & Fields, 1992). A useful study of U.S.-Mexico relations during this period is Alfred Jackson Hanna and Kathryn Abbey Hanna, *Napoleon III and Mexico: American Triumph over Monarchy* (Chapel Hill: University of North Carolina Press, 1971).

CHAPTER FIVE

Felipe García and the Real Heroes of Guelatao

Patrick J. McNamara

Guelatao, a station on the new cherry-colored metro (line A), conveys vivid images of the exotic mountain landscapes of Oaxaca. With its rich ethnic heritage, including more than sixteen distinct indigenous cultures, the southern state of Oaxaca has long captured the imagination of Mexicans and foreigners alike. Unlike the central highlands, where Spanish conquistadors imposed a firm political and economic domination, Native American communities retained considerable autonomy in this remote and rugged land. Yet as a result, many still question the loyalty to the nation of these largely unassimilated pueblos, even though one of the foremost figures in Mexican history, President Benito Juárez, was a Zapotec Indian from Guelatao. Indeed, since 1994, the state has joined Chiapas as an important center of the Zapatista rebellion against the government in Mexico City. Nevertheless, as this essay shows, the common people of Guelatao and their local leader, Felipe García, fought to protect Mexico during one of its greatest crises, the civil war of the Reforma and the subsequent French invasion.

The origins of Zapotec patriotism, and the historical memory of these nineteenth-century conflicts, present a challenge to traditional interpretations of the modern nation-state. Liberal ideology, with its emphasis on personal freedom, emerged from the European Enlightenment in defiance of the power of absolute monarchs. Nations were therefore seen as communities of individual citizens unified by common political ideals or ethnic origins. In order to forge such a society, nationalist ideology sought to displace rival loyalties to a social class or a local community (known as a patria chica *in Mexico). The people of Guelatao, by contrast, imagined the nation as a collection of ethnic communities rather than of individuals, a view that had roots in colonial struggles with their Spanish and mestizo neighbors. Moreover, the Zapotecs' experience serving in the National Guard gave them both solid claims to Mexican citizenship and good reasons to distrust outsiders who tried to act as political intermediaries between them and the national government.*

Patrick J. McNamara received his Ph.D. from the University of Wisconsin and is now assistant professor of history at the University of Minnesota. His research focuses on Indian peasant communities in the Sierra Zapoteca of Oaxaca and rural political culture during the late nineteenth century. He is currently preparing for publication "Sons of the Sierra: Benito Juárez, Porfirio Díaz, and the Zapotec People of Ixtlán, Oaxaca, 1855–1911."

𝓑enito Juárez, Mexico's most celebrated hero of the nineteenth century, was born in the small Zapotec village of Guelatao, Oaxaca, on March 21, 1806.[1] Mexican schools still teach children the epic story of his life: impoverished and orphaned as a young boy, Juárez left his village at the age of twelve, walking the narrow mountain road from Guelatao to Oaxaca City. He found employment in the city and began attending school, where hard work and natural intelligence soon brought him success. He studied briefly for the priesthood but opted instead for a legal career. As a lawyer, Juárez became active in the tumultuous world of nineteenth-century Mexican politics. He joined the liberal cause, which sought to reform society by protecting the rights of individuals against the power and wealth of corporate institutions like the Catholic Church. He eventually became governor of his home state, federal Supreme Court justice, and in 1858 president of the republic. But Juárez presided over a deeply divided country and had to lead the liberal campaign against conservatives during the Three Years' War (1858–1861) and during the French Intervention (1862–1867). Liberals proved victorious in the end and, despite continuing conflicts within their own ranks, Juárez would eventually be recalled by Mexicans as a monumental figure, as the man who saved Mexican sovereignty from foreign aggression and restored constitutional order. Hundreds if not thousands of Juárez statues still stand in town plazas throughout the country. His image is intended to inspire all Mexicans to rise above poverty, ethnic discrimination, political opponents, and foreign interventions. While other heroes have captured the Mexican imagination, no individual has endured for as long or as deeply as Benito Juárez, the Indian president from Guelatao.

Two years after Juárez's birth, in 1808, Felipe García was also born in Guelatao. There are no statues to García and no one outside of his community knew his story or his importance to the liberal cause. Nor did García ever actually meet Juárez, though they spent nearly a decade in the same remote part of Oaxaca. Felipe García remained in Guelatao throughout his long life. He farmed a small plot of land, held a series of local administrative positions including municipal president, joined the regional National Guard battalion, and eventually became a local war hero and village elder. He last served his community in 1903, at age ninety-five, as the president of the Guelatao organizing committee charged with planning local Juárez celebrations, the *Mesa Directiva de la Junta, "Juárez y Progreso."*[2] Throughout his life and in every official capacity in which he served, García pointed to a series of relationships within his community as his source of inspiration and identity. His life offers a glimpse into the ways in which rural Mexicans understood their own contributions to nation-state formation during this turbulent time in Mexican history. Significantly, we see in Felipe García a rejection of the liberal individualism that Juárez came to represent and a deeper emphasis on the communal ties that bonded people together. These ties were strengthened during the nineteenth century through the formation of a rural National Guard battalion and the broad participation of ordinary men and women in defending the nation.

We should also be aware from the beginning of our discussion that the case of Felipe García and Guelatao may call into question the organizing assumption of this volume. Individual life stories of ordinary people in Mexico can offer important and far-reaching insights into the ways in which most people lived their lives. But the focus on particular individuals also runs the risk of overlooking the broader context in which people acted and consciously understood those actions. In that sense, the human tradition in Guelatao was primarily formed around a communal experience.

GUELATAO AND THE RURAL NATIONAL GUARD

Much of Felipe García's adult life was shaped by decisions and policies Benito Juárez made as state governor and then as national president. And in a more indirect way, García's decision to join the National Guard and support the liberals shaped the course of Juárez's life as well. In 1846 the Oaxaca state government initiated a series of reforms that began, according to historian Marcello Carmagnani, the "second conquest" of Indian communities.[3] Ironically, the major advocate of these reforms was Benito Juárez, the Zapotec Indian from Guelatao. But Juárez thought of himself as a liberal, not as an Indian. Although political eulogies would refer to Juárez as the redeemer of Indian Mexico, and the people of Guelatao would always assert that he was one of them, Juárez himself did not embrace his native origins. On the contrary, throughout his political career Juárez enacted policies that sought to diminish the influence of native cultures and local village customs. He sought instead a new set of laws that guaranteed the rights of the individual and challenged the powers of corporate institutions. From his perspective, community control over land and the overwhelming influence of the Catholic Church infringed on the rights of the individual in society.

As governor, Juárez initiated two major reforms designed to limit communal autonomy. First, he determined that a new military establishment was needed to respond to internal unrest. In order to protect "public security" and prevent Indian communities from rebelling, Juárez proposed the formation of "a military force, that by its morality, its discipline, and its training can quickly respond by giving aid in any corner of the state."[4] He was particularly concerned about unrest in Zapotec communities in the Isthmus of Tehuantepec (historically and culturally distinct from the Sierra Zapotecs of Ixtlán district), and about Triqui Indian communities that had rebelled along Oaxaca's western border with the state of Guerrero. After 1847, the U.S. invasion and occupation of Mexico demonstrated that foreign intervention was an equally dangerous threat. In 1848, Juárez began organizing and training National Guard units to defend his regime. In the next two years, state expenditures for the new military establishment grew to more than 25 percent of the entire state budget. And by 1850, 800 permanent National Guard troops were stationed around the state, and another 2,500 were available for rapid mobilization.[5]

Juárez initiated a second reform that ran parallel to his military plans. He reorganized administrative responsibilities in the state, creating a new office of subprefect to oversee local community affairs. Juárez instructed that subprefects "should not limit themselves to counting heads and dictating official letters, but rather they should do something nobler and more difficult: they should govern the people."[6] To govern the people implied a more interventionist approach to local politics than had previously existed. By controlling municipal budgets through tax collection and allocation of public funds, subprefects intended to displace the moral and political authority of communal elders. The "second conquest" of indigenous Oaxaca was quick, resulting from barely a decade of reforms designed to reconstitute the state according to a liberal vision of policymakers. A new era began in Oaxaca, but it bore the familiar traits of the colonial order: a small land-owning and political class determined to extract Indian labor and resources for the benefit of wealthy citizens.

Felipe García's particular response to these reforms remains unknown. In general, however, the people of Guelatao, along with Zapotecs from communities throughout the region, used the new institutions of state control as an opportunity to construct a new relationship with the state and federal governments. By 1855 men from Guelatao joined their neighbors and the subprefect of the district in organizing the Ixtlán National Guard. Unlike economic or political change, which could happen slowly and unevenly in nineteenth-century rural Mexico, the introduction of a new military structure and the recognition of a new role for Zapotec peasants became a catalyst for a rapid and fundamental transformation in the ways in which peasants situated themselves in terms of the nation. For the first time since the European encounter, peasants from the Sierra Zapoteca began to think of themselves as a part of—not apart from—the ruling regime in Mexico City. As a result, the political alliance that pushed through the reforms of the 1840s and 1850s had to contend with a militant and aggressive indigenous population from the central highlands. By adapting to these new institutions, the people of the Sierra Zapoteca repositioned themselves as allies of the state, as loyal citizens invested with certain rights. In this way, adaptation made it easier for Zapotec communities to resist complete domination and ultimately muted the intended consequences of the "second conquest."

Significantly, the subprefect in Ixtlán district in 1855 was also a man who would play a major role in nineteenth-century Mexican politics—Porfirio Díaz. Díaz entered the political stage as a twenty-five-year-old mestizo from Oaxaca City; he would exit at age eighty when faced with a nationwide rebellion that led to revolution. In 1855, however, Díaz was just getting started, learning for the first time how to maneuver within the complex Mexican political landscape. One of Díaz's first acts as subprefect was to train, equip, and mobilize the men of the region into the state's most effective National Guard battalion. Díaz organized the Ixtlán National Guard as a quasi-private army. He drilled his recruits according to his own personal regimen of calisthenics and gymnastics. He began rudimentary education for his men, encouraging them to learn at least how to sign their names. And he spoke to them about the liberal principles that motivated him to serve the nation—his doubts about the interventionist tendencies of the Catholic Church and his disdain for the antidemocratic practices of President Antonio López de Santa Anna.[7] From 1855 to 1876, Zapotec villagers from Guelatao and the rest of the region would be called upon to fight in Mexico's civil wars. Their experiences on the battlefields allowed them to reimagine themselves as belonging to the Mexican national community.[8]

To be members of that metaphorical community did not imply complete agreement or harmony with other members. Zapotec peasants understood from the experiences of forming their own communities how conflicts and tensions divided the collective and required constant negotiation. These disputes emerged within individual communities and between villages over access to the best agricultural land, control over the most reliable water resources, and influence in local political affairs. While disputes within a particular community were always a serious issue, conflicts between villagers posed an even greater threat to regional stability.

For Felipe García and his neighbors in Guelatao the major rival was the nearby town of Ixtlán, the district *cabecera* (administrative head town). To a certain extent, their conflicts in the nineteenth century over land, water, and political power went back to the original decree that formally separated Guelatao from Ixtlán in 1636. In the early seventeenth century, delicate negotiations between the two communities and the Spanish *encomendero* Diego Sánchez Ramírez resulted in a long-term land rent agreement. Guelatao agreed to pay an annual fee of 6 pesos in gold for access to land that Ixtlán claimed as its own. Ownership of the land did not change hands, only the right to use it. The land itself was good for farming, but more important, Guelatao's primary water source, the Xoo Vetó River, ran through this tract. The decree effectively gave Guelatao its economic independence from Ixtlán. But Guelatao did not receive official status as an autonomous political entity until 1900, when Felipe García lobbied state officials and Porfirio Díaz for this recognition. Not surprisingly, Guelatao's political autonomy provoked another round of disputes with Ixtlán over the same tract of land set aside in 1636. Still, for a brief moment in the nineteenth century, from about 1860 to 1890, Guelatao's conflict with Ixtlán appeared less volatile than before. Civil war and foreign intervention posed more dangerous threats to García and his fellow Serranos, and the formation of the National Guard appeared to have a temporary soothing effect on intervillage conflicts.[9]

The structure of the Ixtlán National Guard took into account the potential obstacles to forming a unified and effective military force by reproducing preexisting hierarchies within and between communities. In effect, Díaz and the Zapotec community elders reorganized those distinctions according to a more "rational" structure of military protocol. Once the battalion had been formed, individuals used military rank as markers of local leadership and authority; even during times of peace, captains, colonels, and generals maintained their titles, indicating their status within the community and the region more broadly. In this way, local privileges and distinctions became more institutionalized, adhering to the established norms of military relationships. At the same time, the National Guard became a mediating element within communities, a formalization of privilege and hierarchy that reinforced status according to ethnic, class, gender, and generational identities. These tensions, which had always existed within the communities, were not challenged by the new military order. Rather, preexisting differences were merely incorporated into the body of the National Guard units.

Felipe García benefited from this organizational structure of the National Guard battalion. Díaz determined that community-based regiments led by local elders would offer the best chance at maintaining control over the new soldiers. In addition, community regiments would also offer each town a relative sense of autonomy within the entire corps, and possibly reduce tensions between villages. For these reasons, the forty-seven-year-old García received a commission as a captain in the National Guard, charged with leading a company of men from Guelatao. His leadership within the community and the respect he had earned serving in various municipal offices made him a reliable choice as an officer. García was already a *pasado* in his community, a man who had served in every administrative post within the municipal government. This generational status enhanced García's ability to lead his neighbors into combat and protected his community from manipulation by rival villages. He was not too old to fight; he was the right age to lead. But he did not come from the "right" ethnic group to command the entire corps.

The formation of the Ixtlán National Guard was more complex than simply naming elder men from particular communities to the officer ranks. Ethnic and class divisions within the region complicated the overall structure at the battalion level. Young mestizo men related through ethnic, marriage, and business ties to important politicians and mine owners from the region were named senior officers of the battalion, assuming positions as colonels and eventually generals. Miguel Castro orchestrated many of these arrangements, though he did not perform any military functions himself. For example, Castro secured officer positions for his wife's nephew, Francisco Meixueiro Pérez, and for Fidencio Hernández, another mestizo born in the town of Ixtlán. Meixueiro and Hernández pursued military and political careers until 1876 and then dedicated themselves to using those contacts for business purposes. Like Castro, both men eventually became state governors and both would become tremendously influential in statewide and national politics. In the process, they also became relatively wealthy. Meixueiro and Hernández shared one other thing in common. They married into the same family, the Delgado family of Xiacuí, and became brothers-in-law. Their sons, Guillermo Meixueiro and Fidencio Hernández (*hijo*) were first cousins. These two generations of Hernández and Meixueiro men would become the mestizo caudillos of the central highlands, whose influence extended into the state government in Oaxaca and the federal government in Mexico City. Still, Zapotec community leaders could limit their arbitrary use of power by recalling the contributions everyone from the Sierra had made during Mexico's civil wars. All men had had an opportunity to join the National Guard, and they all could claim to have played an important role in defending the nation.

Thus the Ixtlán National Guard formalized social relationships in the following ways: in general, mestizo men held ranked positions above Indian men, and elder Zapotec men commanded their younger neighbors in community-based regiments. In effect, merit and performance mattered little toward promotion since preexisting factors determined where one entered the system. The National Guard also dealt directly with gender relationships in the region. Women were excluded from any official status within the battalion, though their contributions to the war effort represented an integral part of the organization and maintenance of the troops. In the same way that men reserved for themselves the political offices of municipal administration, the Ixtlán National Guard became another patriarchal domain where gender and generational status determined one's rank. The irony or tragedy of this female exclusion meant that the crucial roles women played during war times went virtually unrecognized by officials in Mexico City during times of peace. But Zapotec men like Felipe García realized that they had not gone into battle alone. Women from Guelatao and other communities made sure that local and national leaders understood that everyone had suffered and sacrificed for the nation.

THE IMPORTANCE OF COMMUNITY

Felipe García's first opportunity to fight came in 1855, when a group of men from Guelatao joined a force of 400 National Guard soldiers in a march to the outskirts of Oaxaca City.[10] Placing his men under the general command of Porfirio Díaz, García and his fellow Serranos were walking into the violent world of mid-nineteenth-century Mexican politics. In this case, the Ixtlán National Guard sought to return a liberal state government to power after conservatives had staged their own coup. As the National Guard troops came over the last mountain pass, the valley of Oaxaca opened before them. But instead of beginning the final descent, military leaders decided that the men should rest one more night before they went into battle. These soldiers had been trained but they had not been tested in real combat. In a scene reminiscent of Miguel Hidalgo's encampment around Mexico City, the soldiers gathered in small groups around campfires, trying desperately to fend off the chilly mountain air. Some of them, perhaps all of them, must have been worried about the next day. Would they die on the battlefield? Would they ever see their families again? Would their sacrifices hold any meaning? They could see the city beneath them and the stars above and they did what soldiers do most often—they waited.

For the people living in Oaxaca City, the flickering orange glow that lit up the night sky threatened the calm and civility of urban life. Valley elites had grown accustomed to negotiating political disputes on their own terms and the introduction of armed Indian peasants added a new and unpredictable dynamic into the political mix. Fearful of the Indian element that could overtake the city, the governor switched sides once again. He promised that liberals would continue to control the state government if the National Guard troops returned to the Sierra. Rather than risk the unknown, the valley elite surrendered to the Zapotec army of Ixtlán district. Without firing a shot, these Indian peasants had swayed the political process. And though no one knew it in 1855, these soldiers and their leaders would influence directly and indirectly the course of statewide and national politics for the next two generations. Felipe García had numerous other opportunities to lead the men from Guelatao into battle; in fact, they fought in every major campaign in Oaxaca during the 1850s and 1860s. After remaining relatively unorganized during 300 years of colonial rule, Zapotec communal leaders argued that citizenship rights were not granted and guaranteed by the state, but defined and defended by communal participation in struggles over nation-state formation.

While Juárez eventually became the symbolic link between Zapotec notions of ethnic identity amid an emerging sense of Mexican nationalism, Felipe García and his neighbors from Guelatao always understood that they were fighting for the nation and not the more limited *patria chica* (local fatherland). In July 1864, two months after Emperor Maximilian of Hapsburg had arrived to assume the throne in Mexico City, García helped organize a town meeting in Guelatao. The men realized that soon their National Guard battalion would be mobilized to defend Mexican sovereignty. And they situated their struggle in terms of Mexico's 1810 independence movement against Spain. They were not fighting for Juárez; they were defending "the precious inheritance that our fathers have passed to us from the town of Dolores." As they declared their opposition to Maximilian and foreign domination, they swore their allegiance to "our form of government, which is a representative, popular republic."[11]

Joining the National Guard units was a privilege reserved for men only, though women fed and bandaged the soldiers and spied on the enemy during key moments of the war effort. Peasant women often traveled with the armies, providing essential support roles just behind the front lines. And women became both the objects and the subjects of war as men argued that they were protecting their homes by going into combat. In fact, the desire to protect "innocent women" provided a justification for calling men to war in the first place. But Mexican women also became the targets of war, the objects of capture, torture, and rape inflicted by the enemy. Although they were excluded from the formal structure of military service, women clearly experienced their own hardships during Mexico's civil wars.[12]

One of the most important functions women performed in times of war was spying. In 1859, while José María Cobos occupied Oaxaca City with a conservative army, the liberal government abandoned the city, establishing a provisional capital in the town of Ixtlán in the Sierra Zapoteca. Liberal officials lived in the mountains for months without any formal means of communication with Oaxaca City. The wives, mothers, daughters, and sisters of liberal politicians began an intelligence network within the city in order to provide information about the actions and movements of the conservative army. The women used their female servants, many of whom came from Guelatao and the surrounding towns, as couriers. When conservative sentries discovered these correspondences, the women were jailed and beaten.[13] In later years, during the French Intervention, women made up nearly 10 percent of the prisoners held in Oaxaca City by Maximilian's government. Along with 213 army officers, twenty-two women were released in honor of Empress Carlota's birthday in June 1865.[14] But outside of the formal organization of the National Guard units, women did not have a place within Mexico's military history. Without that institutional structure, the acts of bravery performed by women went unrewarded. During the Porfiriato (1876–1911), widows, mothers, and daughters would demand compensation for the sacrifices of their male relatives, but few women would claim to have served the nation in any military capacity of their own. The National Guard units reinforced male control over the conduct of war, and later over the ways in which war was remembered.

It is hard to say whether Felipe García shared this interpretation immediately after the wars. But over time, as he grew older, he clearly recognized that everyone in his community had sacrificed to save Benito Juárez's government. In a series of letters to Porfirio Díaz and other officials, García expressed a broader, more inclusive interpretation of the sacrifices made by men and women in Guelatao during the civil wars of the nineteenth century. These letters prompted officials to grant García a pension, but that was not enough for the oldest veteran in Guelatao. Toward the end of his life, in 1903, a national committee approached García with a proposal to build a new elementary school in Guelatao in honor of Benito Juárez. García quickly endorsed the project but he insisted on expanding the original idea to benefit more people. The school should not only serve children, García asserted, it should also be a place where adults, men and women, could learn to read and write. The people who had been deprived of an education in the past, those people who sacrificed for the nation, should not be dismissed as a lost generation in the present. To participate more fully in the political and cultural affairs of the community and the nation, all people should have access to education. This access was a "right" conferred on all Mexicans by Juárez, the "unconquered Indian Redeemer, who proclaimed our rights and secured the second Independence of the Mexican people."[15] Unfortunately, the plan to build a new school in Guelatao generated tremendous opposition by the people of Ixtlán. Villagers from the larger town argued that they should receive the lion's share of state-sponsored development projects. The old land agreement from 1636 was called into question and a new series of conflicts mounted. In the end, Felipe García was unable to save the school project.

Later generations of men and women from Guelatao would follow Felipe García's example. They lobbied almost continuously for some tangible sign of the importance of their town in national history—"the glorious cradle of the Caudillo of the Reforma."[16] But postrevolutionary regimes under Alvaro Obregón (1920–1924) and Plutarco Elías Calles (1924–1928) remained ambivalent about recreating the Porfirian cult around Juárez.[17] In December 1920, less than six months after revolutionary fighting had officially ended in Oaxaca, villagers from Guelatao proposed the construction of a major Juárez monument as a way of creating a national tourist attraction. They envisioned a grand statue, a school, and an interpretive center that would convey the profound importance of Juárez's ideas and accomplishments. In addition to their request for a monument, the letter writers also noted that their village required aid for rebuilding after "the civil dispute," a careful characterization of revolutionary upheaval in Oaxaca. Obregón shuffled the request between various ministries, reluctantly going through the motions of supporting the plan or at least not rejecting it outright. Manuel Vargas, Obregón's secretary, eventually wrote back that there were no funds available for rebuilding villages, though he was keenly aware that Guelatao was Juárez's birthplace. As for the Juárez monument itself, an engineer was finally assigned to the project in 1923, more than two years after the initial request.[18] Throughout his administration, Obregón refused all requests to attend Juárez memorials in Guelatao.[19] He also opposed creating Indian schools that might celebrate Juárez's ethnic origins. In 1922 he rejected this overall approach, stating, "I believe it would be a grave error to turn the Indian into a separate caste with separate laws and advantages; it was an error carried out for many years and one that I intend to eliminate. The Indian should already be considered only as a Mexican citizen."[20]

Throughout the 1920s and 1930s, villagers from Guelatao made repeated requests for financial assistance to raise the level of commemorative events around Juárez to national prominence. Mexico City officials almost always denied these requests. Celebrations and memorials recalling fallen heroes of the 1910 Revolution received more direct support from the government.[21] A turning point came in 1937, when President Lázaro Cárdenas traveled to Guelatao on the anniversary of Juárez's birth, establishing a custom that subsequent presidents have often followed. More important, Cárdenas came to inaugurate a new boarding school that would serve the region's Indian populations.[22] As the Mexican government began pulling away from more radical social policies, the Revolution itself would be reinterpreted as the fulfillment of the Liberal Reform of the nineteenth century.[23] Adoration for Juárez and Guelatao could officially resume.

This kind of recognition for Guelatao continued throughout much of the twentieth century. In the late 1990s an expansion of the Mexico City metro, the A line, added a stop named Guelatao (there has always been a stop on line 3 named Juárez). Even as it honors Guelatao as Juárez's birthplace, this symbol should also be read as an expression of gratitude for the entire community. As with all national symbols, however, the connection between Guelatao and Juárez is much more complicated than the imagery conveyed by a monument, a school, or a metro stop. In fact, a major Juárez biographer, Ralph Roeder, argued in the 1940s that Juárez meant nothing to the people of Guelatao. Frustrated in his pursuit of original memories of Juárez, Roeder concluded, "the road to San Pablo Guelatao leads nowhere."[24] But Roeder was lost in his own preconceived notions of historical memory and myth. The Zapotec men and women of Guelatao indeed held strong memories of Juárez, but those memories were meshed with stories about themselves. From their perspective it has always been inadequate to talk only about a poor Indian boy who walked the dirt road from his community and later became one of the nation's greatest presidents. For the people Juárez left behind, the real heroes of Guelatao were men like Felipe García, the soldiers he led, and the women who risked their own lives to defend their homes and nation.

NOTES

1. About 150 people lived in Guelatao at the time of Juárez's birth; in 1878 the population had grown to just over 300 people. See Mexico, Dirrección General de Estadística, *Estadística de la República Mexicana de 1877 a 1878*, ed. Emiliano Busto (Mexico City, 1880).

2. See Colección Porfirio Díaz (hereafter CPD) 26-2 573-574, Felipe García and Anastasio García to Porfirio Díaz, January 4, 1901. See also CPD 26-3 1027,

Juan Juárez, Municipal President of Guelatao to Porfirio Díaz, January 4, 1901. For military background on Felipe García, see CPD 27-12 4586, Salvador Bolaños Cacho, *jefe político* of Ixtlán to Porfirio Díaz, April 23, 1902. Bolaños Cacho also included a list of the soldiers García led as captain.

3. Marcello Carmagnani, *El regreso de los dioses: El proceso de reconstitución de la identidad étnica en Oaxaca. Siglos XVII y XVIII* (Mexico: Fondo de Cultura Económica, 1988), 229–32.

4. "Exposición al Soberano Congreso de Oaxaca, 1849," in Benito Juárez, *Documentos, discursos y correspondencia*, vol. 1 (Mexico: Ed. Libros de Mexico, 1972), p. 659; and "Exposición al Soberano Congreso de Oaxaca, 1848," in Juárez, *Documentos*, 1:579.

5. See Brian R. Hamnett, *Juárez* (London: Longman, 1994), 37–38; and Carmagnani, *Regreso*, 234. Other state governors formed National Guard battalions around this same time. Alicia Hernández Chávez, "La Guardia Nacional y movilización política de los pueblos," in *Patterns of Contention in Mexican History*, ed. Jaime E. Rodríguez O. (Wilmington, DE: Scholarly Resources, 1992), 207, argues that the National Guard units offered peasant communities "new forms of political legitimacy and representation."

6. "Exposición 1852," in Juárez, *Documentos*, 1:781.

7. See Rosendo Pérez García, *La Sierra Juárez*, Part II (Mexico: Gráfica Cervantina, 1956), 16–17, 122–27. Díaz first learned about liberalism from Marcos Pérez, a university professor who had been imprisoned for defying Santa Anna in the 1840s. Pérez was himself a Zapotec Indian born in San Pedro Teococuilco in Ixtlán district.

8. See Benedict Anderson, *Imagined Communities: Reflections on the Origin and Spread of Nationalism* (London: Verson, 1991 [1983]). For a critique of Anderson's notion of the fraternal bonds implied by nationalism, see Patrick J. McNamara, " 'That Time of Unspeakable Hardship': Narratives of War and Popular Nationalism in Mexico, 1855–1911," American Historical Association Annual Conference, Boston, Massachusetts, January 5, 2001.

9. In addition to letters by and about Felipe García cited in note 3 see Archivo General del Estado de Oaxaca (hereafter cited as AGEO), Secretaría de Gobierno 116-9, resolution sent to Porfirio Díaz from the *Mesa Directiva de la Junta, "Juárez y Progreso,"* Guelatao, June 29, 1903. See also CPD 29-32 12438-12442, Felipe García et al. to Porfirio Díaz, October 12, 1904; CPD 29-32 12589, Guelatao villagers Martín Ramírez, Estéban Pérez, Pánfilo Pérez, and Tomás Martínez to Porfirio Díaz, October 15, 1904; CPD 30-38 15194-15197, Emilio Pimentel to Porfirio Díaz, October 28, 1905; CPD 30-24 9315-9316, Emilio Pimentel to Porfirio Díaz, July 8, 1905; CPD 30-32 12452, Lázaro Ruíz, Ixtlán *jefe político* to Porfirio Díaz, February 3, 1905, and the separate letter on the same date from Daniel Ramírez, Ixtlán's municipal president; and CPD 35-2 889, Tomás Soto, municipal president of Guelatao et al. to Porfirio Díaz, January 21, 1910.

10. The account given here comes from Porfirio Díaz, *Memorias*, vol. 1 (1994) and Pérez, *La Sierra Juárez*, 2:15–20.

11. AGEO, Gobernación, Paquete 1, Guelatao, Felipe García et al., July 10, 1864.

12. See, for example, CPD 31-17 6414-6415, María Marzana to Porfirio Díaz, June 18, 1906.

13. See the "Sumarias" against fifteen women and ten men collected by Manuel Martínez Gracida in *Gobierno Reacionario, conservador o mocho* [original documents, no date]. Incredibly, the confiscated letters are also included in this loose collection of documents within the Biblioteca Pública de Oaxaca, Sala Genaro Vásquez.

14. Archivo Municipal de Guelatao, Fundación Comunidad, Manuel Martínez Gracida, Caja 3, Expediente 10, June 7, 1865.

15. AGEO, Secretaría de Gobierno, 116-9, Felipe García et al. to Porfirio Díaz, Guelatao, June 29, 1903.

16. This phrase comes from a letter signed by more than 150 men from the Sierra Zapoteca at the time of Juárez's death; Biblioteca Nacional, Archivo Juárez, Supl. 527, July 20, 1872.

17. See Charles Weeks, *The Juárez Myth in Mexico* (Tuscaloosa: University of Alabama Press, 1987), 100–103.

18. Archivo General de la Nación (hereafter cited as AGN), Obregón y Calles 816-J-1, Natalio Ramírez et al. to Alvaro Obregón, December 20, 1920. Other documents in the same folder address the Guelatao request, including Amado Aguirre telegram to Alvaro Obregón, April 21, 1923. See also AGN, Obregón y Calles 805-I-4, Natalio Ramírez et al. to Manuel Vargas, February 8, 1921; AGEO, Período Revolucionario 21a-72, "El Presidente y miembro del Ayuntamiento de Guelatao felicitan al C. Gobernador del Edo," February 1, 1923; and AGN, Obregón y Calles 816-J-13, Isaac Ibarra to Alvaro Obregón, April 6, 1923.

19. AGEO, Período Revolucionario 21a-68, "El Agente municipal de Guelatao invita al gobierno para la ceremonia que tendrá . . . con motivo del natalico del Benemérito de las Américas," March 3, 1923; AGEO, Período Revolucionario, 25a-20, "Asuntos relacionados con las fiestas patrias celebrados en el ex-Dto Ixtlán," 1924; and AGEO, Período Revolucionario, 25a-105, "Relativo a la conmemoración del LII Aniversario de la muerte del ilustre reformador Lic. Benito Juárez," 1924.

20. AGN, Obregón y Calles 805-I-19, Alvaro Obregón to B. Flores, director of "Junta Protectora del Indio," state of Mexico, May 10, 1922.

21. See, for example, AGN, Abelardo Rodríguez 328-38, "Amado Pérez y otros solicitan ayuda pecuniaria para la celebración del CXXVIII aniversario del natalico del Lic. Benito Juárez," March 13, 1934.

22. Like the new school, other manifestations of government support came slowly to Guelatao. A potable water system was built in 1941, and the village did not receive access to electricity until 1946. See Pérez, *La Sierra Juárez*, 4:196–202.

23. For this interpretation, see especially Jesús Reyes Heroles, *El liberalismo mexicano*, 3 vols. (Mexico: UNAM, 1957–1961).

24. Ralph Roeder, *Juárez and His Mexico* (New York: The Viking Press, 1947), 1–10.

SUGGESTED READINGS

Countless biographers of Benito Juárez have told more or less the same rags-to-riches story. For a recent biography that emphasizes the personal challenges Juárez had to overcome, see Fernando Benítez, *Un indio zapoteco llamado Benito Juárez* (Mexico: Taurus, 1998). Brian R.

Hamnett, *Juárez* (London: Longman, 1994) provides a thorough analysis of Juárez's political career. And for an explanation of the cultlike status Juárez achieved following his death, see Charles Weeks, *The Juárez Myth in Mexico* (Tuscaloosa: University of Alabama Press, 1987). Juárez wrote his own biography in *Apuntes para mis hijos* (Mexico: Centro Mexicano de Estudios Culturales, 1968). He briefly mentioned the anguish he felt upon leaving his village in 1818, though his real remorse was that the region did not have adequate schools for teaching children how to read, write, and think in Spanish. Apart from this brief reference to his Indian past, Juárez rarely made public his feelings about Guelatao. Indian intellectuals today have no illusions about Juárez and the use of his image by state officials. According to the Zapotec poet Victor de la Cruz (originally from the Isthmus of Tehuantepec), "The so-called national heroes are fabrications of the dominant society." See Natividad Gutiérrez, *Nationalist Myths and Ethnic Identities: Indigenous Intellectuals and the Mexican State* (Lincoln: University of Nebraska Press, 1999), 175. For the importance of revolutionary icons after 1920, see Ilene V. O'Malley, *The Myth of the Revolution: Hero Cults and the Institutionalization of the Mexican State, 1920–1940* (New York: Greenwood Press, 1986). See also Samuel Brunk, "Remembering Emiliano Zapata: Three Moments in the Posthumous Career of the Martyr of Chinameca," *Hispanic American Historical Review* 78 (1998): 457–90.

As I argue in "Sons of the Sierra: Juárez, Díaz, and the Zapotec People of Ixtlán, Oaxaca, 1855–1911" (unpublished manuscript), memories, histories, and celebrations of Mexico's military past formed an essential part of rural political culture. For more on the Porfirian military, see Alicia Hernández Chávez, "Origen y ocaso del ejército porfiriano," *Historia Mexicana* 39, no. 1 (1989): 257–96. For a more complete exploration of the role of women during Mexico's wars of the 1850s and 1860s, see Florencia E. Mallon, *Peasant and Nation: The Making of Postcolonial Mexico and Peru* (Berkeley: University of California Press, 1995). See also Elizabeth Salas, *Soldaderas in the Mexican Military* (Austin: University of Texas Press, 1990). And for a more universal treatment of war and women, see Nancy Huston, "Tales of War and Tears of Women," *Women's Studies International Forum* 5 (1982): 271–82. The formation of a National Guard battalion in Ixtlán, Oaxaca, offered Zapotecs a way to simultaneously resist and adapt to the liberal state. For more on the notion of "resistant adaptation," see Steve J. Stern, "New Approaches to the Study of Peasant Rebellion and Consciousness: Implications of the Andean Experience," in *Resistance, Rebellion, and Consciousness in the Andean Peasant World*, ed. Steve J. Stern (Madison: University of Wisconsin Press, 1987), 3–25.

$\mathcal{A}$lejandro $\mathcal{P}$rieto

Científico from the Provinces

GLEN DAVID KUECKER

RICARDO FLORES MAGON

The Grand Canal, one of the great engineering projects in Mexican history and originally designated as a station on the silver subway (line B), illustrates the peculiar relationship of Mexico City to its environment. In their siege of the Aztec capital of Tenochtitlán, Spanish conquistadors destroyed the dikes that protected the island city from flooding. Once the natives had surrendered, however, they were forced to build a new capital on the ruins of their old metropolis. When the floods returned with devastating effects, particularly in the 1620s, the Spaniards determined to build a great canal to drain the shallow lakes in the Valley of Mexico. The work continued intermittently for the next three centuries, amid recurring floods, until the project was finally completed in 1900, draining Lake Texcoco completely. Mexico City thereupon began a century of unprecedented urban growth, culminating with a population approaching 20 million people. With the valley's ecological resources straining to the limits already in the 1970s, prominent scientists began calling for the recreation of Lake Texcoco, but the plan was never carried out.

The completion of the Grand Canal at the turn of the last century exemplified the modernizing vision of President Porfirio Díaz and his administrative corps of científicos. *Steeped in the positivism of French philosopher Auguste Comte, the* científicos *hoped to instill in Mexico the twin ideals of "order and progress." The Porfirian project also entailed social engineering, as the* científicos *sought to make the lower classes more efficient and productive, just like the machines that were imported from industrialized countries. Yet as this essay shows, the blueprints of progress elaborated in Mexico City often fit poorly with life in the provinces. The Faustian fate of Alejandro Prieto mirrors the historical memory of the Grand Canal; in 2002, following a political controversy about plans to construct a new airport on village land, the metro station was discreetly renamed for Ricardo Flores Magón, a revolutionary critic of Porfirian modernization.*

Glen David Kuecker received his Ph.D. from Rutgers University with a dissertation entitled "A Desert in the Tropical Wilderness: Limits

*to the Porfirian Project in Northeastern Veracruz, 1870–1910." He is
currently assistant professor of history and coordinator of conflict studies at
DePauw University in Greencastle, Indiana. His efforts to coordinate
human rights policies have taken him to Chiapas, Mexico, Bogotá, Co-
lombia, and many other trouble spots in Latin America.*

𝒥n August 1887, Alejandro Prieto stood at the crossroads of modern
Mexican history, between two symbiotic yet conflicted forces—the desire for progress and the need for order. The forty-six-year-old engineer
knew about progress, having been appointed by President Porfirio Díaz
to a vital infrastructure project, the construction of a railroad across the
Isthmus of Tehuantepec. A transcontinental line had operated for decades in Panama, but the Mexican project was far more ambitious; Prieto
envisioned nothing less than a system of three parallel tracks that would
combine to transport entire oceangoing ships between the Atlantic and
the Pacific. If completed successfully, this scheme promised to make
Mexico a hub of world commerce, but the technical difficulties of carrying cargo ships weighing thousands of tons more than a hundred kilo-
meters overland quickly became apparent. As the project literally bogged
down in tropical forests and swamps, Prieto received news from friends
back home, asking him to run for governor of the northern Gulf coast
state of Tamaulipas in the upcoming elections. He abandoned the quixotic railroad project and served two terms as governor, from 1888 to
1896, providing Tamaulipas with a shining example of the Porfirian slogan, "plenty of administration and not too much politics."[1] His gover-
nance personified the idea of order, especially the strategy of using the
state to guide Mexicans through the great transformations needed to
achieve progress.

Historians often consider the 1890s as the decade when the Porfirian
project became a reality. This was a time when past instabilities gave way
to order and progress, a moment when Mexicans focused on the task of
building what they imagined to be a modern nation-state. The Porfirian
project was an attempt at modernization from above, an initiative thrust
upon thousands of Mexican localities by national political and economic
planners operating from the capital, Mexico City. These planners, known
as *científicos*, sought to organize Mexico's political and economic development under the "scientific" political philosophy of positivism. Modernization was a process of long duration marked by incremental steps
toward the establishment of free-trade capitalism, a free-wage labor system, cultural values of a market economy and a capitalist work ethic, and
a political system in which the moderating power of the state would be
invested in a constitution and not in the individual. Although the inner

circle of *científicos* dominated the Porfirian cabinet, other planners, such as Alejandro Prieto, often worked from positions of power in the provinces, as governors or overseers of important projects.

This essay explores Alejandro Prieto's career in order to reveal the contours, meanings, and significance of this important time in Mexican history. It concentrates on three basic themes, first describing several of his development projects to show how he imagined modern Mexico. Second, it examines his larger conception of order and progress to illustrate the Porfirian view of good government as a necessary tool for navigating Mexico through the transformations and dislocations of modernity. Finally, the essay focuses on the capstone of Prieto's engineering career, an attempt to sanitize the port city of Tampico. This final section highlights the deep limitations to the Porfirian project. Running through these themes is the attempt by Porfirians to modernize Mexico by reworking space. Before engaging these themes and ideas, however, this essay offers a brief overview of Prieto's life.

Alejandro Prieto was born in 1841, the son of a wealthy family with extensive properties in southern Tamaulipas. His father, Ramón, was a local notable in the city of Tampico, Mexico's second most important Gulf coast port. Ramón served as Tampico's municipal president in 1839, 1849, and 1850. Alejandro completed his primary education in Tampico, then went to Mexico City for additional schooling, like the children of many local notables. He received a degree in topographical engineering from the National School of Agriculture in Mexico City and specialized in sanitation projects and railroad development. He later became a member of several prestigious Porfirian institutions, including the Mexican Geography and Statistical Society and the Mexican Mining Society. These memberships allowed Prieto access to the inner circles of the *científico* elite and provided a means for securing patronage for projects he imagined. Thus, the young Prieto undertook expeditions on behalf of the Mexican government to Guatemala City, Guatemala, and to San José, Costa Rica, as a consultant to development projects between 1876 and 1877.

Prieto's public service was also rooted in his participation in the resistance against the French Intervention (1862–1867). During the war he was captured by the French but avoided execution when a sympathetic Mexican serving with the French helped him escape. After the war he became a judge of the civil registry and city engineer in Tampico. His service in Tampico earned Prieto selection to the national congress in 1873, and he served as a deputy until his travels to Central America in 1876. After working on the Tehuantepec project during the 1880s, Prieto held office as governor of Tamaulipas between 1888 and 1896. His state political leadership continued even after the end of his second term, for a hand-picked successor, Guadalupe Mainero, served as governor until 1901. During the Mainero administration, former governor Prieto acted as President Díaz's unofficial representative in Tamaulipas, thus making the governor a de facto subordinate to Prieto.

Strong connections to Tampico played a fundamental role in Prieto's biography. Family ties in the port city provided an anchor for Prieto within the Porfirian patron–client system. His sister, Carolina Prieto, was the wife of Antonio Obregón, one of the port's leading political and business leaders. Their daughter, Esther, married Emilio Garza Robert, who was the son of Adela Robert and Rafael Garza Cortina. The Cortinas, Garzas, and Roberts were all leading merchants in the port. Within this family network, Gregorio Cortina Basadre, a nephew of Prieto, received special patronage during his uncle's tenure as governor. Gregorio served as municipal president in 1888 and 1890, and received a lucrative contract for building a new city market in Tampico, as well as one of the first concessions for supplying the city with potable water.

The combination of Prieto's engineering and political experience in turn provided Tampico with a connection to the Porfirian drive toward modernization. While governor, Prieto directed some of the most important modernizing projects in Tampico's history, including the introduction of railroad service, the removal of a sandbar that impeded shipping, the construction of new markets, and improvements to the port's piers and warehouses. After his tenure as governor, Prieto was called upon by Díaz to lead the battle against yellow fever by overseeing a sanitation project in Tampico.

Alejandro Prieto, like many within the governing elite, left firm statements about the Porfirian vision of modern Mexico. He articulated this imaginary Mexico in several publications, including a survey of the history, geography, and statistics of Tamaulipas (1873) and a study of colonization projects in the Isthmus of Tehuantepec (1884). The vision he produced was a combination of the discourse of a naturalist laying claim to raw nature and the measuring project of an engineer preparing to transform the lived environment. Prieto illustrated the Porfirian desire to capture nature through the use of science. In particular, he attempted to harness nature through a painstaking process of description, cataloging, measuring, accounting, placing, and finally possessing. In the Tehuantepec study, Prieto accomplished his goal of identifying suitable land for colonization projects by analyzing the region's climate, water systems, agricultural potential, land prices, tax laws, and process for claiming vacant lands. His goal in these studies was to make the natural world known through engineer's science so that nature could be claimed for modernity.

For his audience of administrators, politicians, diplomats, venture capitalists, and naturalists, Prieto provided a guide for taking the primary space of raw nature and transforming it into the secondary, man-made spaces of modernity. In delineating natural, primary space, Prieto located the target of the Porfirian project. The vision cast by Prieto was a restructuring of the spaces of Mexico through macrostructural transformation of the economy. The structural change would be accomplished by connecting local and regional production centers to global markets. In the vision of Porfirian planners, connecting spaces was to be accomplished by building new and better roads and modern port facilities, but the key to the project was construction of a national railroad grid.

Similar to other Porfirian planners, Prieto was a believer in the railroad and, in particular, a major promoter of the Tampico branch of the Mexican Central Railroad. He had originally proposed the project in the early 1870s and was instrumental in pushing for its completion during his governorship. He viewed the railroad as crucial to the development of Tampico. Speaking to a gathering of Tampico merchants in 1888, Prieto asserted, "Tampico's progress depends much on the termination of this project." With completion of the branch line, he claimed, "This city will completely wake-up from its prolonged lethargy of inaction in commercial activity and in the industries of agriculture, mining, and factories." The Porfirian awakening was rooted in an alteration of space, linking the port city—with its connections throughout the Caribbean, the East Coast of the United States, and Europe—to production centers and markets deep in the Mexican interior. The railroad dramatically reduced transportation costs and time, which altered the spatial logic of Mexico's place within global capitalism. Producers in faraway places like Aguascalientes or San Luis Potosí would now have access to previously unavailable markets in Europe and the United States.[2]

The reworking of space between ports and market centers was not the only transformation set off by railroad development. In the example of Tampico, planners like Prieto knew that infrastructure projects were necessary to handle the increases in economic activity. To meet the demand, Prieto called for a reworking of Tampico's physical space to better serve the needs of global commerce. The river system connecting Tampico to the Gulf of Mexico needed to be cleared and deepened so that modern steam vessels could call at the city docks and deposit cargoes near the new railroad tracks. New jetties were needed to protect vessels approaching the port from the strong winds and rough waters of Tampico's infamous northers. Wharves had to be built, as well as new storage facilities, a customs house, and new buildings for shipping line offices and merchant houses. A wave of migrants came to meet the labor demand. They built new housing whose neighborhoods pushed city limits well beyond the pre-railroad boom spaces. As modern Tampico was born, its urban space was transformed.

While Porfirian planners were preoccupied with building modern Mexico, they were equally concerned about maintaining social and political order. Prieto once stated, "Peace is the indispensable cement that serves as the foundation of the social edifice." Like other Porfirians, he believed "it is the departure point for all administrative work, of all civilizing influences." The absolute need for order as a precondition to progress was clearly implanted in the minds of Prieto's generation. These Mexicans were born into the tumult of the early national period. They had experienced war firsthand and knew the devastation civil strife had caused the progressive development of the nation-state. Prieto and his generation were eager to put aside politics in order to construct the edifice of the nation on firm economic foundations. For them, the experience of war and the heated passions of the previous era's partisan politics were balanced by the scientific reasoning of positivist philosophy. Prieto's training as an engineer transformed the slogan of "order and progress" into basic propositions of good government. The proposition was simple: politics meant enhancing the powers of the state in the areas of public administration. Such power ensured stability and gave Porfirian planners the capacity to contain the forces of change unleashed by their modernizing projects. As progress in economics stimulated dislocations in society and culture, good administration offered the ability to order the dislocations and shape Mexicans into docile, disciplined, sober, and hardworking servants of modernity.[3]

During two terms as governor of Tamaulipas, Prieto dispensed plenty of administration. His semiannual reports to the state legislature reveal a progressive development of a modern state apparatus from a dysfunctional shell of government. Prieto oversaw a dramatic expansion of the state's jurisdiction over the lives of Tamaulipecos. Three areas of statecraft were especially important: raising revenues, infrastructure development, and the regulation of the body. State finances were necessary to increase the power of the state. Likewise, increased revenues were vital for providing political stability, as the state was better able to satisfy discontented parties through distribution of benefits to the disgruntled. Prieto reworked revenue collection systems, including the undertaking of a property census, and used tax incentives to promote the development of mining and agriculture in Tamaulipas. He also worked to build new roads and railroads, with special concern for integrating Tampico with interior cities and markets. Under Prieto's rule, state power over the individual increased. New prisons were constructed, public health projects were instituted, and education became more commonplace. State control over the body also came with new methods of counting people and with improvements in the civil registry. Further defining the administrative function of the Porfirian state, Prieto, ever the engineer, settled a boundary dispute with Nuevo León. Each measure of administration was believed by Porfirians to be a manifestation of progress and a concrete demonstration of Mexico's arrival in the ranks of modern nations.

Signs of progress were obvious to many folks in Tamaulipas. On September 15, 1899, for example, Tampico's municipal president, José María Maraboto, wrote a memorandum to the federal government praising Governor Prieto. "The whole country can see, with unanimous applause, the persistence with which [the governor] has pursued the country's development and progress. The beneficial protection of peace has generated innumerable and important industries, expanded commerce, improved all public services, [and] secured the solid basis for the national credit." Maraboto compared Tampico's material progress—the arrival of the Mexican Central Railroad, the dredging of the bar of Tampico, the new jetties, the construction of the customs house, and the new wharves and piers—to the projects under way in the rival port of Veracruz. Maraboto, however, moved beyond a celebration of the modernizing accomplishments. He addressed the problem of the port city's health and sanitation, presenting them to be the most significant challenge to Tampico's capacity to sustain "progress and civilization."[4]

Although Prieto's works helped to transform Tampico from a stagnant backwater into a modern port, they did not automatically invest Tampico with permanence in the larger Porfirian project. Modernization created new problems that threatened to undermine Tampico's place in modern Mexico. The completed projects, according to Maraboto, had "not actually offered the advantages that are desirable in regards to hygiene and health. In Veracruz yellow fever is endemic and in Tampico . . . various bouts with yellow fever have appeared, which in the last year caused considerable havoc." Disorder resulted not solely from the terror and panic associated with epidemics, but from the disruption yellow fever wrought upon Tampico's role within the regional economic system. "It is important to note," Maraboto cautioned, "that every appearance of yellow fever in Tampico constitutes a serious threat to all of Tamaulipas." As people and cargo moved to and from the port, yellow fever traveled along. An outbreak of yellow fever in Tampico consequently held the potential for infecting interior regions serviced by the port.[5]

Responding to Maraboto, the federal government perceived Tampico's yellow fever problem in even larger terms. "I only want to add," replied the Interior Minister, that "I have been taught that when yellow fever invades Tampico, not only do we see Tamaulipas and its other *tierra caliente* (low country) neighbors seriously threatened, but through the connection of railway lines with those of the American nation, it also affects international traffic." Yellow fever, therefore, challenged Tampico's place in the Porfirian project by threatening to convey a deadly disease throughout Mexico, the borderlands with the United States, and the entire Caribbean region. The scope of the problem was immense from all perspectives—local, state, national, and international.[6]

The alterations to Tampico's urban geography caused by modernization had unintended consequences for the port's disease environment, making it vulnerable to sudden and unpredictable yellow fever outbreaks. Increased migration to the port not only augmented its nonimmune population but also led to the growth of new neighborhoods that increased the number of mosquito vector habitats and breeding grounds, such as cisterns, gutters, and standing water. The increased density, poor living conditions, and high turnover of the port's population combined with Tampico's enhanced communication with endemic centers to push the city beyond a critical point that made the sustained transmission and propagation of yellow fever a reality in Tampico by 1898. To overcome yellow fever's threat to Tampico's modernization, Porfirians had to undo the nexus of factors making yellow fever possible in the port. This was a complicated proposition, as health officials did not know for certain what caused yellow fever or even how it was transmitted.

The core of the problem was the port's lack of basic sanitation. Maraboto speculated that yellow fever was "caused by the lack of sewers . . . the deficient quality of water that the majority of the people drink, and the porous nature of the streets that allow gases to evaporate into the atmosphere from the puddles made by the boorish." Local doctors, he continued, "have indicated that to annul the effects of these physical conditions the establishment of a complete system of sewers, the paving of the streets, and the introduction of drinkable water" were all necessary.[7]

Porfirio Díaz called upon Prieto to cure Tampico of yellow fever. The former governor returned to the engineer's drawing board and devised the final modernizing scheme of his public life. Prieto's sanitation project was an ambitious and expensive effort to transform the port into a healthy, modern city. He outlined the project in an aggressive plan of action published in a 116-page prospectus. The detail of the publication, including descriptions of everything from the smallest pipe needed to the exact location of sewer connections, was exceeded only by the project's audacity. It took a modernizer like Prieto to imagine such a bold restructuring of the port's urban geography. He called for a complete sewer system, the supply of drinkable water to every household and building, and the elevation of low-lying sectors of the city above river level. Prieto's aim was to break the port's connection to yellow fever by transforming the physical spaces of Tampico. In his vision, a sanitized Tampico would be a modern, self-regulating mechanism, an urban environment with a defused yellow fever nexus.

Despite having a plan in place by 1898, Prieto did not manage to finalize a contract for the work until 1901. The delay was not uncommon for Porfirian planners, as they confronted very real limitations in their abilities to implement grandiose development schemes. All too often, the perfect visions of the engineers' drafts were compromised by Mexico's dependent position within global capitalism, which offered Porfirian planners more vision than capital. In Prieto's case, although he negotiated several contracts between the city and federal governments, he failed to find the money necessary to start work. True to the Porfirian pattern of progress, he then turned to foreign businesspeople. Prieto negotiated a contract with two New York capitalists, Markus W. Conkling and William Astor Chanler. The budget of 3,066,000 pesos was to be paid in twenty-five years out of the local share of the port's customs receipts. In exchange, Tampico was to receive a system capable of supplying fresh water to 50,000 people and 1,154 properties. A sewer system would also be built, but only in the better neighborhoods. If money permitted, fire hydrants were to be included. The contract sacrificed the extensive landfill plans as well as the much-needed sewers in the working-class neighborhoods.

It was not until January 1902 that ground was broken on the project. Enthusiasm for the sanitation project ran high among Tampiqueños. Prieto, of course, led this boosterism with an album compiled in July 1903 for the St. Louis Exposition. He presented to the world a hygienic image of Tampico as a safe, clean, secure, and healthy place of modernity. It was a place where capitalists could invest their money and where the commerce of the world could find an accommodating place of business. He stated to President Díaz, "The next exposition in St. Louis, Missouri is without question an opportune occasion to let the civilized peoples of the world know of the progress of Mexico."[8] Prieto's enthusiasm was matched by Gustavo A. Populus, an owner of an office furniture company in Tampico. "In Tampico," he wrote to a friend, "there is much talk of great works, they are planning large projects of sanitation, drainage, and the introduction of drinking water." He continued, "we Tampiqueños as you will surely understand desire that this work is completed, because we do not doubt that it will mean great progress for our city."[9]

Tampico's sanitation solution, however, was riddled with problems that came to a breaking point in 1905. Budget restraints meant that Tampico's "perfect sanitation" could be only imperfectly fulfilled. Inadequate resources also meant that much of the construction was improperly done. Contractors and city officials struggled to cut corners in order to make budgets. These limitations imperiled city dwellers, especially those unfortunates living in areas designated for elevation. The experiences of O. Del Grottes, R. Ramírez, and M. García were typical of how Tampiqueños lived the promise of sanitation. Problems began when city officials ordered them to take down fences on their property, which they did at "considerable expense." Once work was done, their property was a full meter lower than before work began and flooded out with even modest rains. They complained to President Díaz, "when it rains, water rushes in from the street." Even worse, Grottes, Ramírez, and García borrowed money to fill in their land and prevent flooding. "The authorities as well as the contractor are not ignorant of this situation, nevertheless our petitions are not heard by them, and there is not one voice risen for our cause." They concluded, "through these sacrifices we have been left in conditions not at all hygienic."[10] Likewise, Lauro Martínez explained to Díaz that there was "great trouble not only for the property owners, but also for the public in general, to the extent that [the work] has endangered citizens' lives due to the pools of water that form as a result of bad work." At least 500 properties had been damaged, and he concluded that "what this trouble represents is the ruin of a town."[11] Among the 500 injured property owners was Nicolás López, who secured a court order against the contractor's right to excavate the city's communal property. The property remained outside of the contractor's use until 1908, when the Mexican Supreme Court overturned the injunction.[12]

Local discontent over the poor quality of work and the abuses of the contractors focused on the planner, Alejandro Prieto. For example, a local newspaper, *El Cronista*, ran stories highly critical of his role in the project, accusing him of giving away municipal property to the contractors. By March 1905, Prieto found it necessary to address the newspaper attacks by writing a long, public letter to Governor Argüelles. In it he explained to Tampiqueños that the federal government was to blame for giving land use rights to the contractors, and that he had nothing to do with these negotiations. Now a controversial figure, Prieto was of little value to Conkling and Chanler, who "without notice nor explanation" stopped paying Prieto's salary in January 1906.[13] The former governor wrote to Chanler several times, asking for an explanation, but never received a reply. In February, the New Yorkers officially fired Prieto. Having soon fallen into financial difficulty, Prieto wrote to his patron, President Díaz, desperately asking for a job as the administrator of taxes in Tampico. He explained that "I am left with very little hope that I will be retained by the contractor."[14] Prieto sent the president all of his correspondence on the sanitation project and said he was very concerned that rumors and attacks against him would reach the president. When juxtaposed against the energy and vision of Prieto's original sanitation plan, his rapid and inglorious downfall of 1905 provides a remarkable statement about the ephemeral nature of modernization in Porfirian Mexico. The bottom line was that the goal of securing a place in modernity was more distant than the Porfirian planners' ability to reach. In the case of Prieto, the sanitation project outpaced reality and destroyed its promoter.

Consideration of Prieto's fate recalls the portrayal by Marshall Berman of Goethe's tragic modernizer, Faust. In the final episode of the epic poem, Faust finds meaning in his world by engaging in a grandiose development project to tame the oceans at a terrible human cost. Faust, not unlike Porfirian planners, is willing to make others pay this price because of his firm conviction that their suffering will pay dividends of happiness in the future. His utopian vision, however, crumbles due to the recalcitrance of the premodern world, represented by Philemon and Baucis, "a sweet old couple" who own land exactly where Faust wants to build the final project of his modernization scheme. Unwilling to give way, Faust has the couple killed, but he falls into a period of remorse for his actions. The story, Berman believes, reveals the modernizer's deepest fears of insecurity about the trade-offs of modernity: the extensive human costs of destroying the old to make the new, the discontents caused by the modern creation, and the problem of modernity's reproduction. The modernizer's empty fate ultimately is revealed in a disturbing irony: "once the developer has destroyed the pre-modern world, he has destroyed his whole reason for being in the world." Prieto's fate paralleled that of Faust, but for an important exception. The Porfirian project in Tampico was imperfect in its ability to complete the destruction of Tampico's premodern world of floods, epidemics, and lack of control over nature. Prieto, using Berman's terms for dependent development, was a pseudo-Faust pursuing the original's model of development.[15]

NOTES

1. Quoted in Alan Knight, *The Mexican Revolution*, vol. 1, *Porfirians, Liberals, and Peasants* (Lincoln: University of Nebraska Press, 1986), 15.

2. Alejandro Prieto, "Discurso pronunciado en Tampico la Noche del 1 de Febrero de 1888 en el Circulo electoral Tampiqueño," *Discursos leidos por el Señor Gobernador del Estado de Tamaulipas* (Victoria: Imprenta de "El Eco del Centro," 1891), 21 and 22.

3. Alejandro Prieto, "Manifiesto que Dirige el C. Ingeniero Alejandro Prieto a los Pueblos del Estado de Tamaulipas," *Discursos leidos por el Señor Gobernador del Estado de Tamaulipas* (Victoria: Imprenta de "El Eco del Centro," 1891), 16.

4. José María Maraboto to Ministero del Estado, September 15, 1899, Caja 26, Legajo 24, FS: 012601, Colección Porfirio Díaz, Universidad Iberoamericana, Mexico City (hereafter cited as CPD C/L/FS).

5. Ibid.

6. Secretaria de Gobernacion to Ayuntamiento de Tampico, September 15, 1899, CPD/C26/L24/FS: 012600.

7. Maraboto to Ministero del Estado, CPD/C26/L24/FS: 012601.

8. Alejandro Prieto to Porfirio Díaz, CPD/C27/L28/FS: 010633-34.

9. Gustavo A. Populus to Francisco Esteves, October 20, 1901, CPD/C8/L28/FS: 002939.

10. O. Del Grottes, R. Ramírez, and M. Garcia to Porfirio Díaz, March 15, 1905, CPD/ C10/L30/FS: 003996.

11. Lauro Martínez to Porfirio Díaz, October 17, 1905, CPD/C36/L30/FS: 014382-3.

12. Suprema Corte, Caja 619; Expediente 42, Archivo General de la Nación. Mexico City.

13. Alejandro Prieto to Alfredo Chavero, June 8, 1906, CPD/C18/L31/FS: 006974-77.

14. Alejandro Prieto to Porfirio Díaz, February 21, 1906, CPD/C9/L31/FS: 003316.

15. Marshall Berman, *All That Is Solid Melts into the Air: The Experience of Modernity* (New York: Penguin Books, 1988. First published in 1982), 70.

SUGGESTED READINGS

Berman, Marshall. *All That Is Solid Melts into the Air: The Experience of Modernity*. New York: Penguin Books, 1988. First published in 1982.

Knight, Alan. *The Mexican Revolution*, vol. 1, *Porfirians, Liberals, and Peasants*. Cambridge: Cambridge University Press, 1986.

Prieto, Alejandro. *Historia, geografia y estadistica del Estado de Tamaulipas*. Mexico: Tip. Escalerillas num. 13, 1873.

_____. *La colonizacion del Istmo de Tehuantepec*. Mexico: Imp. de I. Cumplido, 1884.

_____. *Discursos leidos por el Señor Gobernador del Estado de Tamaulipas*. Victoria: Imprenta de "El Eco del Centro," 1891.

_____. *Proyectos de mejoras materiales de salubridad é higiene en el puerto de Tampico*. Mexico: Oficina Tip. de la Secretaría de Fomento, 1899.

CHAPTER SEVEN

Juana Belén Gutiérrez de Mendoza

Woman of Words, Woman of Actions

SUSIE S. PORTER

 *Normal, the Mexico City teachers'
school, located on the blue metro line
(number 2), epitomizes the promise
of universal education that was a
primary focus of nineteenth-century liberalism. In the life of Juana
Gutiérrez, a prominent teacher and journalist, we see yet a third version
of that basic ideology, distinct from both the communal citizenship demanded by the campesinos of Guelatao and the obsession with material
progress of the* científico *elite, which were described in the previous two
selections. Gutiérrez's early life on a hacienda and her escape through the
fortuitous opportunity to gain an education contain some parallels with
the experiences of that classic liberal hero, Benito Juárez. Neverthelesss,
she came to understand the costs to ordinary Mexicans of the Reform laws
that he helped enact. She and other journalists who dared to attack the
dictatorship of Porfirio Díaz spent considerable time in prison and, as a
result, their liberal beliefs became radicalized over time. For a time she
collaborated with Ricardo Flores Magón, but her feminist convictions soon
led to an acrimonious split with the prominent anarchist. This essay highlights the unique difficulties faced by women opposition leaders as they
attempted to reconcile political activism with the traditional demands of
family life. Their sacrifices were not in vain, however, for they expanded
the opportunities for future generations of Mexican women as teachers
and in other professions.*

*Susie S. Porter received her Ph.D. from the University of Califor-
nia, San Diego, with a dissertation entitled "In the Shadows of Industrialization: The Entrance of Women into the Mexican Industrial Work
Force, 1880–1940." She is assistant professor of history at the University
of Utah.*

The life of Juana Belén Gutiérrez de Mendoza, while in ways uncommon, fits within important trends in the lives of Mexican women of the
late nineteenth century. This generation of women, informed by the
political tradition of liberalism that emphasized individual rights and

citizenship, took advantage of new opportunities for women in education, politics, and employment. They built upon these experiences, fash-
ioning an understanding of liberalism that better reflected their goals
and changed Mexican society not only for women but for all Mexicans.
Their individual experiences of radicalization occurred within the context of the Porfiriato (1876–1911) and the coming and process of the
Mexican Revolution. Juana Gutiérrez de Mendoza was among those
Mexicans who held a radical interpretation of the liberalism of Benito
Juárez. Her belief in individual rights, education, and the separation of
church and state eventually led her to early participation in the Partido
Liberal Mexicano (Mexican Liberal Party). Her participation in politics—and time spent in prison because of this participation—resulted in
the radicalization of her politics and her support of a socialism tailored
to the realities of Mexico. Gutiérrez de Mendoza and women like her
could be described as feminists inasmuch as they both celebrated the
role of women in Mexican history and worked to improve the position of
women in the future of Mexico. This generation of women followed
different career paths as teachers, doctors, and journalists, and many participated in Mexican politics; some, like Gutiérrez de Mendoza, became
revolutionaries.

Women's increasing participation in Mexican political life occurred
within the context of economic modernization associated with the
Porfiriato and the political ferment that development engendered. Juana
Belén Gutiérrez was born the year before Porfirio Díaz became president of Mexico for the first time. As she grew up, Gutiérrez would come
to understand that her social condition, and that of many Mexicans like
her, was that of those marginalized from the benefits of the Porfirian
project. On the one hand, the Díaz government facilitated many of the
things associated with modernization. Since Independence, the presidency had changed hands seventy-five times, and so in some respects his
government brought political stability. Porfirio Díaz imposed the rule of
law with the expansion of the rural police and the cultivation of a web of
regional alliances to consolidate his power. His government inherited an
overwhelmingly rural country with an empty treasury, poor credit on
the world market, a long list of foreign debts, a trade deficit, and a mining sector outdated and languishing from neglect. Díaz passed legislation favoring foreign investment, the expansion of transportation,
banking, industrial development, and the mining sector. Steam, water,
and electricity began to replace animal and human muscle; the government expanded its capacity to improve public health and sanitation, transportation networks, and communication infrastructure. Mining became
profitable once again, commercial agricultural production expanded, industry developed rapidly, and certain of the arts flourished. On the other

hand, though, modernity came at a cost to many. Agricultural workers, for example, were worse off financially than their rural ancestors a century before. While average daily wages remained nearly steady, the cost of basic goods such as corn and chile more than doubled, and beans cost six times more in 1910 than in 1800. Gutiérrez was born into these contradictions characteristic of modernity. The unique mix of circumstances of her life—a woman of modest origins who was able to receive an education—gave her the insight and the power to speak about and fight against these very contradictions.

The Gutiérrez family came from the Mexican countryside. Their history mirrored that of many Mexicans in the mid- to late nineteenth century. The series of laws known as La Reforma facilitated the transfer of land from indigenous communities and the Catholic Church to new hands. This transfer of land both resulted from and facilitated the expansion of commercial agricultural production, further benefiting large landholders. Men and women migrated from rural areas to haciendas and provincial cities to work as day laborers and factory workers. Born in Jalisco, her father, Santiago Gutiérrez Lomelí, left his homeland as a young man in search of work. Gutiérrez decided to head north and came to settle in the state of Durango where work opportunities were opening up in newly established manufactories. There he met and married Porfiria Chávez, with whom he had three children. Santiago Gutiérrez and his wife eventually settled in San Pedro Gallo, Durango, where he worked for some time on Roncesvalles hacienda, both in his trade as blacksmith and in odd jobs as a day laborer. Porfiria worked in their home.

Juana grew up on the hacienda where her father worked, along with the children of other campesinos and workers, and like those children she did not expect to go to school. The Mexican government made some advances in the provision of education in the second half of the nineteenth century; however, the beneficiaries of these advances were limited in number and by sex. The 1867 Juárez Declaration made primary education obligatory, and mandated that municipal governments and hacendados provide schools for residents. Nationwide, however, few Mexicans received a formal education. In 1874 there were 8,103 schools, which tended to be located in cities. Educational opportunities for girls were limited: fewer than 550 schools were coeducational, and of the remainder, about four to one were for boys only.

The Díaz government encouraged the education of girls when it passed the Regulation for Girls' Primary and Secondary Schools in 1878. Female education at this time retained much of its emphasis on preparing women to be better wives and mothers. Educated women, their supporters argued, would be better equipped in their primary responsibility of raising future citizens—implicitly male citizens. They were not taught history or civics, but were instructed in "obligations of the woman in society and of the mother in her relations with the family and state."[1] This emphasis on citizenship fit within larger patterns of secularization and signaled shifting authority from the Church to the state, and the desire to imbue women with a civic-minded morality that, while still founded in spirituality, was less informed by the Church and more by liberal thought. At the same time, the government encouraged education for lower- and middle-class women that led to employment. The Women's Normal School opened in 1890, largely enrolling women from the growing middle class. For women of more humble means, the government established the School of Arts and Vocations in 1892. By the end of the century over 1,000 students enrolled in this school, which instructed women in sewing, embroidery, and other sorts of handiwork tied to industrial production. These schools were urban institutions and had no impact on the lives of women like Gutiérrez.

The story of how Juana Gutiérrez came to receive an education is one of unusual opportunity. As a child, Juana spent her days working in the house with her mother, running errands, playing with friends, and occasionally finding time to herself. One day she was walking along an isolated part of the hacienda when she saw a piece of paper flitting along, carried by a dry breeze. Beneath the dirt she could see that something was printed on the paper. Seeing the printed letters made her dash after the dancing fragment until she caught it up in her hand. Juana found a grove of trees and settled in among the trunks to examine the enigmatic lines of print. But the letters continued to dance in front of her eyes just as they had when carried by the wind, almost taunting her with their incomprehensibility. The more she concentrated, the more her desire grew to penetrate their world, and the more she felt herself sink into the darkness of the tree trunks and the dryness of the earth beneath her. Then she heard a voice asking, "Is it hard for you to read?" It was Don Felipe, the owner of the tree trunks, the dust, the tattered piece of paper she held in her hand, and the hacienda that contained them all. Juana believed that it was a crime to read and felt as if she had been turned into dust herself.[2]

"Yes," Juana answered tentatively.

"Well, then why don't you go to school?" It was a response that greatly surprised Juana. His question was so startling that she could not think to answer.

"Why don't you go to school?" he asked again.

Juana burst into tears both from the confusion of the situation and her frustrated desire to go to school. As the tears filled her face and took away her words, Don Felipe continued to look at her and repeat his question.

Finally, Juana responded, "Because they won't let me."

"They will let you go. I will speak with your father and he will let you go."

"Dad yes, but Mom no."

"Your mother too. Tomorrow I will go see them." And with that Don Felipe went on his way, leaving Juana in the fold of the tree trunks, the dusty letters grasped tightly in her hand.

The rest of the day was heavy with anticipation. Juana continued with her chores at home and remained silent about her encounter. The next day after breakfast her father told her that in the coming month she would begin going to school. Her mother, in an angry voice, told Juana to clear the table, wash the plates, and get on with her household chores. The heavy burden of female labor in the countryside, particularly the onerous task of grinding corn by hand to make the daily tortillas, contributed to the traditional lack of schooling for women.

The education Juana Belén Gutiérrez received at the hacienda school proved to be an important influence in her life. Words would continue to shape her sense of herself and of the world. In 1892, at the age of seventeen, she married Cirilo Mendoza, a miner ten years her senior, in Sierra Mojada, Coahuila. She taught him how to read and write. Cirilo and Juana had three children together: Santiago, who died in infancy, Julia, and Laura Mendoza. Soon thereafter, Cirilo died, leaving Gutiérrez de Mendoza a young widow with two children to support. At twenty-two years of age she began working as a newspaper correspondent. Her work as a journalist writing about social injustice occurred at a time when many adherents of liberal thought were developing a critique of the Mexican government. She wrote for two opposition newspapers, *El Diario del Hogar* (established by Filomeno Mata in 1881) and *El Hijo del Ahuizote* (established by Péres Bibbins and later acquired and directed by Daniel Cabrera). Her interest in the working conditions of miners and in the presidency of Porfirio Díaz, which she held responsible for inhumane work conditions, became a focal point of her writing. Her articles landed her in prison in 1897. As would be a pattern in her life, the time she spent in prison would shape her thinking and lead her to new action. After leaving prison, she reaffirmed her commitment to fighting against the social and political conditions upon which she reported.[3]

In 1901, Juana moved to Guanajuato with her children. There she decided to publish a newspaper as a means of continuing to give voice to her views and to liberal and anti-Porfirian ideas. She named the newspaper *Vesper* after the star she had spent evenings watching with her son Santiago before he died. The title suggested hope and keeping an eye toward the horizon. To the title she added the slogan "Justice and Liberty" to capture her political priorities. In a short time the cost of running the press took up all her savings. In order to continue her work, she sold what at that time was not only her most precious possession but an important means of generating household income: her goats. "My goats! I confess that when I arrived at this critical moment I felt the impulse to return to the mountains, a desperate urge to hug Sancha, my favorite goat, to once again climb the hilltops and see the sun, that burning sun which reverberated in the hills, and burned the face. Yes, return to the mountains."[4] At the time, her personal life vied for importance over the stacks of paper and words directed against the things she saw and wrote about. Despite these feelings, Juana decided that Porfirio Díaz had committed serious injustices and that while he was president she would not return to the mountains. With the money she earned from the sale of her goats and the modest contributions of political sympathizers, Juana continued printing *Vesper*. Her attacks against Porfirio Díaz and his political allies did not sit well with the governor of Guanajuato. Late in the evening of December 9, 1901, a friend called on her to warn her that the governor had ordered her arrest. The idea of being sent to El Castillo de Granaditas prison, which sat up on a hill overlooking the city, led her not to wait for a second warning. Juana left the city immediately.

On January 2, 1902, Juana awoke in the City of Palaces (Mexico City). She recalled, "I couldn't sleep, because when I tried to do so I thought I saw kidnappers carrying off my children. I couldn't even figure out how to go about in the streets for fear that they would rip the little ones from my hands." Such fears of a woman from the provinces soon faded and she took up her political work once again, including reinitiating publication of *Vesper*.

Gutiérrez de Mendoza was one of many Mexicans who formed organizations for reasons of politics, religion, fellowship, and mutual support. Mexican women had a tradition of their own, all-female organizations that they continued to support, and they began to join with men in mixed-sex organizations as well. Gutiérrez de Mendoza became a member of the lodge Liga Republicana (Republican League), which advocated fellowship in contrast to Catholicism and whose members included Doña Laureana Wright de Kleinhans and Doctor Matilde Montoya. The latter two women were important figures in this generation of women. Laureana Wright de Kleinhans (1846–1896) was born in Taxco, Guerrero, and was active in various social organizations such as the Liceo Hidalgo, the Scientific Society "El Porvenir," and the Liceo Mexicano. She was the director of and an active contributor to the women's magazine *Violetas de Anáhuac* (1887–1889), which concerned itself with charitable activities, social conditions, and women's position in Mexican society, including the right to vote. Wright de Kleinhans was also the author of *Mujeres notables mexicanas*, which celebrated Mexican women's accomplishments. Matilde Montoya (1859–1938) was the first woman to receive a degree in medicine in Mexico. She practiced obstetrics in the early 1870s and received a degree as a surgeon in 1887, despite great opposition to her attendance at medical school.[5]

The years 1901 to 1903 were important ones in the movement against the presidency of Porfirio Díaz and transformative ones for Gutiérrez de Mendoza. She joined the group of men and women who came together around Camilo Arriaga. A mining engineer by training, Arriaga joined the anti-Díaz movement because of the president's modus vivendi with the Catholic Church. He organized the Club Liberal Camilo Arriaga (Camilo Arriaga Liberal Club), which held its first congress in 1901 in San Luis Potosí and would come to be identified as a central early contributor to the ideological foundations of the Mexican Revolution. At this congress, Gutiérrez de Mendoza served as First Committee Member on the organization's manifesto. The manifesto adopted a series of narrowly conceived resolutions that were largely anticlerical in nature. From these limited beginnings, men and women who supported the liberal cause began to come together in recognition of their common goals and to organize in increasing numbers.

Women formed their own, all-female organizations and also joined with men in mixed-sex organizations. Some of the women's organizations included Admiradoras de Juárez (Admirers of Juárez) (1904), Sociedad Protectora de la Mujer (Society for the Protection of Women) (1904), and the Hijas de Anáhuac (Daughters of Anáhuac) (1907). Many of the women who joined the Partido Liberal Mexicano (PLM) were also active in newspaper publishing, organizing women, and fighting in various capacities during the Revolution. One member, Sara Estela Ramírez (1881–1910), was a teacher, writer, and labor organizer from Coahuila who at age twenty-four edited the newspaper *La Corregidora*. The name for this newspaper, which appeared in 1901, acknowledged Josefa Ortiz de Domínguez—La Corregidora—as a heroine of the struggle for Mexican Independence. Ortiz de Domínguez, the wife of the *corregidor* (Spanish magistrate) of Querétaro, communicated the message that sparked the call to arms in September 1810. In choosing the name for her newspaper, Ramírez associated her publication with that most legitimate of causes, Mexican Independence, while honoring women's role in that history. Teacher, writer, and political activist Elisa Acuña y Rosete (?–1946) also joined the PLM. She later published *La Guillotina*, directed against the dictatorship of Victoriano Huerta (1913–1914), and helped to organize the feminist organization Las Hijas de Cuauhtémoc (The Daughters of Cuauhtémoc) and the First Feminist Congress of the Pan-American Women's League in 1923.

The spread of antigovernment activities soon became the object of scrutiny and persecution by the Díaz government. In 1903 the Díaz government had several opposition journalists arrested, including journalists for *Excelsior*, *El Hijo del Ahuizote*, and *Vesper*. Gutiérrez de Mendoza was among those sent to prison. Her extended stay in prison was a revelatory experience; it was a moment of reevaluation of her relationship to the law and how she thought of her struggle to improve the circumstances of her fellow Mexicans. In later reminiscences, Gutiérrez de Mendoza recalled:

> Prison, with its cruel realities, informed me of my distance from reality. I no longer believed that the downfall, death, or any sort of suppression of the President of the Republic was sufficient to resolve all problems. That multitude of human beings, tortured in the name of the law, all at once changed my criteria; that immense pain, that misery as deep as a chasm, would not be cured with democratic bandages. There in prison there were beings torn from the human condition, transformed into I don't know what kind of monstrosity of abjection and pain. It would have been impossible to end all that with a simple and exact application of the law, especially given that it was precisely the application of that odious instrument which had transformed humanity into a monster.
>
> The law had been applied to the little ones buried in the snow at Roncesvalles (hacienda); the law had been applied to the miners who remained buried in the cave-in at La Sirena mine; the law had been applied to those peons I had seen work from four in the morning to six in the evening, all for a hand full of corn. The law had been applied to all those I had seen suffer.[6]

When Gutiérrez de Mendoza was released from prison in December of 1904, the Flores Magón brothers and other PLM members—who had also been in prison—invited her to accompany them into exile. At first Gutiérrez de Mendoza hesitated. She resisted the idea of fighting against conditions in Mexico from exile in the United States. Nevertheless, after receiving several encouraging letters from those who had gone ahead, Juana decided to join them. Together they engaged in a variety of political activities including reinitiating anti-Porfirian publications, fundraising, and political demonstrations in Mexican American and Mexican exile communities. Disputes soon split the group. Juana Gutiérrez de Mendoza, Elisa Acuña y Rosete, and Sara Estela Ramírez eventually moved to Laredo, Texas, and made efforts to reinitiate publication of *Vesper*. They also published *La Protesta Nacional*, which appeared as if printed in Saltillo, Mexico, in order to avoid arrest.

Political and ideological disputes emerged among members of the PLM over the radicalization of some members and their diverging alliances to liberalism, socialism, and anarcho-syndicalism. The disputes, which split the exile community, turned increasingly personal. Ricardo

Flores Magón made aggressive attacks against Gutiérrez de Mendoza, focusing not on her politics but on her personal character. In attempts to discredit Gutiérrez de Mendoza and her allies, he claimed that she and Acuña y Rosete had a sexual relationship. Flores Magón referred to their relationship in a private letter as "disgusting." He wrote, "When we were in San Antonio we found out, this is disgusting, that Doña Juana and Elisa Acuña y Rosete gave themselves to a putrid lesbianism—which we found repugnant. . . . We were repelled by this, and consider it shameful to maintain contact with these women. As is always the case, we who were the most intimate of friends of these liberal women were the last to find out about their vile habits (*porquerías*). . . . Truly disgusting details are told about all this and many sympathizers have withdrawn their support from these propagandists of lesbianism."[7]

Flores Magón did not leave such accusations to private correspondence but published similar attacks against the person of Juana in the PLM newspaper, *Regeneración*. In making public accusations of a same-sex relationship, Flores Magón relied on a powerful rhetorical means of discrediting Gutiérrez de Mendoza and Acuña Rosete. In turn-of-the-century Mexico, sexuality was central to public definitions of female morality, and morality was the key to public credibility and social standing. By questioning her sexuality, Flores Magón attempted to discredit her politics and her voice in public arenas. His construal of lesbianism as a perversion was meant to characterize her politics as equally perverted.[8]

Gutiérrez de Mendoza, in stark contrast, remained focused on the topic of politics in her explanations of her separation from the group. She criticized the Flores Magón brothers for charging an admission fee for public rallies meant to spread the word of the liberal cause among Mexicans living in the United States. Furthermore, she argued, the Flores Magón brothers and their followers practiced a rigid socialism, overly influenced by Americans who paid them to do so. Rather, she argued, any political philosophy had to be adapted to the particular realities of Mexico.[9] It was within the context of these disputes that Gutiérrez de Mendoza, who was never fully satisfied doing her political work from across the border, finally decided to leave the United States and return to Mexico in 1905.

Upon her return to Mexico, and through 1909, Gutiérrez de Mendoza continued her work in journalism and organizing. Her activities during this time attest to the breadth of her vision for the transformation of Mexican society, which included the rights of workers, campesinos, and women. In 1905 she brought together a group of workers under the name Socialismo Mexicano (Mexican Socialism), the official newspaper for which was *Anáhuac*. In 1907 she had met Dolores Jiménez y Muro (1848–1925), a poet, teacher, socialist, and feminist from a prominent

Aguascalientes family. With Jiménez y Muro she founded Socialistas Mexicanos (Mexican Socialists). In 1909 she founded two organizations that worked for the improved status of women—the Club Político Feminil Amigas del Pueblo (Friends of the People Female Political Club) and, along with Acuña y Rosete and several other women, the club Las Hijas de Cuauhtémoc. The women in these organizations carried out various activities. In behavior rare for women at the time, they staged protests in central locations, such as under the statue of Columbus on Reforma Avenue, and carried placards on their chests and backs. For this they were known as *mujeres sandwich* (sandwich-board women). They petitioned Francisco Madero for the vote for women during his electoral campaign and demanded political rights equal to those afforded to men. In September 1910, Las Hijas de Cuauhtémoc sponsored a huge anti-Díaz demonstration that also encouraged women to claim the rights and responsibilities of public life.[10]

Earlier that year, on May 8, 1910, Juana Gutiérrez de Mendoza published an article in *Vesper* that gives us a better understanding of her politics. In this article we see that her political philosophy originated in mid-nineteenth-century liberalism at the same time it looked to the future of modern Mexico. In the article, Gutiérrez de Mendoza compared Díaz's thirty years in power with the Plan de Noria. The Plan de Noria was the manifesto written by Porifirio Díaz against the presidency of Benito Juárez when the latter sought reelection for a fourth term of office in 1871. Díaz had run against Juárez and Sebastián Lerdo de Tejada in what turned out to be highly contentious elections, ultimately decided by a congress dominated by Juárez supporters. The Plan de Noria was a declaration against unlimited reelection of the chief executive and against Juárez who, for Díaz, had repudiated the principles of the liberal Plan de Ayutla. Gutiérrez de Mendoza reiterated her accusations of hypocrisy on the part of Díaz by using a clever device; she quoted the Plan de Noria and then commented on Díaz's own words from the perspective of thirty years of his presidency.

A central aspect of the Plan de Noria was a criticism of the successive reelection of Benito Juárez to the presidency, which, Díaz argued, endangered national institutions. Gutiérrez de Mendoza asked why, if national institutions were endangered by reelection, Díaz had not hesitated in reelecting himself for more than thirty years. Díaz also accused the Juárez-era congress of lacking independence and characterized its senators as "obsequious courtesans" who continuously came to the same conclusions as the chief executive. The *Vesper* article claimed this to be quite an exaggeration, and more appropriately a description of Díaz himself. This point she followed with a quote from the Plan de Noria that stated, "The Constitution of 1857 and free elections will be our banner, less government and more freedoms our program. If no citizen imposes and perpetuates himself in the exercise of power, this will be the last revolution." To this, Gutiérrez de Mendoza simply replied, "No Comment."[11]

While Gutiérrez de Mendoza accused Díaz of not living up to the ideals he claimed in the Plan de Noria, she made clear that the problem lay not just with an individual leader and illegitimate elections but with an unjust system of rule that extended to a corrupt senate. "The fall of a tyrant is not the fall of tyranny," she wrote.[12] More was required than simply ousting the president. She called upon her compatriots to look at the condition to which Díaz and his followers had brought the country. Gutiérrez de Mendoza saw a nation drowning in endless calamity. The public debt, a lack of education for the people, the occupation of Mexican territory by the United States, economic concessions given to foreigners to the detriment of the country, and a disenchanted youth all sapped the country. Monopolies meant the starvation of the people and wealth only for *científicos*, the elite group surrounding Porfirio Díaz.[13]

Juana's love of words led her not only to journalism but to poetry as well. Few Mexican women wrote poetry, and those who did tended to be women of upper-class society. Their poems celebrated natural beauty, religious sentiment, and the virtues of women they admired. Gutiérrez de Mendoza was one of a few women whose poetry was, like her journalistic articles, politically oriented. Her poem "The Last Offering to Juárez" described celebrations of the birthday of Benito Juárez, which she would celebrate differently, and served to critique those who had betrayed the Juárez legacy. The poem was dated March 6, 1906, the day of celebration of the birthday of Benito Juárez. She wrote,

> The latest offering to Juárez
> Let them approach your altar, I cede to their footsteps
> Let them profane the sacredness of your temple
> The traitors who mutilated your works
> And your beliefs and your teachings defiled
> The cowards who have forgotten your example.

Gutiérrez de Mendoza continued to publish *Vesper*, a loud and clear voice in the all-out attack against the Díaz regime during the time leading up to the elections of 1910. As a correspondent for the newspaper *El Partido Socialista*, Gutiérrez de Mendoza interviewed the opposition candidate, Señor Francisco Madero. It was during these interviews that Gutiérrez de Mendoza became convinced of Madero's motives and decided to support his cause. After Díaz stole the election, she followed Madero's Plan de San Luis Potosí, dated October 1910, which called for armed rebellion against the Díaz government, and participated in the Tacubaya conspiracy.

Francisco Madero ascended to the presidency in 1911. While many Mexicans celebrated, for others the triumph of Madero brought less change than that for which they had hoped and struggled. Gutiérrez de Mendoza was among those who felt Madero had not done much to alleviate the situation of poor Mexicans, especially that of campesinos. In 1911, Gutiérrez de Mendoza moved to the state of Morelos to ally herself with the followers of Emiliano Zapata. Both she and Jiménez y Muro became colonels in the Zapatista movement.[14]

After General Victoriano Huerta staged a military coup overthrowing Madero, he had Juana, along with Dolores Jiménez y Muro and several other women, thrown in Belén prison for being Zapatistas. *Excélsior* newspaper reported that when the police arrested Gutiérrez de Mendoza they found in her home the Zapatista hymn, propaganda, and safe conduct papers.[15] She was released when Constitutionalist forces overtook Huerta and forced him out of the country in July 1914. However, the change in the presidency meant little to Gutiérrez de Mendoza. The subsequent occupant of the presidency, Venustiano Carranza, never recognized Emiliano Zapata and his followers as anything more than bandits. The divide between Constitutionalists and Zapatistas put Gutiérrez de Mendoza in the position of outlaw as well. In 1916 she and her daughter, Laura Mendoza, who at seventeen years of age was also active in the Zapatista cause, were sent to prison.

Gutiérrez de Mendoza, though, was untiring. Despite repeated stays in prison she continued her work to improve the living conditions of campesinos. In 1919 she founded the Colonia Agrícola Experimental Santiago Orozco (Experimental Agricultural Colony Santiago Orozco) on land formerly belonging to the Temixco Hacienda. Despite several small subsidies and generous words of praise from the federal government, the colony failed to sustain itself. Gutiérrez de Mendoza returned to Mexico City in 1922. At this time she formed the group Acción Femenil (Female Action) and participated in organizing the Consejo Nacional de Mujeres Mexicanas (National Council of Mexican Women), an organization dedicated to raising women's consciousness, aiding miners and young people, and working toward the emancipation of the people. When he became Minister of Public Education, José Vasconcelos named Gutiérrez de Mendoza to work as a rural teacher in Jalisco and Zacatecas. This position allowed her to work with the Mexican Indian population, a longtime interest of hers in part, she noted in her writings, because she was descended from Caxcanes Indians on her mother's side of the family, and in part because of the injustices committed against them that she hoped to remedy.

Juana Belén Gutiérrez de Mendoza died on June 13, 1942. In February 1933, President Abelardo L. Rodríguez had granted Gutiérrez de Mendoza a pension of a few pesos a day for "services to the Revolution." One of her last known actions gives us insight into her continuing dedication to the human condition, above and beyond her love for the power of words. A niece was seriously ill and in need of medicine her family could not afford. Juana Belén Gutiérrez sold her last possession, her printing press, to purchase the medicine.

NOTES

1. Julia Tuñón Pablos, *Women in Mexico: A Past Unveiled* (Austin: University of Texas Press, 1999), 79.

2. All direct quotes, unless otherwise indicated, are taken from autobiographical notes written by Juana Belén Gutiérrez de Mendoza in 1913 and collected in Angeles Mendieta Alatorre, *Juana Belén Gutiérrez de Mendoza (1875–1942). Extraordinaria precursora de la Revolución Mexicana* (México, 1983), 16–18.

3. Scholars do not coincide on the dates of various events in the life of Gutiérrez de Mendoza, including her marriage and imprisonment. The dates given here come from Alicia Villaneda, *Justicia y Libertad. Juana Belén Gutiérrez de Mendoza, 1875–1942* (México: Documentación y Estudios de Mujeres, 1994), 20.

4. Ibid.

5. Alatorre, *Juana Belén Gutiérrez*, 20–21.

6. Ibid.

7. Letter from Ricardo Flores Magón to Crescencio Múrquez, 10 June 1906. Archivo Histórico de la Secretaría de Relaciones Exteriores, LE 918. Cited in Villaneda, *Justicia y Libertad*.

8. Flores Magón thought of women as victims of capitalism, not co-participants in revolutionary struggle. Rather than encourage women to participate in public political activities, he urged them to strengthen the resolve of the men in their lives in their fight against capitalism. In his 1910 essay, "A la mujer," he wrote, "Humiliated, degraded, bound by the chains of tradition to an irrational inferiority, indoctrinated in the affairs of heaven by clerics, but totally ignorant of world problems, [woman] is suddenly caught in the whirlwind of industrial production which above all requires cheap labor to sustain the competition created by the voracious 'princes of capital' who exploit her circumstances. She is not prepared as men for the industrial struggle, nor is she organized with the women of her class to fight alongside her brother workers against the rapacity of capitalism." Flores Magón was against female suffrage, claiming that capitalism, not the denial of rights within a democratic political system, was the cause of women's subjugation. *Regeneración*, September 24, 1910, cited in Martha Eva Rocha, *El Álbum de la mujer*, vol. 4, *El porfiriato y la Revolución* (México: INAH, 1991), 224.

9. Villaneda, *Justicia y Libertad*, 43–44.

10. Among the women who joined Gutiérrez de Mendoza in the struggle for female suffrage were Dolores Jiménez y Muro, Dolores Arana, Manuela Peláez, María

Trejo, and Rosa G. de Maciel. Jiménez y Muro also played a central role in establishing Regeneración y Concordia (Regeneration and Harmony), a women's rights organization that also strove to improve the situation of rural and urban workers and Indians; its members were principally women writers and teachers. Shirlene Soto, *The Emergence of the Modern Mexican Woman; Her Participation in Revolution and Struggle for Equality, 1910–1940* (Denver: Arden Press, Inc., 1990), 39, 47, 48. Alatorre, *Juana Belén Gutiérrez*, 50. In 1914, Gutiérrez de Mendoza founded a worker discussion group in Mexico City, Labradores Mexicanos Instituto Popular (Mexican Laborers Popular Institute), which was led by her daughter, Laura Mendoza. In 1919, Gutiérrez de Mendoza collaborated with Elena Torres, teacher, feminist, and representative from the Partido Socialista de Yucatán.

11. Villaneda, *Justicia y Libertad*, 52–54.
12. Ibid.
13. Ibid.
14. Jiménez y Muro also wrote the introduction to the Plan de Ayala (1911), the defining document of the Zapatista movement. Soto, *Emergence of the Mexican Woman*, 47. Villaneda, *Justicia y Libertad*, 59, 69.
15. *Excélsior*, September 3, 1913.

SUGGESTED READINGS

Arrom, Silvia Marina. *Women of Mexico City, 1790–1857*. Stanford: Stanford University Press, 1985.

Franco, Jean. *Plotting Women: Gender and Representation in Mexico*. New York: Columbia University Press, 1988.

Mendieta Alatorre, Angeles. *Juana Belén Gutiérrez de Mendoza (1875–1942). Extraordinaria precursora de la Revolución Mexicana*. México, 1983.

Radkau, Verena. *Por la debilidad de nuestro ser*. México: Cuadernos de la Casa Chata, CIESAS, 1989.

———. *"La fama" y la vida; una fábrica y sus obreras*. México: Cuadernos de la Casa Chata, CIESAS, 1984.

Ramos Escandón, Carmen. "Mujeres trabajadoras del porfiriato, 1876–1911." *La Revista Europea de Estudios Caribeños y Latinoamericanos y del Caribe* 48 (June 1990): 27–44.

———, and Ana Lau. *Mujeres y Revolución, 1900–1917*. México: INHERM, 1993.

Rascón, Maria Antonieta. "Preocupaciones coincidentes." *Fem* 3 (noviembre–diciembre 1979).

Rocha, Martha Eva. *El álbum de la mujer*, vol. 4, *El porfiriato y la Revolución*. México: INAH, 1991.

Siller, Pedro. "Testimonios: Juana Belén Gutiérrez de Mendoza." *Historia Obrera* 5 (junio 1975): 4.

Soto, Shirlene. *The Emergence of the Modern Mexican Woman: Her Participation in Revolution and Struggle for Equality, 1910–1940*. Denver: Arden Press, Inc., 1990.

Towner, Margaret. "Monopoly Capitalism and Women's Work during the Porfiriato." *Latin American Perspectives* 4, nos. 1 and 2 (Winter and Spring 1977).

Tuñón, Julia. *El álbum de la mujer*, vol. 3, *El siglo XIX (1821–1880)*. México: INAH, 1991.

Tuñón Pablos, Enriqueta. *El álbum de la mujer*, vol. 2, *El siglo XIX (1821–1880)*. México: INAH, 1991.

Vallens, Vivian M. *Working Women in Mexico during the Porfiriato, 1880–1910*. San Francisco: R and E Research Associates, Inc., 1978.

Vaughan, Mary Kay, and Heather Fowler-Salamini, eds. *Women in the Mexican Countryside, 1850–1990*. Tucson: University of Arizona Press, 1995.

Villaneda, Alicia. *Justicia y Libertad. Juana Belén Gutiérrez de Mendoza, 1875–1942*. México: Documentación y Estudios de Mujeres, 1994.

Villegas de Magnón, Leonor. *The Rebel*. Edited by Clara Lomas. Houston: Arte Público Press, 1994.

PART III

REVOLUTIONARY GENERATIONS, 1910–1940

*W*hen Francisco I. Madero issued the Plan de San Luis Potosí in 1910, calling for armed rebellion against the Porfirian dictatorship, the contradictions within Mexican liberalism emerged to drag the country into a decade of civil war followed by twenty years more of reconstruction and reform. Madero had first tried to unseat the eighty-year-old president through the ballot box, but Díaz jailed the opposition candidate and stole the election of 1910. Although the rebellion sputtered at first, pervasive dissatisfaction with the regime caused the movement to spread beyond the original antireelection party. Pascual Orozco, a muleteer reader of the anarchist newspaper *Regeneración*, took the field in Chihuahua to the north, while in the southern state of Morelos, Emiliano Zapata demanded "land and liberty" for campesinos. Even sometime bandits like Francisco "Pancho" Villa found legitimacy in the revolutionary ranks. In May 1911 the insurgents drove Díaz into exile, and that fall, Madero won the first free election in a generation. But as president, Madero delayed the implementation of land and labor reforms that many had fought and died for, driving former allies such as Orozco and Zapata into renewed rebellion. To suppress these new threats, the president relied on the army of the old regime, an unwise move, as became apparent in February 1913, when a Porfirian general, Victoriano Huerta, seized power during an outbreak of fighting in Mexico City known as the Ten Tragic Days. Police murdered the deposed president a few days later.

The military coup began an even bloodier phase of fighting that annihilated the Porfirian regime and laid the foundations for a new government with the Constitution of 1917. Shortly after Huerta claimed the presidency, the Maderista governor of Coahuila, Venustiano Carranza, declared himself the First Chief of a Constitutionalist revolution, although he had little actual authority over the diverse rebel factions. The insurgents had defeated Huerta by the summer of 1914, but the coalition promptly split between the more numerous popular forces of Villa and Zapata, on the one hand, and the better-trained troops of Carranza and his able general, Alvaro Obregón, on the other. Obregón defeated his opponents in a climactic campaign in 1915, reducing Villa and Zapata to the level of guerrilla chieftains on opposite ends of the country. The United States intervened twice during the Constitutionalist revolution, occupying the port of Veracruz in 1914 and invading Chihuahua in a Punitive Expedition that failed to capture Pancho Villa, who had raided

Columbus, New Mexico, in 1916. When the new constitution was finally promulgated in 1917, it represented a compromise between the conservative Carranza, who wanted merely to add nationalist provisions to the liberal 1857 charter, and radicals who demanded far-reaching social reforms to benefit campesinos and industrial workers. Although the revolution saw the most extensive fighting in Mexico since the wars of independence, it remained a profoundly regional movement, particularly violent in some areas and virtually absent in others. Even in the Villista stronghold of Chihuahua, many remembered the decade more for its disruptions than for its heroism (Chapter 8).

During the 1920s, rival factions fought for the spoils while at the same time attempting to reconstruct the economic damage suffered during the previous decade of fighting. Revolutionary activists endeavored to organize peasants and workers to demand their rights under the Constitution of 1917, which had been flagrantly ignored by Carranza (Chapter 9). Land reform began under the presidential administration of Alvaro Obregón (1920–1924), who also sought to incorporate the indigenous masses into the Mexican nation through a vigorous program of rural schools. Education Minister José Vasconcelos likewise sponsored an ambitious program of public art intended as propaganda for the revolutionary government (Chapter 10). President Plutarco Elías Calles (1924–1928) turned his attention to the labor movement, seeking to forge a broad national confederation of unions, but the corrupt leadership deprived workers of genuine benefits. In the 1928 election, Obregón ran again, recalling for many the origins of the Porfirian dictatorship. He won the ballot but fell to an assassin's bullet, and rather than risk a similar fate, Calles announced the creation of a revolutionary party to institutionalize government and avoid a return to caudillo politics. Nevertheless, the increasingly conservative Calles adopted the unofficial title of Maximum Chief of the revolution and held power behind the scenes by controlling a succession of three puppet presidents in a period known as the Maximato (1928–1934).

The presidential administration of General Lázaro Cárdenas (1934–1940) finally sought to carry out the revolutionary promise of social justice. Considered at first to be simply another stooge of Calles, Cárdenas built a coalition of popular organizations and army officers that drove the former president into exile. Having assured the power of the presidency, he then implemented a sweeping program of agrarian reform, distributing nearly 50 million acres of land to campesinos. The president also supported union activism, particularly in the petroleum industry, which remained in the hands of Standard Oil and other foreign corporations decades after Díaz had awarded the first concessions. When the Anglo-American companies refused to comply with Mexican law,

Cárdenas ordered the expropriation of their property on March 18, 1938, a move that was widely applauded as a declaration of Mexico's economic independence. Cárdenas also sought to transform the official party from a collection of revolutionary chiefs into a genuinely popular organization, including labor unions and agrarian leagues. Nevertheless, his efforts to incorporate indigenous communities into the nation through a comprehensive program of rural development fell victim to pressures for industrial development in the cities (Chapter 11).

CHAPTER EIGHT

*"Te Amo Muncho"**

The Love Letters of Pedro and Enriqueta

William E. French

Lagunilla, the thieves' market on the new silver metro (line B), is no place to linger at night, but during the day it recalls the flavor of the traditional Mexican tianguis, *with vendors selling all manner of second-hand goods, from used books and old postcards to pirated cassettes and miscellaneous hardware. Yet one staple of the markets of old that has virtually disappeared is the* escribano, *a person who made a living by reading and writing for those who could not. Although now unemployed by the spread of literacy, such professionals had a vital role in Mexican society just a hundred years ago by giving people without an education access to legal documents, by reading correspondence from family members engaged in migrant labor, and especially, by crafting love letters.*

Courtship is by nature a private and ephemeral activity, not readily open to the historian's prying gaze, but through the documentary evidence of love letters, this essay reconstructs romantic life in northern Mexico at the turn of the last century. The letters reveal how difficult it could be for two young lovers to build a relationship of trust in an honor-bound world plagued by malicious gossip. Such a task was made all the more difficult by the double standard inherent in a patriarchal society. Although both lovers had to provide tokens of their affection, for the woman, the ultimate proof of her love lay in a willingness to engage in sexual relations. In doing so, a woman surrendered her honor while trusting her lover to fulfill his promise of marriage, but a refusal to submit could be interpreted as a challenge to his honor, often leading to tragedy.

*This is exactly how the phrase appears in a love letter in early twentieth-century Parral, Chihuahua. Use of the word "muncho" in place of "mucho" is significant for a number of reasons. It reminds us that northern Mexicans spoke Spanish with a distinct regional accent and of the close connection between the spoken and written word. Love letters were exchanged even between people who could not read or write, by making use of intermediaries with one or both of these skills. Love letters themselves are often better understood when read out loud.

William E. French, an associate professor of history at the University of British Columbia, is the author of A Peaceful and Working People: Manners, Morals, and Class Formation in Northern Mexico *(1996) and coeditor of* Rituals of Rule, Rituals of Resistance: Public Celebrations and Popular Culture in Mexico *(1994).*

𝓜any love letters can be found among the papers and legal files of the judicial archives in the town of Parral, the center of a once-prosperous mining district in the northern Mexican state of Chihuahua. In some cases, they have been submitted to judicial authorities to prove the existence of a written promise of marriage. In others, they have been copied into the judicial record or appended to the transcript of a criminal investigation after being retrieved by judicial officials from the scene of a crime—either from the pocket of one of the corpses or neatly piled on a table near the dead couple—the crime being that of murder-suicide, an event that sometimes accompanied the end of a courtship gone terribly awry. Such was the fate of Pedro and Enriqueta, a young courting couple from Villa Escobedo, another mining town in the Parral district that was struggling to sustain mining operations during the upheaval and uncertainty of the revolutionary decade that began in 1910. The sounds of the two gunshots shattered the stillness of that February afternoon in 1919, leaving Enriqueta murdered, Pedro dead by his own hand, and family members to wonder how the courtship of five months could end in such a horrific fashion. While brothers, sisters, and other family members knew little about the relationship, other than that the two were suitors, the thirty-one letters found at the crime scene—fourteen from Pedro to Enriqueta and seventeen from Enriqueta to Pedro—allow us to piece together the progression of their relationship, from its tender beginnings to its bitter end, and to draw our own conclusions about the volatile mix of love and violence that could characterize courtship in Porfirian and revolutionary Mexico.[1]

STAGES IN A COURTING RELATIONSHIP

The arrival of a letter from a male to female usually announced the beginning of a courtship. A surprising number of people sent love letters, as literacy in Chihuahua may have been about 30 percent and love letters have been found that were written by artisans such as blacksmiths and tailors and by mine workers (*operarios*), such as Pedro. Literacy, however, was not a requirement for writing or exchanging these missives. In one case in Huejotitan, a small, predominantly agricultural village near the mining towns, a *novio*, or suitor, who could neither read nor write, had sent a series of love letters to his *novia*, or intended, who also could neither read nor write, with the intention of convincing her to leave her paternal home to live with him happily ever after. Essential to this matchmaking was the suitor's sister, who acted not only as messenger, delivering the letters, but also, employing her skills as a reader (she testified that she could only read, not write), as interpreter and advocate, reading her brother's heartfelt prose to his credulous though hesitant true love. While it is not known who wrote these letters, testimony reveals that the suitor had a literate relative who served as a state functionary in a nearby town.[2]

In the case of Pedro and Enriqueta, both signed their names to the letters they exchanged. Pedro's initial letter, as was the case with many at this first stage of courtship, was full of formal and polite language, with "*Usted*" (You) marking almost every line. With this initial missive, the male opened himself up, revealing his feelings and asking if they were reciprocated. "How fortunate I would be if you should give shelter to this love that for some time has wandered about and only in you hopes to find its happiness; but how miserable I would be if you should reject my good wishes with a cruel refusal of your love." The male usually excused such a forthright admission as driven by passion, a passion of such vehemence in his heart, Pedro declared, "that it is no longer possible for me to suffer any longer." Another young male suitor was equally moved: "[F]rom the first time I saw you my heart felt a terrible passion that consumed me and not being able to stand it any longer I resolved to declare these clumsy words to you."[3] Only in this way could going so far beyond the bounds of propriety be justified. Yet male suitors still ran the risk of offending the recipient, of staining her honor. To offset this danger, Pedro was quick to combine honorable intentions with his passion: "I speak to you with frankness and without offending your dignity, I love you with the intention of an honorable man (*hombre honrrado*) when he directs himself to a Señorita of your high moral qualities." The fears of another suitor are similar: "If in my words I should offend you with some mistake you should have the kindness to forgive me because the love I offer you is so great that you can't imagine it."[4]

Enriqueta, the object of Pedro's affections, prefaced her initial response with a statement as to her own frankness or openness, a quality, she said, that was always in her. By doing this she was staking a claim to being honest and truthful in matters of the heart—the central issue in a courting relationship. Enriqueta also needed more convincing. "If you really love me with a true and pure love, my heart will reciprocate, but before anything I desire that you should swear to me that yours is a true love (*amor sincero*) not one just for passing time. Disillusion me of this and the feelings of your heart will be reciprocated." Other women also expressed their concern that males might be interested in something other than courtship leading to a future commitment. A disillusioned *novia* complained to judicial officials that she had been reluctant to accept her suitor's attentions from the beginning because she feared that he had already been married or perhaps that he was only trying to satisfy a whim.[5] So began a process central to the relationship of most couples, the task—accomplished through the exchange of love letters—of convincing one's intended of the truthfulness and sincerity of the love that was being offered. Nor was this task easily accomplished. As we will see, both sides had much to lose, often making courtship a time of doubt, gossip, and mistrust.

After their mutual declaration of love, suitors typically escalated their protestations that the love they offered was indeed true, while at the same time demanding increasing proof of the other's sincerity and commitment. "It seems to me that what you say indicates that you don't love me, that another woman has robbed me of your love," pleaded Enriqueta in one letter. In two others, she closes, "if you don't have affection for me tell me in order to kill with one blow my illusion." In yet another: "If you always will love me with the sweet expressions that you write to me I would consider myself happy but I don't know at times because it seems to me that the love you say you profess isn't true—dissipate this doubt that envelopes my soul and I will be happy." And, finally: "Tell me again that your love is only mine." For his part, Pedro reassured her: "You are the only owner of all the love of your passionate Pedro." In another letter (although this is somewhat open to interpretation): "[T]he love that I declare to you is as pure and true as is your [*sic*]—and even more." Finally, "Enriqueta: If I'm not yours I won't be anyone's and I would rather lose my life than lose you." In the letters exchanged by another pair of suitors, Jesus and Carlota, this same dynamic prevailed. He pledged his love to her while at the same time doubting her commitment to him. When she failed to give him her photograph, an important means of proving sincerity and commitment, he asked what he was supposed to think—for him, an obvious conclusion was that her intentions were not good. Even when she swore on the blood of her mother that she had been faithful to him, he remained unconvinced.[6]

Constant written protestations of reassurance were never enough, however, and suitors soon began demanding more tangible proof of commitment and intent. The next step, then, was to send a *prenda*, a gift or token of one's love. A *prenda* could take many forms. For example, Jesús, introduced in the previous paragraph, was demanding a photograph as a kind of *prenda*. For other couples, a religious picture or rosary served the purpose, and so could a handkerchief embroidered with the initials of one's love. *Prendas* were important signs of intent that served as proof of the commitment of those involved and that the courtship was progressing along toward an eventual marriage. Pedro asked for such an item, specifically, a lock of Enriqueta's hair: "I would like to have a token of yours in my possession—tell me if one day I should be able to get one or not." As for Enriqueta, when a symbol of Pedro's love arrived in the mail she was beside herself: "I don't doubt now Pedro this love that in your words, in your eyes, I have seen and even more so now that I have incomparable proof—your photograph. In the sad hours of your absence it will calm the agonies of my soul and dissipate the doubts that sometimes assault me." Some suitors even kept count, as did the *novia* of a 19-year-old tailor in Parral, much to his disgruntlement: " . . . you say in your letter that you have already given me three things and I haven't given you even one—what more do you want from me? Do you want me to rip out me [*sic*] heart to give it to you—I can give you soul, life and heart."[7]

Love letters themselves also served as tokens or a kind of *prenda*. When Enriqueta composed a poem with the first word in each line beginning with a letter from Pedro's name, she described the letter as a "humble memento" in which she had "engraved on paper the tender complaints of the soul in love with you." The first stanza of the poem in her letter reads:

> Pasión veemente abraza el alma mía
> (Fervid passion embraces my soul)
> En este corazón vive enserrada
> (In this heart it lives enclosed)
> Divinos ojos de mi prenda amada
> (Divine eyes of my loved darling)
> Retira de mi alma esta agonía
> (Take from my soul this agony)
> Orgullosa de amarte enamorado
> (Proud to love you my loved one)

Eventually, however, even *prendas* were not enough. The ultimate demonstration of commitment that the male often asked for directly was for the woman to begin sexual relations with him, often in exchange for a promise of marriage. After three months of courtship, Ysidro wrote to his intended bride, María Anastacia, specifically asking her to accept such a bargain: "Libradita: This letter is my last in which I swear to you and obligate myself to marry you if you accept my desires—today I wait for you at the hour that you should arrange and I hope that no one will know what is going on."[8] The disgruntled tailor from Parral also demanded this proof of love (*prueba de amor*), as he called it. In three separate letters he pressured his true love to leave her home to be with him, promising to "cover her honor," in other words, to marry her, within three months. Many males regarded proof of a woman's virginity as a necessary prerequisite to marriage. As one stated directly, by beginning sexual relations it was possible to "try her out to know what kind of character she was," in other words, to know if she were a virgin.[9] In another case, the woman yielded to the demand for sexual relations after her *novio* told her that he knew she was not chaste and that, if she were, she should prove it to him.[10]

Failing to prove this state to the satisfaction of the *novio* could have drastic consequences for women. After five months of correspondence, a twenty-five-year-old blacksmith, as he himself admitted, convinced his sixteen-year-old *novia* to sleep with him after swearing that he would marry her. By morning, however, he had changed his mind, claiming that she had not been a virgin and that, instead of husband and wife, the two could remain together only as lovers (*queridos*).[11] Other women were simply abandoned; one trusting bride-to-be was deposited in a brothel.[12] The law extended protection only to previously chaste women, so in court women were placed in the difficult position of insisting on their previous virginity while admitting that they had slept with their prospective husbands. The pressure for women to submit, however, was tremendous, and many, having begun sexual relations, ended up before judicial authorities in hopes that they would help convince men to follow through on their promises of marriage. Although nineteen-year-old Feliciana initially informed her *novio* that she did not want to continue their courtship because she could not accede to his request for sex, she eventually gave in.[13] When Pedro suggested that Enriqueta yield to his desires, however, she responded in a different manner: "With the same love as always I answer your letter. . . . At the same time I say to you that I never will consent to that which you desire because you know that it is for me an offense—never again pronounce these words. If you do I will never answer another one of your letters. I will not stop loving you because of this because my heart is only yours." While his request went past her acceptable bounds, the proposition was not enough to end the relationship, suggesting that women expected such behavior from men during courtship.

BETRAYAL, DECEPTION, AND VIOLENCE

Male preoccupation with proving virginity as the ultimate proof of love also brought *novios* into conflict with the male relatives of their *novias*, given that men were also intent on maintaining the sexual purity of the female members of their families. Love letters reveal that suitors often kept the fact of their relationships hidden from parents and other family members, communicating by signals as well as letters and in hasty conversations out windows and back doors late at night. One case reveals why: a brother killed the young man who was attempting to court his sister.[14] Not all relationships were so secret, however: one suitor wrote to ask his *novia* at which window of her house the band he had hired should serenade her. There were also dances and walks home from the houses of friends or relatives or from places of work; and the parental home itself could not be made impregnable. In one instance, a woman's mother allowed the courting couple to meet in her home. Yet, in general, the limits on the ability of couples to get together made the letters all the more important—everything that needed to be said had to be expressed in them.

The need for secrecy highlights some of the intergenerational struggles that took place over choice of a marriage partner, struggles well documented in love letters. Frustrated by stipulations in the Mexican Civil Code that required both males and females under the age of twenty-one to obtain parental permission to marry, young lovers lamented their fates and plotted their freedom. When Jesús's father refused to give him permission to marry Maurita, saying that he was inexperienced and should wait three more years, Jesús wrote to her: "[I]f you should want to go with me to Monterrey or wherever you want I am ready any time you want. . . . I am ready to give you your house wherever you want it." He promised that in Chihuahua or Monterrey, both larger cities with more anonymity, they could get married because he would say that he did not have a father. He pointed out that when Lucas, perhaps a brother or mutual friend, had been denied parental permission to marry, he carried off Amelia and they had married later.[15]

The feeling of panic in his letter is palpable. He not only feared that Maurita would end the courtship ("[I]f you should not want to continue with my relations, just tell me. I don't want to waste your time"), but given the context of relationships as sketched here, Jesús feared that Maurita would interpret this turn of events as an attempt on his part to deceive her: "I am telling you the truth. . . . I love you and I am not trying to deceive you" and later, "[M]y love for you is pure and I only want you." In this short letter he returned to the theme of deception no fewer than eight times. In another letter, he revealed why he was so insistent about not being taken for a deceiver—his father's refusal had made it impossible for him to follow through on his promise of marriage, which had possibly been given in exchange for the beginning of sexual relations. For Jesús, failure to follow through on his promise and stand up to his father threatened his very manhood: "I am convinced that we can't get married here . . . you will say that I am not a man (*no soy hombre*) but I'll give you your house where you want it and I'll support you all your life."

Another suitor highlighted the tension between the filial role and that of the male suitor: "One day my greatest hopes will be realized even though you say that in my house they don't want you. Well, this isn't true, you're not right and even if it were this way I am very independent of them and nobody controls my will or intentions."[16] While he stressed his independence, Manuela, his *novia*, revealed that she had been warned many times never to run off with a suitor. Yet in the face of parental opposition and despite the great danger that the male would not follow through with his promise of marriage, here was a way for a woman to force the issue of marriage on her reluctant family. Only by agreeing to the marriage could honor be restored after the woman had left, or been forced from, the parental home.

At times the power of the family was its control over the money necessary to get married, an event that could be an expensive proposition. The local press lamented how much artisans spent on lavish wedding celebrations. Jesús made it clear to Maurita that it was not money that prevented him from marrying her: "I don't want you to think it is because of lack of money because I have twenty times more than I need to get married." His need to reassure her about this fact only helps to illustrate how commonly it was the reason for holding off on marriage. As Ismael, a twenty-two-year-old mine worker (*operario*), explained to Atanacia, his eighteen-year-old *novia*, they should live together now and then get married when he had sufficient money to afford the expenses of a wedding, which he promised, in writing, in a very simple letter: "I address these lines to the Señorita Atanacia N. I give my word that I will marry her as soon as I get the money. Signed, Ismael M." Her parents, not finding their honor sufficiently covered by this note, brought him before judicial authorities, hoping to force an immediate marriage.[17]

Not everyone expected that living together would lead to marriage, however, revealing that standards of sexual behavior differed according to class and even within class. Men who labored in the mines and their women often agreed to an arrangement that was explicitly stated: the woman would provide domestic service and begin sexual relations in exchange for support by means of the male's paycheck. This type of long-term relationship—known as an *amasiato*—was relatively common. One mine worker even questioned the entire institution of marriage in a letter to his *novia*, perhaps because he was already legally married and did not intend to return to his wife, yet wanted fifteen-year-old Ramona to live with him: "[W]e don't need witnesses . . . why do you need the Sr. *jefe* (boss or district political authority) or the Sr. priest as you say to me you want . . . do you think with the words that they speak we will be happier . . . because I believe that none of these Señores will induce me to search for your well being . . . they are very separate from our relationship."[18]

Attempts to maintain the sexual purity of the female members of families as well as to lay claim to honorable or decent status through the proper celebration of weddings often pitted male family members against *novios* interested in obtaining the ultimate proof of love in encounters that were occasionally fatal. Male preoccupation with deception and betrayal at the hands of a woman could also make courtship deadly. While Jesús was preoccupied in his love letters to Maurita that she would take him for a deceiver, in the relationship between Pedro and Enriqueta it was Pedro who felt deceived. In fact, all the written pledges and *prendas* were not sufficient for Pedro. Although he allowed himself to be temporarily reassured of Enriqueta's love, his doubts inevitably resurfaced. Once in love, the fear that a suitor's love was feigned or false was a constant preoccupation and, when realized, was accompanied by feelings of betrayal and deception that sometimes proved fatal. Both males and females feared this fate, revealing that they viewed the world around them as a dangerous and hostile place. "I used to think that in life all one would find was treachery," stated Enriqueta, "but you have convinced me that your love is immense and pure and now I am happy."

The predominance of the theme of betrayal must be understood against the backdrop of the power of gossip and the importance of maintaining one's reputation in the community. One young man asked for a letter back from a *novia* who had broken off relations so that it could not be used to make fun of or mock him. Pedro reported to Enriqueta that people were saying she had said of him: "You are my toy" (*tu eres juguete mio*). Although she insisted that he should never believe what they said about her because it was a lie, he countered: "How can I not believe it when it comes from the mouths of people who are such intimate friends of yours." Friends, or *amigas*, were also at fault according to Jesús: "There are friends in this world (*amigas*) who don't exist for any other reason than to disgrace others." As he explained it: "I have sworn to myself that she will never deceive anyone ever again."[19]

It was at this stage when the figurative protestations of love unto death, so common in these letters, took on ominous, literal connotations. "Only through death will I forget you"; "only in death will my desires become still"; "I would rather lose my life than lose you"; "Yours until the grave"; and "I am ready to give even my life to prove to you my love is pure" are a few of the passages in love letters expressing this common theme. Although not all men who felt they had been deceived killed the women they were courting (indeed, some broken courtships were even rekindled), the murder-suicide of a *novia* and *novio* was not an unexpected outcome of betrayed love. The event itself took on almost ritualistic overtones, as the couples met, *prendas* in their possession and love letters in hand. Indeed, one common reason for a final meeting between the two was to return love letters. When Andrés M. attempted to kill María and then took his own life, eleven love letters, a pink ribbon, and her photograph were found on his body.[20] As Jesús explained in a suicide note to his sister, "No one is to blame except that woman who took me from your side . . . it seems impossible that this woman should have robbed me of my heart because for me it seems I won't love any other like this. . . ."[21] In all cases in the Parral archives, the *novio* shot his lover and then himself, usually in the head.

The lives of Pedro and Enriqueta, whose love letters have formed such a prominent part of this essay, ended in such a manner. As the breakup of their relationship is clearly documented in their letters, it is worth discussing in greater detail. In this case, alcohol was a contributing factor. As she found herself accused of being untrue and having to deal with Pedro's insecurities every time he got drunk, Enriqueta made him promise not to drink any more; in other words, she set limits on his behavior and on how he was to treat her. This was somewhat unusual, as a constant theme of the middle-class press and popular almanacs of the time was that women, especially wives, were to offer love and understanding, not limits, as the means of keeping men away from vice. Pedro, admitting that he was the most humble and vice-ridden man alive, initially agreed to stop drinking. When he returned to the bottle, however, and she ended the relationship, demanding the return of her love letters, he was astounded. "How can you say I am the only one responsible for the end of the relationship," he protested, "when you knew all along I was a drinker?"

Whereas Enriqueta blamed alcohol, Pedro himself identified another intoxicant as the source of his problems: love. "You can't imagine that which this poor heart suffers for your love," he proclaimed, "and as I can't find the means of dissipating my passion, I constantly find myself with my mind drunk with your love that only with death will I forget you. . . ." And, in another letter: " . . . you do what you want, I can't force you to love me, but I love you and if because I love you it's going to cost me my life, I lose it with all my will, that which I beg of you is that you shouldn't belittle me for another." He signed this letter "your deceived Pedro" and the previous one "your inconsolable Pedro." These, the last two letters written by Pedro, must have been sent shortly before he murdered Enriqueta and killed himself. Judicial authorities found the letters on the corpses along with a number of *prendas*, a white handkerchief embroidered with the name "Pedro" in one corner on her body, and a button containing Enriqueta's picture on his. This final scene and others like it, which would not have been out of place in a turn-of-the-century Mexican novel like *Santa*, were front-page news: they served to instruct women in the consequences of sullying male honor and to define men as willing at all costs to act, either in order to take what was theirs or to preserve their reputations.[22]

REFLECTIONS

The explosive mix of honor and passion revealed in love letters exchanged by suitors in Porfirian and revolutionary Chihuahua helps explain why courtship could sometimes be a dangerous time. Revealing one's true feelings and convincing another of one's sincerity in a world full of treachery and deceit were hard enough to accomplish. To do so in a context in which reputation and honor were to be protected at all costs was all the more difficult. Fear of betrayal formed the backdrop for increased protestations of love and the exchange of *prendas*. Courtship culminated in the sexual act itself, which served as the ultimate proof of love, often offered in exchange for the promise of marriage. If male honor depended upon safeguarding the chastity of the female members of the family, then love could be proven only by delivering up this same commodity. Both male relatives and upset *novios* could be dangerous, even lethal. In addition to revealing the intricacies of courtship and the hopes and fears of young men and women, love letters were important as aesthetic objects. Like *prendas*, they were proof of a courting relationship and symbols of trust, commitment, and permanence. Accepting one implied the beginning of a courtship, while handing them back marked its end. Moreover, the act of writing helped not only to express but to construct the very feelings being expressed. As Pedro stated: "You should know what immense tranquility your passionate Pedro has received by returning to write to you with such growing and sweet love." But there was more to it than that. In a society that privileged the written word over the spoken, love letters staked a claim to permanence and authority that went well beyond that which could be asserted verbally. The more self-reflective letter writers, such as Enriqueta, expressed the importance of writing and, in this, she has the final word: "I would like only to see you to be able to explain to you what is going on in this heart that only is yours but verbally I don't do it because that's worth missing in order to leave imprinted on paper all the impressions that my soul feels for you."

NOTES

1. All love letters are located in the Archivo Judicial, Hidalgo del Parral, Chihuahua, Mexico, (hereafter referred to as AJHP), and were written between 1870 and 1924. The specific case of Pedro and Enriqueta is entitled: "Averiguación: con motivo á la muerte trájica de Pedro y la joven Enriqueta," 25 February 1919, AJHP. In this and all other notes, as in the body of the chapter itself, all last names have been omitted.

2. "Criminal contra Liberato por rapto y contra José por complicidad en dicho delito," 26 September 1894, Huejotitan, AJHP.

3. Lino to Soledad in "Criminal instruida con motivo del delito de homicidio," San Francisco del Oro, 4 October 1925, AJHP.

4. Lino to Soledad, 1925, AJHP.

5. "Querella presentada por Feliciana en contra de Joaquín," Parral, 12 April 1924, AJHP.

6. "Averiguación criminal en contra de Jesús, por rapto y estupro," Parral, 30 October 1912, AJHP.

7. "Criminal contra Eleno, por rapto," Parral, 23 March 1893, AJHP.

8. "Criminal contra José por el delito de estupro," Parral, 11 April 1903, AJHP.

9. "Criminal contra Marcos por el delito de rapto," San Antonio del Tule, 8 February 1908, AJHP.

10. "Querella presentada por Feliciana en contra de Joaquín," Parral, 12 April 1924, AJHP.

11. "Averiguación criminal en contra de Jesús, por rapto y estupro," Parral, 30 October 1912, AJHP.

12. Presidente municipal, Torreón, Coahuila to jefe político, Distrito de Hidalgo, 19 October 1911, in Archivo Municipal, Hidalgo del Parral, Chihuahua, Mexico, caja 1911B.

13. "Querella presentada por Feliciana en contra de Joaquín," Parral, 12 April 1924, AJHP.

14. "Criminal instruida con motivo del delito de homicidio," San Francisco del Oro, 4 October 1925, AJHP.

15. "Averiguación con motivo de querella presentada por Maximiam por rapto y estupro en contra del Acusado Jesús," Parral, 28 May 1909, AJHP.

16. "Criminal contra José, acusado del delito de estupro," Santa Bárbara, 9 March 1912, AJHP.

17. "Criminal contra Ysmael, acusado por delito de estupro," Parral, 1891, AJHP.

18. "Averiguación por el delito de rapto en contra del Teofilo," Santa Bárbara, 27 June 1910, AJHP.

19. "Averiguación con motivo de la muerte de Jesús y Josefa," Parral, 16 February 1912, AJHP.

20. "Averiguación con motivo de las lesions que sufrió María y suicidio de Andrés," Parral, 17 February 1912, AJHP.

21. "Averiguación con motivo de la muerte de Jesús y Josefa," Parral, 16 February 1912, AJHP.

22. Written by Federico Gamboa in the late nineteenth century, *Santa* was first published in 1903. It tells the story of a young woman from the countryside who exchanges her virginity for a promise of marriage. Deceived by the suitor, she becomes pregnant and is cast out by her family, ending up by working in a brothel in the city. See Federico Gamboa, *Santa* (Mexico: Grijalbo, 1979).

SUGGESTED READINGS

French, William E. *A Peaceful and Working People: Manners, Morals, and Class Formation in Northern Mexico*. Albuquerque: University of New Mexico Press, 1996.

Johnson, Lyman L., and Sonya Lipsett-Rivera, ed. *The Faces of Honor: Sex, Shame, and Violence in Colonial Latin America*. Albuquerque: University of New Mexico Press, 1998.

Knight, Alan. *The Mexican Revolution*. 2 vols. Cambridge: Cambridge University Press, 1986.

Twinam, Ann. *Public Lives, Private Secrets: Gender, Honor, Sexuality, and Illegitimacy in Colonial Spanish America*. Stanford: Stanford University Press, 1999.

CHAPTER NINE

Rosa Torre González

Soldadera and Feminist

SARAH A. BUCK

 *Although the official monument to the Revolution of 1910 is located on the blue metro line in Mexico City, statues of revolutionary heroes—invariably represented as men on horseback—can be seen in plazas throughout the country. Indeed, historians have described the Revolution as one of the high points of Mexican patriarchy, in which masculine heroes such as Emiliano Zapata and Pancho Villa fought climactic battles to determine the nation's fate. Even after the soldiers had put aside their rifles and cartridge belts, postrevolutionary governments distributed the benefits of land reform and labor protection primarily to men.*

Nevertheless, women also made vital contributions in the decade of fighting as soldaderas, *both camp followers and female soldiers, who cooked for the troops and in some cases actually carried weapons in combat along with men. Female activists took an equally important role in organizing labor unions and agrarian leagues to force the government to fulfill the reforms promised by the Constitution of 1917. As this essay shows, women used their patriotic service to demand equal rights of citizenship, in particular, the vote. Yet because of the prevailing gender roles and the scorn for camp followers held by many revolutionary commanders, women were forced to assert their voices in ways that perpetuated their inferior social status. Even the general monument at Revolución has become a crypt honoring great men and helping to bury the historical memory of the* soldaderas *who also gave their lives for the Mexican nation.*

Sarah A. Buck received her Ph.D. from Rutgers University with a dissertation examining women's activism and suffrage politics in the decades following the Mexican Revolution. She is assistant professor of history at Allegheny College in Meadville, Pennsylvania.

𝒥n March 1924, Rosa Torre González proudly wrote of her achievements as an elected representative to the *ayuntamiento* (city council) of Mérida, Yucatán. She celebrated her position as the first woman to "arrive to a councilman's post" in the Mexican republic, at a time when women did not even have the right to vote. Although her two-year term was cut short by a military rebellion, she nevertheless worked to extend public services to the poor of Mérida, who had been largely ignored by the Porfirian regime. Torre González recognized that her experience held great significance for women seeking to gain equal rights of citizenship. Her career demonstrates how some Mexican women took advantage of the professional opportunities, political transformations, and social changes presented by the Revolution to expand the boundaries of women's action.

Biographers and chroniclers of the Mexican Revolution, who have followed Torre González in celebrating her position as one of the first women to hold political office in Mexico, have asserted that she was an early adherent of Francisco I. Madero's uprising against the Díaz dictatorship, a standard claim among revolutionary veterans, who used their service during the decade of fighting to justify their subsequent political power. This long-held republican connection between military service and citizenship led the same biographers to assert, in addition, that Torre González served as a *soldadera*, a term encompassing both camp follower and female combatant. Such sources have stated, without significant supporting evidence, that she acted as a spy, *soldadera*, and nurse in the first Yucatecan battles of the Mexican Revolution in the region of Mérida.[1]

In fact, all revolutionary armies depended on women to forage for food, and in battle, many women picked up weapons and fought alongside the men. Because so many women died in service to the Revolution, Torre González and other feminists (including some of her biographers) drew the natural conclusion that women had earned the rights of citizenship. Torre González dedicated the rest of her life to working as a teacher and political organizer to help forge a new revolutionary consciousness among Mexican men and women. Therefore, even if she or others had inflated her own military service record—like so many contemporary male politicians—she well earned the title of *soldadera*, if that term is defined simply as a combatant for the Revolution.

Like many other feminists of her age, Torre González mediated the desire to gain equal rights and opportunities for women with an emphasis on the benevolent, moralistic, and nurturing aspects of her political and social activities. Notwithstanding her claims to military service, she cultivated a maternal image of herself as a public mother working for the common welfare. Writing about her accomplishments in the *ayuntamiento*, she recalled having worked to censure immoral movies, to regulate Mérida's municipal department of health and hygiene, and to develop educational and social welfare projects, and cooperating with teachers to ensure children's school attendance, to organize literacy campaigns, and to create new children's parks. She also emphasized her work on behalf of women, reeducating prostitutes and female prisoners for new occupations and more honorable life-styles. Torre González claimed that as a woman, she could administer public welfare, education, and women's issues as well as men could, and perhaps more effectively.

Torre González and many other women involved in revolutionary reform and feminist organizing built upon the professional, political, and social opportunities presented by the Revolution in the state of Yucatán to advance feminist goals on a regional and national level. They used maternalism, a political strategy glorifying women's maternal qualities, to expand their own spheres of action as well as the bounds of acceptable behavior for all women in Mexican society. Maternalism helped such women to secure legal changes ensuring their equal civil, labor, and political rights with men. Yet at the same time, this strategy limited the expressions of feminism and the style of women's action for years to come, by linking women's public behavior as civic actors to their private roles as mothers and caregivers. Consequently, up to the present day, women's wage labor and political participation have been largely relegated to areas that conform to an ideal vision of wives and mothers.

Rosa Torre González was born in the southeastern state of Yucatán in 1896. Although she never wrote about her early childhood and even her exact birthplace remains unknown, she probably grew up in a comfortable middle-class family in Mérida—a surprising but relatively common experience for future social revolutionaries. By the turn of the century, Porfirian development projects had endowed the Yucatecan capital with all the accoutrements of a modern metropolis, from banks and newspapers to theaters and opera houses and from telephone and tram lines to sewers and trash collection. To bolster the city's reputation as the "Paris of Mexico," prominent residents hired French and Belgian architects to design elaborate mansions along the premier boulevard, Paseo de Montejo. The elite could afford such luxury thanks to revenues from Yucatán's primary export industry, henequen, a form of hemp used to make agricultural binding twine by the International Harvester Corporation.

While the estate owners passed most of their time in Mérida, peons labored beneath the beating sun to tend the endless rows of henequen. The work reached its peak at harvest time, when they chopped the stalks and, after removing the sharp spines, carried them off to mills to be shredded into raw fiber for export. The hacienda workforce included indentured servants from China and Korea as well as Yaqui Indians deported from the northern state of Sonora to toil as virtual slaves. Most of the workers, however, were indigenous Mayans who had once farmed the land in village communes, raising corn to support their families. As the market for henequen grew, wealthy hacendados used the liberal reform laws to take over village lands and force the residents to become peons on the expanding estates. Despite their sense of grievance over the hard labor and lost land, these hacienda workers took a relatively minor role in the resistance against the Porfirian regime.[2]

The most active political opposition surfaced among urban sectors excluded from power by Yucatán's own *científico*, Governor Olegario Molina. During the early years of the Porfiriato, local elites had contended for administrative office, sharing the patronage of the state government among themselves while promising loyalty to President Díaz. Molina, however, had amended the state constitution to allow his own reelection in 1906, at the same time he used his contacts with International Harvester to monopolize revenues from the henequen bonanza. But the following year the export boom went bust, and in the depression that followed, urban workers ranging from longshoremen and teamsters to printers and teachers began to protest their declining real wages. Their discontent soon merged with Francisco Madero's antireelection campaign against the aging dictator. Madero attracted considerable popular support when he visited Yucatán in June 1909 on a national tour encouraging local opposition parties. These new political clubs, although tied to elite clans excluded from power by the Porfirian inner circle, nevertheless became an outlet for the political aspirations of the middle and working classes. Members published anti-Díaz newspapers, posted manifestos in public spaces, and discussed the need for democratic reform. It was probably by disseminating revolutionary propaganda that the fourteen-year-old Rosa Torre González joined the Maderista movement in 1910.

Yet the claim that Torre González served as a *soldadera* in the first battles against Díaz seems far more problematic, notwithstanding the Yucatecan tradition that the *primeras chispas* (first sparks) of the Revolution flared in the peninsula. In the fall of 1909, in response to increasing political repression, leaders of the two main rival factions plotted a regional uprising against the Molina administration. Known as La Candelaria, the conspiracy was soon infiltrated by police, who arrested hundreds of partisans. The following summer, at the height of the election campaign, a rebellion broke out in the town of Valladolid, but the Porfirian army quickly crushed this movement as well. Historians Allen Wells and Gilbert Joseph have shown that the real beginnings of the Revolution in Yucatán came not from elite conspiracies but among campesino insurgents from free villages on the fringes of the henequen zone. Although financed at first by opposition elites, these smallholders in the southern hills of Puuc and east of Temax provided the bulk of revolutionary activity in the peninsula, thereby carrying on a Maya tradition of resisting Spanish control that dated back to the colonial period and the nineteenth-century Caste War. These peasant soldiers seem highly unlikely to have needed the service of a middle-class *soldadera* like Rosa, who perhaps could not even cook a decent tortilla.[3]

Meanwhile, the main current of the Revolution proceeded in northern and central Mexico, where Madero first drove Díaz from power and then failed to consolidate a stable administration. When the dictator refused to allow a free election in 1910, Madero called for a revolutionary uprising that spread widely in the spring of 1911. Unable to contain the insurgency, Díaz left for exile in Europe, allowing Madero to win a new election held that fall. Nevertheless, the incoming president failed to redress the grievances of peasants who had lost land to the old oligarchy, and nowhere more so than in Yucatán, where the planter elite quickly regained control of the state government. As a result, former partisans such as Emiliano Zapata declared themselves in revolution once again, and Madero ordered the federal army to suppress them. His trust in the Porfirian establishment proved fatal, however, when General Victoriano Huerta seized power in a military coup in February 1913. Revolution again spread through the countryside, except in Yucatán, as insurgent forces under Zapata, Francisco Villa, Venustiano Carranza, and Alvaro Obregón took arms to restore constitutional government. They deposed Huerta in July 1914, but the revolutionary coalition fell apart soon thereafter. The civil war reached a climax in the spring of 1915 as the popular forces of Zapata and Villa struggled against the professional armies of Carranza and Obregón to determine the future of the Mexican Revolution.

Throughout these campaigns, both federal and rebel soldiers alike depended on the work of *soldaderas*, as Torre González and her biographers recognized. The name derived from the *soldada* (wage) given to common soldiers, and historically these camp followers were often paid servants. Many volunteered to join the revolutionary armies, following husbands or other family members, but others were conscripted; the federal army, in particular, rounded up women as well as men in their *leva* drafts. The troop trains of the Villista army contained large numbers of women, prompting historian Friedrich Katz to describe it as a "folk migration."[4] Indeed, the *soldaderas* often formed the vanguard of the army, foraging ahead of the troops, as an Englishman observed: "Like locusts they descended upon the outraged villagers, robbing the roosts, capturing squawking fowls and even squealing piglets, gathering the scanty sticks for the fire over which to have a black pot simmering and flat maize 'tortillas' heating on the embers as soon as the dust-masked troopers might be ready for their fare."[5] Preparing those tortillas was one of the most onerous duties in the army, for women still ground the corn by hand while kneeling over the three-legged metates (grinding stones), a backbreaking chore that took hours each day. Elena Poniatowska writes: "without the soldaderas there is no Mexican Revolution: they kept it alive and fertile, like the land. . . . Without the soldaderas, the men . . . would have deserted."[6]

A few bourgeois and urban working-class women contributed to the Revolution in more professional ways. The Villista army, for example, maintained a modern medical service with trained doctors and nurses who were equipped with the latest surgical appliances and housed in four railroad boxcars. Women also spread propaganda for the Revolution, as did Juana Gutiérrez de Mendoza, described in a previous selection, who was arrested several times for supporting the Zapatista cause. At the same time that they encouraged people to support the cause, women provided intelligence information that might be useful to rebel armies in the field. Apart from those who served as nurses, spies, and propagandists, some middle-class women simply posed for the cameras with the bandoleers, rifles, and sombreros of revolutionary troops. Such images had a clear, if often overlooked, political purpose, staking a claim to the rights of citizenship for women. Nevertheless, it was the anonymous, working-class *soldadera*, like the common soldier, who made the Revolution.

Although camp followers have supported armies throughout history, the Mexican case is perhaps exceptional for the degree to which *soldaderas* blended the "masculine" roles of soldier with the "female" support services. Zapatista *soldadera* Angela Jiménez demonstrates the fluidity that existed between these duties as she dressed as a man to follow her father into the revolutionary ranks. Her skill in combat eventually earned her the rank of lieutenant; nevertheless, she returned at times to women's clothing to spy on the federal army. When her unit was captured, she ordered fellow *soldaderas* to steal enemy weapons and conceal them in laundry bags, thereby allowing the male soldiers to escape. As an officer in charge of male troops, Jiménez expressed a sense of maternal duty by personally preparing food that they seized from haciendas. She later recalled: "I could not ignore that since I was the only woman around I felt it was my obligation to feed the men who had been near starvation."[7]

The Revolution finally returned to Yucatán in 1915, when Carranza ordered General Salvador Alvarado to occupy the peninsula in order to ensure a steady stream of henequen revenue to pay for the war against Villa and Zapata. The Constitutionalist chief sought to limit Mexican populism, but Alvarado proved far more than simply a conservative proconsul. He carried out wide-ranging social reforms to win popular support for the revolutionary cause, beginning by freeing slaves on the henequen plantations. A middle-class reformer committed to capitalism, he nevertheless formed the Yucatecan Socialist Party and enacted sweeping moral reforms, closing bordellos and banning alcohol. Alvarado also had a progressive agenda for women's rights, including coeducation and a liberal divorce law. Essential to implementing this ambitious program was the process of mobilizing popular support through workers' unions, peasant leagues, women's groups, and political parties. By encouraging such organizations, he consolidated his own regional power base while also helping to reeducate the Mexican masses into revolutionary men and women who would form a productive and loyal citizenry. Alvarado made Yucatán a "laboratory for the Revolution," and many of his reforms were later enshrined in the Constitution of 1917.[8]

Education became a pillar of postrevolutionary reform and state-building projects, yet the revolutionary man and woman had decidedly different roles. Teachers and activists disseminated new social, economic, and political ideas and practices by building urban and rural schools, by organizing civic and political groups, and by holding lectures, showing films, and printing pamphlets for the public's benefit. This revolutionary educational project, like the Constitution and the political-social order that it sought to promote, was shaped by assumptions about proper gender roles. The new Ministry of Education sought to provide domestic education for females, and schools offered classes in crafts that could be practiced independently at home, such as sewing and embroidery, soap-making, cooking, and dessert-making. In contrast, males were educated to work outside the home in manual labor and the professions and to be civic actors. These assumptions reflected gender differences embedded in revolutionary legislation, which assumed that men would be the main wage earners for their families, the main recipients of land reform, the voters and civic actors, while women would be wives and mothers.

Despite these limitations, women teachers and activists often worked consciously and unconsciously to subvert the patriarchal aims of postrevolutionary schooling. As a single, professional woman, Torre González presented an alternative model to the ideal of the wife and mother. In her classes at the state normal school in Mérida, she encouraged change, mobility, and new opportunities for women and youth. She also helped organize the first two feminist conferences in Mexico, which were called by Governor Alvarado in 1916. The general stipulated that delegates must have at least an elementary school education, which limited participation primarily to teachers. Nevertheless, Torre González acted as a propagandist for the conference, traveling around the countryside, encouraging qualified women to attend from towns such as Acanceh, Temax, and Motul, in order to maximize the conference's influence. Not surprisingly, given their backgrounds, delegates focused largely on broadening women's educational opportunities as a means to open other fields of social action. They advocated a rationalist educational curriculum to counter the conservative influence of the Church, and also emphasized social hygiene to improve the living standards of the popular classes. Conference attendees discussed women's suffrage, but could not agree on a resolution supporting the issue.[9]

Upon returning home, delegates implemented the tactics they had discussed at the conferences. They organized female neighbors and helped establish cooperative kitchens to feed working women and their children. In addition to promoting literacy and hygiene, teachers helped implement the progressive family laws that Alvarado had created. The Yucatecan conferences also provided a foundation for disseminating feminist principles throughout Mexico and Latin America. Activists protested the failure of revolutionary legislation to grant women political rights, pushed for increased labor protection for women, and challenged the ways that marriage and divorce laws discriminated against women.

In an attempt to limit the spread of Yucatecan socialism, President Carranza transferred Alvarado to a new assignment in 1918, but this merely set the stage for even more radical reforms under Felipe Carrillo Puerto. A native of Motul, in the heart of the henequen zone, he had been the leading organizer of agrarian leagues and urban unions, known collectively as *ligas de resistencia*, which he spread far more actively than even Governor Alvarado had desired. In 1919, Rosa Torre González had helped found a League of Resistance for women, which was named after Rita Cetina Gutiérrez, a prominent Yucatecan educator. These leagues received a boost when Carrillo Puerto shrewdly became an early supporter of Alvaro Obregón in the presidential election of 1920. Two years later, the young socialist won the gubernatorial election and, even before assuming office, he continued to consolidate the state's revolutionary administration. In 1921, he presided over Yucatán's Second Workers' Congress, held at Izamal, which coordinated the various workers' leagues and called for the state government to socialize the means of production. As treasurer and propaganda officer for the "Rita Cetina Gutiérrez" League, Torre González attended the Izamal Congress along with three other women, including Elvia Carrillo Puerto, Felipe's sister, who was known as La Monja Roja (the red nun) for her radical beliefs. Encouraged by their arguments, conference delegates added women's issues to the agenda and ultimately passed resolutions for the establishment of night schools for women workers and for the creation of rural libraries when local leagues had sufficient funds.[10]

The organizing efforts of Yucatecan feminists not only improved the standard of living for women throughout the state but also earned government support for their long-term goal of suffrage. Torre González and her comrades had helped found nearly fifty feminist leagues by 1923, one-tenth of the total of more than 470 socialist leagues in Yucatán. They established libraries and schools, sponsored literacy and temperance campaigns, and gave lectures on birth control, hygiene, child care, and the evolution of the feminist movement. Torre González personally spent her evenings teaching women to read in the O'Horan Hospital and the Ayala Asylum. The feminist leagues also contributed to the welfare of rural communities by pooling resources to purchase cooperative sewing machines. Members of the "Rita Cetina Gutiérrez" League also visited and inspected schools and hospitals and helped establish a state orphanage.[11] In 1922 they returned to the suffrage question, left pending since the 1916 feminist conferences, and began to petition the state legislature for the right to vote. In response to their lobbying efforts and the many articles published in the socialist press, Carrillo Puerto agreed to grant women de facto permission to hold office. Although he delayed in amending the state constitution, he nominated four women to run in the 1922 election. All four won their ballots, including Elvia Carrillo Puerto, who became a state representative, and Rosa Torre González, who entered the Mérida city council.[12]

In her year of service at the *ayuntamiento*, Torre González worked hard to ensure that the Revolution reached all the people of Mérida, not just the elite who had benefited from Porfirian development programs. Although fin de siècle construction projects beautified some sections of the city with paved streets, sidewalks, hospitals, and theaters, dwellers in poorer neighborhoods had difficulty finding affordable housing and lacked basic sewers and wells. Torre González advocated reforms to the sanitary code to improve basic services to the poor, and proposed a new meat inspection station to prevent the sale of rotten and adulterated food. She also continued her work to provide education and welfare programs for poor children. Meanwhile, at the state level, Carrillo Puerto launched an ambitious land reform initiative intended to provide campesinos with farms capable of sustaining their families.

Yet despite its popular appeal to the laboring classes of Yucatán, Carrillo Puerto's socialist experiment came to an abrupt halt when a military rebellion engulfed Mexico at the end of 1923. Large numbers of federal army officers rose up in favor of a failed presidential aspirant, Adolfo de la Huerta, and the peninsula's planter elite cooperated with the rebels to topple the local regime. Governor Carrillo Puerto and some of his closest allies were captured and executed, and Torre González and other sympathizers were harassed in the belief that they helped to hide socialist leaders. Troops loyal to Obregón ultimately defeated the rebels, but a decidedly more conservative state administration was formed through appointment and election. The women who had been entrusted with government positions were forced to step down from their offices and Yucatecan feminism went underground, not to reemerge for another decade.

This setback notwithstanding, women in Yucatán began organizing openly again by the mid 1930s, but they divided between those who focused on suffrage and political rights and those whose concern was social, welfare-oriented labor. Groups dedicated to welfare provision outnumbered those pushing for suffrage because of the more pressing need for cooperative economic resources, such as corn mills and sewing machines. Social feminists also lobbied for the construction of schools, hospitals, clinics, day care centers, and public dining rooms. Such services could help liberate women and their families economically and provide time for other economic, political, and recreational activities. Welfare-oriented feminist action also tended to highlight women's maternal functions, both as maternalist feminists and welfare activists, and as the wives and mothers who utilized such services to aid them in their roles as providers and caregivers.

Although these activities built upon the foundations established a decade earlier by Rosa Torre González, there is no record of her contribution to this stage of the women's movement, in Yucatán or elsewhere. She does not appear in the archives again until the 1940s, when she belonged to a Mexico City affiliate of the Inter-American Commission on Women, a middle-class group dedicated to world peace rather than class conflict. Maternalist claims that women would exert a positive moral influence on politics also inspired the Technical Feminine Commission, another group in Mexico City, in which she worked to mobilize support for suffrage. Partly as a result of such organizing, the Mexican government finally granted women the right to vote in municipal elections in 1947 and in presidential elections in 1953. Thus, Mexican feminists ultimately achieved the goal of effective suffrage, one of the original reforms demanded by Francisco Madero in 1910.

Throughout her career, Torre González took a leading role in politics and social reform, yet to justify these actions, she tended to use certain kinds of arguments, especially maternalist claims emphasizing women's roles as mothers. As a result, the increased participation of women in politics and the workforce has been concentrated in roles that most closely resemble women's unpaid labor in the house. Women have been most highly represented in service industries, including domestic labor, food preparation, and the expanding professions of education and health care, while men continue to dominate the workforce in industry, manufacturing, and highly paid professions. Political opportunities for women have been similarly constrained, particularly in the executive branch, which has dominated Mexican political decision making. Those women who have gained positions at the cabinet level and as undersecretaries have tended to receive portfolios such as tourism, education, labor, and foreign relations. Yet despite the ongoing gender discrimination, Mexican women have continued to struggle for equality following the example set by Rosa Torre González.[13]

NOTES

1. The *Diccionario histórico y biográfico de la Revolución Mexicana* makes such claims, citing the Archivo Histórico de la Secretaría de la Defensa Nacional, yet failing to point to specific documents in this archive (see "Rosa Torres [*sic*] González," *Diccionario histórico y biográfico de la Revolución Mexicana*, CD-Rom, INEHRM). See also "Rosa Torres [*sic*] González," in Aurora Tovar Ramirez, *Mil Quinientas Mujerse en nuestra conciencia colectiva: Catálogo biográfico de mujeres de México* (Documentación y Estudios de Mujeres, A.C., 1996), 626–27, which cites the former.

2. Gilbert M. Joseph, *Revolution from Without: Yucatán, Mexico, and the United States, 1880–1924* (Durham: Duke University Press, 1988), 71–82; Allen Wells, *Yucatán's Gilded Age: Haciendas, Henequen, and International Harvester, 1860–1915* (Albuquerque: University of New Mexico Press, 1985), chapter 6.

3. Allen Wells and Gilbert M. Joseph, *Summer of Discontent, Seasons of Upheaval: Elite Politics and Rural Insurgency in Yucatán, 1876–1915* (Stanford: Stanford University Press, 1996), chapter 7.

4. Quoted in Elizabeth Salas, *Soldaderas in the Mexican Military: Myth and History* (Austin: University of Texas Press, 1990), 39; see also xii, 36–52.

5. Patrick O'Hea, *Reminiscences of the Mexican Revolution* (Mexico, 1966), 85.

6. Elena Poniatowska, *Las soldaderas* (Mexico: Conaculta/INAH, 1999), 14.

7. Quote from Salas, *Soldaderas in the Mexican Military*, 74. See also Esther R. Pérez, James Kallas, and Nina Kallas, *Those Years of the Revolution, 1910–1920: Authentic Bilingual Life Experiences as Told by the Veterans of the War* (San José, CA: Aztlán Today, 1974), 161.

8. Joseph, *Revolution from Without*, 99–115.

9. *El Primer Congreso Feminista de Yucatán: Anales de Esa Memorable Asamblea* (Mérida: Talleres Tipográficos del "Ateneo Peninsular" Plaza de la Independencia, 1916), 45, 52.

10. Juan Rico, *El congreso obrero de Izamal* (Mérida, 1922), 8–11, 122–28; idem, *La huelga de junio* (Mérida, 1922), 92-94. I thank Piedad Peniche for bringing these passages to my attention.

11. *El Popular*, February 24, 1922; *Tierra*, August 5, 1923.

12. *La Revista de Yucatán*, April 19, December 23, 1924.

13. Teresa Rendón, "El trabajo femenino en México: tendencias y cambios recientes," *El Cotidiano* 53 (1993): 4; Roderic Ai Camp, "Women and Men, Men and Women: Gender Patterns in Mexican Politics," in *Women's Participation in Mexican Political Life*, ed. Victoria E. Rodríguez (Boulder, CO: Westview Press, 1998), 168.

SUGGESTED READINGS

Cano, Gabriela. "Soldaderas and Coronelas." *Encyclopedia of Mexico: History, Society and Culture.* Michael S. Werner, ed. Chicago: Fitzroy Dearborn Publishers, 1997.

Fallaw, Ben. *Cárdenas Compromised: The Failure of Reform in Postrevolutionary Yucatán, Mexico.* Durham: Duke University Press, 2001.

Joseph, Gilbert M. *Revolution from Without: Yucatán, Mexico, and the United States, 1880–1924.* Durham: Duke University Press, 1988.

Knight, Alan. *The Mexican Revolution*, 2 vols. Cambridge: Cambridge University Press, 1986.

Lau, Ana. "Una experiencia feminista en Yucatán, 1922–1924." *Fem* 8, no. 30 (1983): 12–14.

Macías, Anna. *Against All Odds: The Feminist Movement in Mexico to 1940.* Westport, CT: Greenwood Press, 1982.

_____. "Felipe Carrillo Puerto and Women's Liberation in Mexico." In *Latin American Women: Historical Perspectives*, ed. Asunción Lavrín. Westport, CT: Greenwood Press, 1978.

O'Malley, Ilene V. *The Myth of the Revolution: Hero Cults and the Institutionalization of the Mexican State, 1920–1940.* Westport, CT: Greenwood Press, 1986.

Poniatowska, Elena. *Las soldaderas.* Mexico: Conaculta/Instituto Nacional de Antropología e Historia, 1999.

Salas, Elizabeth. *Soldaderas in the Mexican Military: Myth and History.* Austin: University of Texas Press, 1990.

Soto, Shirlene Ann. *Emergence of the Modern Mexican Woman: Her Participation in the Revolution and Struggle for Equality, 1910–1940.* Denver: Arden Press, Inc., 1990.

Vaughan, Mary Kay. *Cultural Politics in Revolution: Teachers, Peasants, and Schools in Mexico, 1930–1940.* Tucson: University of Arizona Press, 1997.

_____. "Modernizing Patriarchy: State Policies, Rural Households, and Women in Mexico, 1930–1940." In *Hidden Histories of Gender and the State in Latin America*, ed. Elizabeth Dore and Maxine Molyneux. Durham: Duke University Press, 2000.

_____. "Rural Women's Literacy and Education during the Mexican Revolution: Subverting a Patriarchal Event?" In *Women of the Mexican Countryside, 1850–1990*, ed. Heather Fowler-Salamini and Mary Kay Vaughan. Tucson: University of Arizona Press, 1994.

Wells, Allen. *Yucatán's Gilded Age: Haciendas, Henequen, and International Harvester, 1860–1915.* Albuquerque: University of New Mexico Press, 1985.

Wells, Allen, and Gilbert M. Joseph. *Summer of Discontent, Seasons of Upheaval: Elite Politics and Rural Insurgency in Yucatán, 1876–1915.* Stanford: Stanford University Press, 1996.

CHAPTER TEN

Nahui Olin

The General's Daughter Disrobes

ANNE RUBENSTEIN

Chapultepec Park, conveniently accessible on the pink metro line and a favorite location for Sunday picnics or visits to the zoo, provides the art lover with a stunning tour of Mexican history. The anthropology museum, one of the world's finest, displays the glories of the pre-Hispanic world, an easy walk from the hilltop castle and its historical museum, highlighted by the nineteenth-century collection of Maximilian and Carlota. The Rufino Tamayo Museum of Modern Art, appropriately located midway between them, mediates these two worlds with some of the finest works of Mexico's twentieth-century artistic renaissance.

The origins of this cultural flowering lie in the social revolution of 1910. Inspired both by modernist painters such as Picasso, who scandalized European society, and by the peasant armies of Zapata, who tramped through the salons of Mexico City, a revolutionary generation of Mexican artists broke free of staid nineteenth-century conventions. Building on changes already under way during the Porfiriato, they began to experiment with new methods of representation as well as with the vernacular traditions of Mexican folk art and the remains of pre-Hispanic art, and they reached out to new audiences who had never before had access to visual art. This renaissance is often associated with the great muralists Diego Rivera, José Clemente Orozco, and David Alfaro Siqueiros, who explicitly intended their monumental, public art as revolutionary propaganda. Nevertheless, the artistic community of the 1920s was not limited to those three; countless other artists, intellectuals, and even primary school art teachers helped create the public image of the revolution and therefore shaped its future meaning. Carmen Mondragón, a Porfirian socialite rebaptized as the Bohemian artist Nahui Olin, engaged the contemporary debates over the significance of the Indian in Mexican society and over the struggle between nationalism and cosmopolitanism. Although she was often dismissed as simply a beautiful muse for male genius, this essay shows how Nahui Olin took an active role in defining her own image, in life and art.

*Anne Rubenstein began her study of popular aspects of postrevolu-
tionary art in her first book,* Bad Language, Naked Ladies, and Other
Threats to the Nation: A Political History of Comic Books in Mexico
(1998). The coeditor of Fragments of a Golden Age: The Politics of
Culture in Mexico Since 1940 *(2001), she is now working on a book
about movies and their audiences in Mexico. She is assistant professor of
history at York University, Toronto, where she won the Dean's Award for
Outstanding Research.*

Nahui Olin led a complicated life. Born with the name Carmen
Mondragón, she inherited the gifts of artistic talent, intelligence, rebelliousness, great beauty, and a personal connection of one kind or another to nearly everyone who mattered in early twentieth-century Mexico.
By the time she was thirty she was a scandalous figure; within a few decades she was nearly forgotten; since her death in 1978, interest in her
work and life has revived. No longer a figure in the gossip columns, she
has become an important Mexican artist.

Carmen Mondragón was born in 1893 in Tacubaya, a wealthy Mexico
City neighborhood. She was the fifth of eight children in an elite, politically well-connected family. Carmen's father served as one of Porfirio
Díaz's generals, but like many Latin American military men of the time,
he also had some training as an engineer. Around the time of Carmen's
birth, her father designed an exceptionally efficient repeating machine
gun; in 1897 he took the whole family to France, where he was to oversee production of the famous new weapon, dubbed "the Mondragón."
The baby of the family, born in Paris, was even named Napoleon in
honor of the Mondragón's sojourn abroad. This gun was so important in
shaping her family and her life that when Carmen Mondragón painted
her father's portrait many years later, she showed him in uniform,
wreathed with laurel leaves, surrounded by tiny floating golden cannons.

The Mondragón family remained in Paris until 1905, when Carmen
was twelve. By then the "New Woman"—intellectually active, ambitious,
physically fit, unfettered by corsets or conventions—had already made
herself visible on the streets of European capitals; such women might
even have entered the consciousness of such sheltered children as Carmen
Mondragón. If we can believe the evidence of the later self-portraits in
which she portrayed herself as a child, she already had her hair in a very
modern bob—albeit with long braids remaining in the back—by the age
of ten. In any case, Carmen Mondragón's Parisian childhood shaped her
adult imagination powerfully. She was to return often to these memories
in drawings and paintings of herself as a little girl. One such painting
shows a scene of outdoor play with her brothers, sisters, and the family
dog. But other drawings and paintings portray her as the largest or only

figure, unsmiling and staring out at the viewer, in settings such as the garden of Versailles palace. Such pictures represent young Carmen as precociously serious-minded and cultured (and perhaps a little lonely); whether or not this was true, she certainly chose to remember herself that way.

When the Mondragón family returned to Mexico City in 1905, they sent Carmen to a convent school whose teachers were French nuns. Carmen soon scandalized the faculty of Colegio Frances with her poetry. Written in an impeccable French that showed a certain precocious interest in the new modernist literature, Carmen's poems made such proclamations as "Illusions are the ailment of the weak" and "Love is creative, love is creation, creation of humanity and of art," which seemed like strong stuff coming from a well-bred young lady in 1906.[1] At the age of fourteen she wrote, "My misfortune is to have but one destiny: to die because . . . the world, men, and the universe . . . are all too small to satisfy my soul."[2] Eighteen years later she published these poems and other writings from her schooldays in a very small edition, under the title *A dix ans sur mon pupitre* ("At age 10 at my school desk"), keeping the original French although printing and distributing the book in Mexico; the cover featured an India-ink self-portrait of "Nahui Olin, age ten"— one more of Carmen Mondragón's backward glances at her childhood.

The young Señorita Mondragón received the education appropriate for a Mexican girl from an elite family during the Porfiriato. Everyone around her assumed that young women such as Carmen would never need to work for a living but would require the kinds of accomplishments that would help her run a large household, keep a husband amused, and do the entertaining and socializing that would further his career. Thus, the nuns at the Colegio Frances and her private tutors carefully schooled her in French and Spanish grammar, drawing and painting, and piano (she played classical duets with her sister Lola). She had inherited the talent for design that her father had learned to use in inventing weapons, but she was encouraged to turn that talent toward drawing portraits of friends and relatives or painting flowers and other innocent objects and scenes.

When Carmen Mondragón became Nahui Olin, at age twenty-nine, she adopted a deliberately naive style of drawing and painting. But the art education she received as a schoolgirl was as sophisticated as that to be found anywhere, as her later portrait drawings reveal. Like all academic art education of the time, it was very likely rigorous and dry, without much encouragement for imagination or invention; but the sisters of the Colegio Frances would at least have ensured that the talented Señorita Mondragón learned to make clear and convincing representations of people and objects in a number of media.

Was Carmen bored by all this? She never said so. Still, it is easy to imagine her relief as she completed her formal schooling and turned her attention toward an increasingly bohemian social life. She caused a mild scandal in 1910, at seventeen years old, by appearing at a high-society costume ball—part of Mexico City's elaborate celebrations of the centenary of Independence—dressed as a male Turk, complete with perfumed cigarette. Carmen and her siblings probably attended many of the 1910 centenary celebrations, including the exhibit of Mexican art curated by the painter Gerardo Murillo, who went by the name Dr. Atl. While higher government subsidies went to the simultaneous centenary exhibits of Japanese and Spanish art, the Mexican show was far more important in the long run: it marked the beginning of modern art in Mexico.

This was the first exhibit ever of Mexican painting and sculpture, and Dr. Atl used it as a platform for his own ideas about art. Painting in Mexico, Dr. Atl said, should use the newest techniques from Europe—which painters should learn by visiting European capitals on fellowships provided by the Díaz government, rather than in the staid art academies of Mexico itself—but they should address topics particular to Mexico. The country needed art to mirror its history, especially its ancient, indigenous past. Thus, when Carmen Mondragón strolled through the centennial art exposition, she would have seen giant canvasses depicting Aztec legends as well as smaller pictures of Mexican volcanoes and rivers, many painted in styles far removed from the stiff techniques she had been studying. This must have appealed powerfully to the young woman's rebellious spirit.

When the Revolution exploded in 1910, Carmen's life probably changed little, at least at first. Much of the fighting took place far away from the capital city. But General Mondragón picked the wrong side to support in one of the dramatic struggles for political power that marked this era. In February 1913 he joined a military coup that came to be known as *la decena trágica*, the Ten Tragic Days. This revolt toppled Francisco Madero from the presidency and installed Victoriano Huerta in his place, after a brutal ten-day battle in the streets of Mexico City. Huerta showed his gratitude by making General Mondragón the head of Mexico's armed forces. But he then fired the general from his cabinet-level position four months later, in June 1913, apparently fearing that Mondragón might take for himself what he had already helped Huerta acquire. (Huerta also complained that Mondragón had not managed to stop the advances of the revolutionary armies who opposed him.) From that point on, the Mondragón clan lived in a cloud of political suspicion that their neighbors' bitter memories of the Ten Tragic Days only compounded. Two aunts came to replace the servants who had done all the cooking for the family, because the general feared poison. At the end of 1913 the general led his extended family—thirty-seven of Carmen's relations, though not Carmen herself—into European exile.

In the middle of all this drama, in August of 1913, Carmen Mondragón married a good-looking and well-connected young man three years her junior. Despite, or because of, the political circumstances, their gala wedding was one of the high points of the season. This young man, Manuel Rodríguez Lozano, was only seventeen at the time, but he was already a graduate of the Colegio Militar and working as an undersecretary in the diplomatic corps. Carmen met him at a State Department dance and was drawn to his handsome looks, his charm, and especially his artistic talent. Manuel Rodríguez Lozano, though very young, may have already understood himself to be gay when he engaged himself to Carmen Mondragón. But in other ways this was a brilliant match between social equals with many common interests. And it was rare in this epoch for a Mexican man to remain unmarried, even if he preferred to sleep with (or *did* sleep with) people, either male or female, other than his wife.

Still, long after the painful end to this ill-fated marriage, Carmen's family reported that she tried to cancel the wedding on the night before it was to occur, but her mother forced her to go through with it. One version has it that Señora Mondragón bluntly offered Carmen the alternative of a wedding or taking vows as a nun; another has the mother explaining to her daughter that, since the general was in political trouble, the family could not also absorb the scandal that would be created by canceling a grand society wedding at the last minute. In any case the photographs from the day of the wedding show both members of the couple looking apprehensive.

In their first year of marriage, Manuel Rodríguez Lozano and Carmen Mondragón de Rodríguez seemed happy enough. They stayed behind when the new bride's family left for Europe and probably enjoyed discovering how the Mexican Revolution was revolutionizing art. Painters, muralists, photographers, and printmakers mostly avoided fighting in the war itself, even if—like Dr. Atl—they embroiled themselves in the politics of the era. But whether or not an artist had political interests, the war provided an excuse to break with the stultifying traditions of academic art that had shaped painting and related fields through the end of the nineteenth century in Mexico. In 1911, belatedly following the example of the French Impressionists, Mexico's first school of open-air painting opened after a thrilling (if unsuccessful) strike by students at the nation's most important and most conservative art school, the Academia de San Carlos; Manuel Rodríguez Lozano was involved with it almost from its inception.

All the same, by the end of 1914 the political situation in the country had deteriorated enough that the newlyweds followed the rest of the

Mondragón clan out of the country. They went first to New York, then to Paris. In France the attractive young couple hobnobbed with Matisse, Braque, and Picasso, while Carmen's fluent French enabled them to keep up with the latest ideas in the world of art and literature. But finally—as the war in Europe, too, grew more dangerous—Carmen and her husband moved into the Mondragón family household in San Sebastián, Spain. They remained there for seven years, though after the end of World War I they could once again visit Paris.

Little trustworthy evidence remains to explain what went wrong between Carmen and her husband in those seven years in Europe. He later claimed that Carmen had borne their child, gone crazy, and murdered the infant, but that her powerful family had covered up the crime. She never responded, neither to defend herself from the accusation of murder nor to explain what the death of her newborn meant to her. Her family told one of her biographers that she never even heard this story, and that the baby died of natural causes shortly after it was born.[3] The various versions of the tale conflict to such an extent that it is not clear whether the child was born in Mexico City, Paris, or San Sebastián. No death certificate for this baby has ever been found, to back Manuel Rodríguez Lozano's story or refute it. And Rodríguez Lozano had two strong motives to lie about his marriage and its ending.

First, he might have been angry and frustrated at the time he spent under his father-in-law's protection and in his father-in-law's house, unable to get a career started in a foreign country. These emotions could easily have found an outlet in slandering his wife and the entire Mondragón family. Second, there was the issue of injured masculine pride. The marriage finally ended when Carmen Mondragón very publicly left her husband for another man—a profound challenge to the public perception of Rodríguez Lozano's honor as a man. In the portraits Carmen made of him during their years in Spain, and which she exhibited publicly after their marriage ended, she always showed him as girlishly pretty; this, too, could have felt like a blow to Rodríguez Lozano's pride. As a gay man (however clandestinely) and a man apparently without children, Manuel Rodríguez Lozano must have felt his masculinity to be especially open to challenge. In 1924 he figured in another scandal when his young protégé, the 19-year-old painter Abraham Ángel, committed suicide shortly after the two men returned from a trip to Argentina. Later, Rodríguez Lozano affiliated himself with members of the literary movement Los Contemporáneos, whose members—most notably Salvador Novo—were viciously gay-baited in the 1930s. Thus, prudence would have suggested to Rodríguez Lozano that he keep his marriage, and his own innocence in its failure, before the public eye. He had good reasons to tell this shocking tale about his former wife and her family, and to go on telling it.

That Manuel Rodríguez Lozano had strong motives to tell the seemingly implausible story that his crazed former wife had murdered their child does not necessarily mean he was lying, but it might encourage us to question the story's veracity. Furthermore, this story bears a strange resemblance to other narratives about women artists, which frequently paint them as crazy. Whether or not such stories are true, they support the idea that making art was a male activity—productive rather than reproductive—and in that sense, a woman who made art was already socially "insane." When Carmen Mondragón remade herself as the artist Nahui Olin, the subject of her art was her own femininity; this could be read as a subtle response to her former husband's insistence on describing her as dangerously, crazily unfeminine.

In any case, the unhappy pair returned to Mexico City in 1921 and resumed their positions in the art world there. Rodríguez Lozano attempted unsuccessfully to join the new mural-painting projects sponsored by the Department of Public Education. Both Carmen and Manuel attended parties and gallery openings, museum shows and lectures. Both participated, too, in the art shows and museum exhibitions held in honor of the centennial of Mexican Independence (this time the events celebrated the end rather than the beginning of the war for independence). Carmen had four portrait drawings in the largest of these exhibitions; her subjects included the painters Roberto Montenegro and Gabriel Fernández Ledesma, a suggestion of the social circles she moved in. Manuel contributed a painting to this exhibit: his *Retrato de mi esposa* (Portrait of my wife) was the only picture he ever exhibited of Carmen, and even then, he named her only "my wife."

During the centennial celebration in Mexico City, Carmen and Manuel would have seen Dr. Atl's most recent success as a curator, a gigantic exhibition of Indian artifacts and crafts. This was the first such exhibit ever held in Mexico, and the catalog—also written by Dr. Atl—was the first scholarly treatment of Mexican indigenous folklore. This marked a remarkable shift in merely eleven years: in 1910 it was avant-garde simply to make oil paintings of Mexico's indigenous people; by 1921, in order to be avant-garde, an artist had to collect and study the objects through which indigenous people represented themselves. This new trend indicated paternalist racism as well as the desire to keep up with the European avant-gardistes such as Picasso, who were collecting African masks at the time. (Years later, as their love affair was ending, Nahui Olin wrote to Dr. Atl that "you believe that you are intelligent because you exploit the talents of others," which might refer to the dynamics of their relationship but might also describe Dr. Atl's "discovery," or appropriation, of the work of indigenous artisans.⁴) But the new interest in indigenous crafts also shows how fast the Mexican art world had changed in response to international modernist ideologies and the specific demands that the Revolution at home made on Mexican artists to join in rebuilding the nation.

Sometime around the opening of the 1921 exhibit, Carmen Mondragón was formally introduced to Dr. Atl at a party she attended with her husband. She never recorded her first impression of the charismatic artist who was to replace Rodríguez Lozano in her life. But Dr. Atl wrote of her that he immediately felt lost in her huge green eyes; and he was impressed enough to invite both her and her husband to visit his studio. She went, her husband did not, and shortly thereafter she moved out of the apartment she shared with Manuel and back to her family's Tacubaya mansion; the marriage was finally over. By the beginning of 1922, Carmen Mondragón and Gerardo Murillo, otherwise known as Dr. Atl, were living together in a former convent, a colonial edifice that was home and studio for them both, in the center of Mexico City. Thus began an affair that led Carmen to create some scandalous scenes, change her style of painting, and change her name.

Gerardo Murillo was forty-seven years old at the time to Carmen Mondragón's twenty-nine, and he had a reputation as a womanizer. He often appears in Carmen's drawings and paintings with a receding hairline, long nose, and short beard emphasizing his immense forehead and piercing gaze. His friend Edward Weston's photographs show Dr. Atl's graying hair, slightly ragged clothes, lanky but powerful build, and slouching posture, as well as the same intensity of expression that Carmen Mondragón captured in her drawings and paintings: he looked the part of the politically engaged intellectual who was, at the same time, a bohemian artist. Like Carmen's abandoned husband, Dr. Atl belonged to both the world of politics and the world of art, but he was substantially more successful in both. Gerardo Murillo combined the talents, interests, sophistication, and drive that Carmen had probably looked for in her husband.

Gerardo Murillo had taken the name Dr. Atl before the Revolution began. The doctorate was conferred, in jest, by a bohemian friend, while *atl* is the Nahuatl word for water. Thus his new name echoed some of the long-term ideas and concerns of the Porfirian elite and the Revolutionary vanguard, too. By calling himself "doctor" he laid claim to the science-and-progress ideology of the *científicos*, but the Nahuatl word "atl"—which no native Nahuatl speaker used as a name—indicated both his admiration for the ancient civilizations of Mesoamerica and his difference from them. That is, he was an *indigenista* rather than an indigenous person: concerned with the creation of the "cosmic race" of Mexicans (as José Vasconcelos had named it) through mingling elements of European and indigenous heritage, he nonetheless retained all the privileges of belonging to the wealthy, pale-skinned minority of Mexicans who made up its intellectual and artistic elite. He would have been furious if anyone had ever mistaken *him* for an indigenous person or claimed that his paintings belonged to a folk tradition.

When Carmen Mondragón changed her name, at Dr. Atl's suggestion, to Nahui Olin, she, too, was indicating allegiance to *indigenista* ideology and interest in the remaking of Mexican national identity, rather than making any claim to an indigenous identity herself. Her new name, like Dr. Atl's, was a Nahuatl word but not an Aztec name: it meant "fourth movement of the sun," referring to a calendrical epoch. (From a Mexica point of view, this would have been rather like renaming oneself "Second Millennium.") But for her, changing her name also meant sacrificing a public association with her famous and powerful family, as she had not had to do in adding her husband's last name to her own at marriage, following the standard Spanish-language practice. Thus, she committed herself more deeply and more publicly to Dr. Atl than she had to her husband. But dropping her family name also might have meant that she was trying to spare her family the scandal that came when she left her husband for Dr. Atl. And she picked an interesting moment for this highly charged act: her father, who had remained in San Sebastián, died in September 1922.

That year also marked the beginning of the decade and a half in which Nahui Olin developed her style as an artist and produced her best work. This was also the era in which she collaborated with some of the most important artists of the day, modeling for photographs and paintings. The poetry and philosophic essays contained in the five books she published between 1922 and 1937 are interesting mainly, as we have seen, as examples of European modernist thought, but the books themselves—printed in tiny editions, beautifully designed, often with hand-drawn covers—are remarkable objects, and the first three also show how closely Nahui Olin and Dr. Atl worked together on these projects.

Nahui Olin's drawings and paintings, which are far more skillful than her writing, are also interesting because they document her life. Taken together, the images make up a memoir of her friends, childhood, family, travels, possessions, and even her pets—detailing her emotional and erotic life. She made countless self-portraits. She often depicted herself in the arms of handsome men, sometimes kissing them, sometimes swooning backward, but always engaging with them erotically. She never represented a sexual act, but one painting does show her, naked, leaping toward a naked man on a Mexico City balcony (her bent leg covers their genitalia). When she painted her cats, she often gave them her own large, light-green eyes; one painting varies the theme of Nahui-with-lover by showing one big tomcat curled up in what seems to be postcoital bliss with a smaller, green-eyed cat. To look at Nahui Olin's paintings, then, was to experience her pride in and enjoyment of her lithe, voluptuous body—even when it was disguised as a cat.

Most of Nahui Olin's paintings had her pleasure in physicality as subject matter; all of them shared a style of painting that expressed that same bodily pleasure in a different way. While in Europe, Carmen Mondragón had made correct, careful pictures with fussy little brush strokes in rich but muted colors. As Carmen Mondragón became Nahui Olin, her style changed, too. She used wetter paint and more rapid, flowing brush strokes, longer and more curving lines, more relaxed compositions, and much brighter colors. (Perhaps this new palette responded to Dr. Atl's love for bright, uncomplicated colors, but the other changes in style as Carmen Mondragón became Nahui Olin seem to be entirely her own inventions.) These new paintings look as if the artist took pleasure in the act of making them. Even when she was painting seemingly innocent and impersonal scenes of village squares or circus tents, Nahui Olin brought something of her own body to the work.

Her work as a model for other artists in this period marked her image indelibly in the canon of Mexican art, for she appears in some of the most important of all the murals of the period. In Diego Rivera's first great mural, for the National Preparatory School, she is the Goddess of Erotic Poetry. Rivera had her pose for a mural at the Teatro Insurgentes as an implausibly blonde indigenous woman aiding a fallen Aztec warrior, but she reappears on the mural's other side as a member of the Porfirian elite, bedecked in pearls. And in his murals for the National Palace she appears twice as a beautiful white woman in fancy party clothes, living the good life—much more Carmen Mondragón than Nahui Olin. Similarly, Roberto Montenegro's portrait of Nahui wrapped in a tasseled Indian blanket nonetheless emphasizes her lipstick, pale skin, and blonde hair by contrasting them with a bright red background, and also makes a point of her elegant manicure and delicate jewelry: he, too, envisioned her as a high-society woman.

Dr. Atl depicted Nahui Olin with more personal, varied imagery. Some of his drawings convey the impression of a body in graceful motion with only a few smudges of charcoal, while others portray her with meticulous verisimilitude but stripped of most external signs of class or ethnicity. In several paintings, Dr. Atl imagined her with a shaved head: by portraying her with neither short nor long hair, hair that was not curly or straight, blonde or black, he deprived Mexican viewers of an important clue to her social status, her race, and even her political position. In Dr. Atl's vision, Nahui Olin was a body inhabited by a mind (he made a lovely drawing of her reading) but without a social or economic context.

Only Edward Weston, the brilliant photographer from California, seems to have believed in the Indian persona implied by Nahui Olin's name. In his photographs, she has thick, short, disordered hair. She glares sullenly out at the camera. Even her delicate features somehow appear coarser. She does not look like an Indian, exactly—but she appears to have been Edward Weston's idea of an Indian. Nahui Olin, in turn, drew a caricature of Weston with puffy red hair and bright pink cheeks, making a point of getting his ethnicity right.

Nahui Olin and Dr. Atl had not lived together long when they began fighting. The intensity of their physical relationship, which his and her artworks bear witness to, apparently could not make up for his pleasure in the company of other women, her jealousy and quick temper, and perhaps a certain competitiveness between them. It must have been very difficult for Nahui Olin to maintain her association with such a powerful man in the male milieu of Mexican art, especially as she avoided associating herself with the many women who did form part of that world.

Women artists existed at the margins of this circle, rarely if ever taking the high-prestige role of mural painting. Still, the Revolution opened up new possibilities for women in the visual arts. They worked in watercolors and drew, media that had long been considered appropriate for women, but they also took up oil painting and printmaking. Perhaps the boom in mural painting for male artists left some room in these other traditionally masculine artistic disciplines for women to work. And photography attracted women artists, too, as it had all over the world: it was too new a field for it to have a male-only tradition. Women played other important roles, too. They provided the publicity for modern Mexican art by collecting and displaying it; they published art magazines and wrote criticism; they ran galleries. Women helped create artists, if not art, by organizing art schools; like Nahui Olin, they taught drawing and painting classes. Some artistically inclined women found themselves relegated to the role of muse, providing emotional support, financial help, sexual satisfaction, critical attention, and other forms of caretaking to male artists, as Nahui Olin did for Dr. Atl. But often, women in the world of Mexican art took care of each other as well as taking care of the men around them. Networks of women artists and their female supporters helped each other open galleries, find patrons, leave marriages, get into museums, and in general go on doing their work.

Nahui Olin, one of the first women artists to have worked in Mexico, never worked with women curators, gallery owners, critics, patrons, models, and artists. Her artist friends, lovers, and teachers—including

Manuel Rodríguez Lozano, Diego Rivera, Dr. Atl, Edward Weston, and Antonio Garduño—all were male. And she collaborated with them in ways that reinforced stereotypical gender roles: she played the wronged spouse or abandoned lover, the nude model, the hopeful starlet. She often included her male lovers in her self-portraits, but she rarely depicted another woman. When she turned to women for aid and comfort, she relied only on her female relatives: her mother, who lived until 1948, and later her sisters and nieces. It is tempting to speculate on how different her life and art could have been had she maintained relationships with her female peers.

Instead, Nahui Olin's most important relationship within the world of art was with Dr. Atl, and it was explosive. Their public battles soon became the stuff of gossip. Decades after their affair ended, rumors still circulated in Mexico City about the time that Nahui Olin supposedly chased a nude model away from the platform where Dr. Atl was painting her into a mural. Guests at a dinner party in the former convent claimed to have seen her serve him *mole* (chile pepper stew) by dumping it on his head. In separate interviews in a newspaper's Sunday supplement, each declared their intention not to marry another artist (though they did not mention each other by name). Dr. Atl eventually published a memoir, complete with excerpts from her letters, in which he included an account of the time he broke a jar of paint over her head. She responded to the incident with the paint by posting a letter to him on the front door, in which she announced that, having cheated on him with twenty men, she had now taken an Italian opera singer as her lover. With that public declaration, the relationship ended as abruptly as it had begun five years earlier.

Dr. Atl and Nahui Olin met again afterward, apparently amicably. One of her last letters to him indicates that she still cared for him: "I love you even while hating you—because love is contradiction, is absurd."[5] He carefully saved her letters, drawings, and poems, even buying paintings from her occasionally when she could not support herself by teaching drawing classes. But they never really resumed their friendship.

In one of her poems, Nahui Olin wrote, "when I pose, I am another."[6] If she meant that, while posing, she was another person—not herself—the range of ways in which artists saw her would attest to that. Depending on the artist, she could seem a high-society flapper, a goddess, a peasant, or simply a beautiful body. But she also meant that, while modeling, she was "another" artist like the artist who was capturing her image: not a muse, but a collaborator. She proved the point when she sent printed invitations to every important artist, collector, and critic in Mexico, asking them to attend *her* exhibit of nudes (pictures of her taken by the photographer Antonio Garduño, as the small print on the invitation noted). Even the Secretary of Education attended the opening of the impromptu gallery in the patio of the colonial-era mansion where Nahui lived in 1927.

This marked the high point of her notoriety. Shortly afterward, she made an unsuccessful attempt to find work as a silent-film actress in Hollywood. Stills from her Metro-Goldwyn-Mayer screen test showed her from behind, draped strategically with a Spanish shawl but otherwise undressed, with the expression and makeup of a vamp in the style of Theda Bara. Perhaps Nahui Olin objected to being made an exotic, racialized "other"; but on the other hand, she allowed *Ovaciones* (then Mexico's best-selling magazine) to print the photos when she returned to Mexico. After this adventure, though, her name gradually receded from the gossip columns.

Mexico's adventure with artistic revolution and sexual liberation was coming to an end; the 1930s would prove to be a much more serious-minded time, in which radical artists still contributed to the reconstruction of the nation and the representation of its history but no longer were invited to make policy or act as exemplary figures of the revolutionary man or woman. For decades after 1929, Nahui Olin continued to paint and to exhibit her works in galleries and museums, and to model for paintings, drawings, photographs, and murals. She took new lovers, and her paintings celebrated each affair: a dreamlike romance with the captain of a Cuban cruise liner tragically cut short by his death at sea, two tempestuous years with the illustrator Matías Sampoyo, and several more. She went on teaching art, mostly at the high-school level. And she received a small stipend from the government in exchange for donating several paintings every year to the national museum's collection. But although what she did with her life remained very much the same, her activities became private; she was no longer infamous.

Eventually, Nahui Olin grew too old to work. She retired to a house— still in the heart of Mexico City—that she had inherited from her parents, and devoted herself to caring for the city's innumerable stray cats. Many city dwellers came to regard the nearly silent old woman surrounded by mewling street cats as an icon of the city, but hardly anyone connected her to the beautiful, notorious New Woman of the 1920s, Nahui Olin. When she could no longer take care of herself, she moved back to the house in which she had been born, and a niece looked after her until she died at age 84, in 1978.

But that was not the end of Nahui Olin's story. Her art survived her, and indeed has become much better known since her death than it was in the decades before. Much of Nahui Olin's art reflected her experience of femininity: her pleasure in her own beautiful body, her attraction to the beautiful men around her, her sense of herself as an object to be looked at. When she looks out of her own paintings, it is herself she stares back at with those huge, startling green eyes; we know she is looking into a mirror, and thus she adopts the masculine position of being the one who looks, only to emphasize the underlying femininity of her position as the object of the gaze. Her art made no feminist statements—she celebrated traditional gender roles rather than critiquing them—unless her viewers read into her rebellious depictions of her own sensuality a specifically political viewpoint that she never espoused in her many writings. Her multiple self-portraits, in sum, could almost have been made by one of the many male artists for whom she modeled; her art asks its viewers to see it as though a man had made it.

Yet Nahui Olin's stature as an artist has risen dramatically in the years since her death *because she was a woman*. After about 1975, the second wave of global feminism helped create interest in women artists. And the period from 1910 to 1950, when Mexico truly was a global center for visual art, continued to intrigue art lovers even as the artists who were not muralists—photographers and surrealist painters, many of whom were women—began to seem more interesting in retrospect. These two processes converged with a boom in studies of Frida Kahlo and reproductions of her work, a process of kitschification so powerful that critics began calling it "Frida-mania."[7] But this interest in Mexican women artists of the early twentieth century has expanded to include Nahui Olin. In 1992 and again in 2000, major museum shows in Mexico City displayed Nahui Olin's paintings and drawings and also exhibited some of the photographs, drawings, and paintings by others for which she modeled. No longer the scandalous *desnuda*, Nahui Olin seemed in retrospect to have been a liberated woman, ahead of her time. Perhaps she had not experienced her own life that way, but it hardly seems to matter; as long as her art has an audience, her restless soul must be at peace.

NOTES

1. Quoted in Tomás Zurian, "Nahui Olin, una mujer de los tiempos modernos," in *Nahui Olin, una mujer de los tiempos modernos* (Mexico City: Museo Estudio Diego Rivera, 1992), 50–51. All translations from French and Spanish are by me unless otherwise indicated.

2. Quoted in Adriana Malvido, *Nahui Olin, la mujer del sol* (Mexico: Editorial Diana, 1993), 20.

3. Ibid., 26–27; see also Beatriz Zamorano Navarro, *Manuel Rodríguez Lozano, una revisión finisecular* (Mexico City: Instituto Nacional de Bellas Artes/Museo de Arte Moderno, 1998), 63.

4. The letter, and an attached drawing, was part of the Nahui Olin retrospective at the Museo Mural Diego Rivera, Mexico City, 2000. See the catalog, *Nahui Olin: Opera varia* (Mexico City: INBA, 2000), 56.

5. Quoted in Malvido, *Nahui Olin*, 81.

6. Quoted in ibid., 54.

7. Claudia Schaefer, *Textured Lives: Women, Art, and Representation in Modern Mexico* (Tucson: University of Arizona Press, 1992), xii–xiii.

SUGGESTED READINGS

Cuevas, José Luis. "The Cactus Curtain," *The Evergreen Review* 2 (Spring 1959): 111–20.

Garduño, Blanca, and Tomás Zurián Ugarte. *Nahui Olin: Una mujer de los tiempos modernos*. Mexico City: Instituto Nacional de Bellas Artes/Museo Estudio Diego Rivera, 1992.

Kaplan, Janet. *Unexpected Journey: Remedios Varo*. London: Abbeville Press, 2000 [1988].

Malvido, Adriana. *Nahui Olin, la mujer del sol*. Mexico City: Editorial Diana, 1993.

Murillo, Gerardo (Dr. Atl). *Gentes profanas en el convento*. Mexico City: Ediciones Botas, 1950.

Olin, Nahui (Carmen Mondragón). *A dix ans sur mon pupitre*. Mexico City: Editorial Cultura, 1924.

_____. *Calinement je suis dedans*. Mexico City: Libería Guillot, 1923.

_____. *Energía cósmica*. Mexico City: Ediciones Botoas, 1937.

_____. *Óptica cerebral poema dinámicos*. Mexico City: Ediciones México Moderno, 1922.

Poniatowska, Elena. *Tinísima*. Mexico City: Ediciones Era, 1992.

Rivera, Diego. *Mi arte, mi vida*. Mexico City: Editorial Herrero, 1963.

Schaefer, Claudia. *Textured Lives: Women, Art, and Representation in Modern Mexico*. Tucson: University of Arizona Press, 1992.

Weston, Edward. *The Daybooks of Edward Weston: Volume One, Mexico*. New York: Aperture, 1961.

Zamorano Navarro, Beatriz. *Manuel Rodríguez Lozano, una revisión finisecular*. Mexico City: Instituto Nacional de Bellas Artes/Museo de Arte Moderno, 1998.

Zurián Ugarte, Tomás. *Nahui Olin, Ópera varia*. Mexico City: Instituto Nacional de Bellas Artes/Museo Mural Diego Rivera, 2000.

CHAPTER ELEVEN

Lic. Moisés T. de la Peña

The Economist on Horseback*

ENRIQUE C. OCHOA

 *Although there are more than a dozen university campuses in Mexico City, no one ever mistakes the subway station Universidad, at the southern end of the green metro line (number 3). The National Autonomous University of Mexico (UNAM), founded in 1553, enrolls more than 300,000 students and is an internationally recognized leader in scientific research. But its striking campus, built on volcanic rock and renowned for the murals adorning its library tower, symbolizes the divided heritage of the Revolution of 1910.*

On the one hand, UNAM graduates such as economist Moisés T. de la Peña dedicated their careers to realizing the revolutionary promises of the Constitution of 1917. Although teachers and activists such as Rosa Torre González (see Chapter 9) had played a crucial role in organizing campesinos to press for agrarian reform, farmers needed more than a parcel of land to support their families, let alone to contribute to national development. In addition to distributing land, the government also had to provide them with access to credit, technical support, and transportation to market their crops. The revolution thus depended on the work of skilled administrators with both knowledge and commitment to social change.

On the other hand, UNAM reached its pinnacle of influence, with a generation of graduates in national leadership positions, at precisely the moment when the revolution seemed to lose its way. The transition between the aging revolutionary veterans, who had ruled Mexico since Francisco Madero, and these young professionals took place during the presidential administration of Miguel Alemán (1946–1952), an alumnus of the UNAM law school who endowed the university with its new campus. Yet having acquired the professional skills needed to carry out social reform, they chose instead to pursue modernization for their own personal benefit.

---

*The title was provided by Lic. de la Peña's son, the late economic historian Sergio de la Peña. From Iván Gutiérrez and Enrique C. Ochoa's unpublished interviews with Sergio de la Peña, March 1992.

Politicians used their legal expertise to divert development projects from the impoverished countryside to rapidly growing cities. Young economists likewise turned their backs on the social mission of the revolution and plotted a course of "trickle-down" industrialization based on capital accumulation for the rich rather than consumption for the masses. Finally, these university graduates put a modern facade on the authoritarian political system inherited from the Porfirian era and abandoned the democratic reforms demanded in 1910.

Enrique C. Ochoa described the rise and fall of Mexico's postrevolutionary welfare system in the prize-winning book, Feeding Mexico: The Political Uses of Food Since 1910 *(2000). His current research examines the historical development of the Mexican economics profession. An associate professor of history at California State University, Los Angeles, he is a member of the editorial collective of* Latin American Perspectives.

*O*n horseback and armed with a notepad and a revolutionary commitment to social change, Licenciado Moisés T. de la Peña traveled throughout the Mexican countryside during the 1930s and 1940s and documented rural economic and living conditions. De la Peña's research forays took him to regions where few Mexico City–based scholars or government officials had gone and to places where the residents often had only a vague awareness of the government in Mexico City. Employing the tools of modern economics and ethnography, and with the assistance of a team of researchers, he provided the first major systematic studies of the geography, economy, and social conditions of several remote states. Influenced by President Lázaro Cárdenas's (1934–1940) efforts to use state power to transform rural Mexico, de la Peña offered his research to policy makers to address poverty and underdevelopment, becoming one of the most prominent, if not most influential, economists of the day.

Through his travels, research, and writing, de la Peña joined the ranks of urban-educated intellectuals who left their classrooms and libraries and entered the vast Mexican countryside to aid in state-building efforts following the revolution of 1910. Mexico at the time of the revolution was hardly an integrated nation-state. Historian Alan Knight has characterized it as "less a nation than a geographical expression, a mosaic of regions and communities, introverted and jealous, ethnically and physically fragmented."[1] An army of political and cultural workers attempted to unify Mexico by constructing a cohesive and culturally homogeneous nation-state that would bring social justice to all Mexicans.

The work of Lic. Moisés de la Peña provides insights into the role of economists in attempting to modernize rural Mexico, integrate various regions into the national market, and improve the lives of all Mexicans. De la Peña's writings addressed a wide array of topics, including rural Mexico, agricultural production, indigenous Mexicans, poverty, the transportation sector, and industry. He wrote profusely about Mexican economic development and underdevelopment and demonstrated a genuine concern for workers' wages and social conditions. Lic. de la Peña's formation as a socially conscious economist during the 1930s and his passionate belief in the role of active state intervention to create a unified and socially just nation made him a maverick as economic policy shifted by the 1940s and 1950s and calls for social justice became mere rhetoric. The professional life of Lic. de la Peña exemplifies some of the contradictions that emerged when revolutionary zeal collided with bureaucratization as social and economic reform was placed on the back burner by the late 1940s.

THE MAKING OF A SOCIAL ECONOMIST

The revolution that erupted in 1910 transformed Mexico and the way its inhabitants viewed their nation. Tens of thousands of campesinos took up arms to demand "Land and Liberty." Popular rebellion challenged years of unequal economic growth during the presidency of Porfirio Díaz (1876–1911) and denounced years of elite usurpation of community lands, exploitation of workers, and the growing influence of U.S. and European capitalists. While calls for social justice were ubiquitous, they varied regionally. The local and national bourgeoisie attempted to hold the revolution at bay by incorporating many popular demands into the Constitution of 1917. As the leaders of the revolution consolidated their power and silenced campesino leaders, Mexicans engaged in a profound national awakening that sought to construct a unified Mexican identity.

It was in this revolutionary era that Moisés de la Peña emerged as an economist with a deep commitment to the social transformation of Mexico. Born in the small northern town of Iturbide, Nuevo León, in 1899, he lived the first thirty years of his life in the states of Nuevo León and Coahuila. The son of latifundistas, de la Peña worked on the family lands and acquired hands-on experience farming, interacting with campesinos, and marketing crops. Growing up in northern Mexico, a region historically isolated from the rest of the nation, he witnessed how the construction of the railroad only partially broke the region's isolation. He was keenly aware, however, that the railroad did not necessarily lead to the expansion of Mexico's internal market and instead benefited a few elite hacendados and foreign investors. The outbreak of revolutionary fighting in 1910 and its continuation throughout much of the decade led to a greater integration of the North with the rest of the country, yet it also brought with it enormous destruction. Coming of age during this era of profound transformation, de la Peña was shaped by the rapid development of national integration and the potential that new technology had for benefiting all Mexicans. By the late 1920s he completed his education at the Ateneo Fuente de Saltillo in Coahuila and moved to Mexico City to continue his study of rural Mexico at the National Autonomous University (UNAM).

The Mexico City that Moisés de la Peña arrived in, circa 1930, was socially and intellectually vibrant. This was a period of state-building, when intellectuals and politicians devised plans for consolidating the central government and creating a hegemonic regime in order to transform Mexico into a modern nation. Since the 1920s a socially conscious social science had emerged that demonstrated a sincere concern for improving the welfare of the poor and sought to understand the structural factors of poverty and backwardness. Its adherents differed from Porfirian-educated intellectuals who were more influenced by social Darwinian notions of human development that excluded the majority of Mexico's poor from the immediate benefits of progress. For the revolutionary social scientists, knowledge and technology were to serve the interests of all Mexicans.

One crucial change that took place just as Moisés de la Peña arrived was the administrative reform of UNAM in 1929, granting it autonomy and helping it to become a first-rate university system that addressed the needs of Mexican society. Several UNAM professors developed the curriculum for an economics program that was initiated within the Law School in 1929. Because it attracted few students at first, Moisés de la Peña and others who entered the program received a significant amount of attention from the young and dynamic professors in the program. Already by 1935 such outstanding scholars as Jesús Silva Herzog, Daniel Cosío Villegas, and Gilberto Loyo had built the program into the prestigious National School of Economics.

Most of the early professors at the new National School of Economics were disillusioned with the policies of previous administrations and argued for the active use of state intervention to address the nation's ills. These scholars, many influenced by Marxism and the remarkable industrial progress achieved by the Soviet Union, believed that the science of economics could be used to help transform Mexico into a modern society for the benefit of all. Sociologist Sarah Babb has demonstrated that for social economists, few alternative models existed. In her content analysis of the theses produced by graduates of the National School of Economics, she found that the first citation of the influential British economist John Maynard Keynes did not appear until 1939 and there were only three citations of him between 1939 and 1945. The first Spanish translation of Keynes's work did not appear in Mexico until 1942. Frequently cited economists included Ernst Wagemann, a European who advocated a greater role of the state in the economy. Marxism and the writings of many European economists demonstrated the weakness of unregulated capitalism and signaled the need for state intervention both to regulate production and to help subsidize consumption.

The expansion of state intervention in the economy created a demand for workers trained in economics at UNAM. Beginning in the second half of the 1920s, the federal government allocated funds for public works programs and established a central bank and an agricultural credit bank to stimulate economic development. These institutions and others collected data on wages, prices, and other economic indicators, and by the early 1930s began to create planning departments. Since the majority of the UNAM professors also held government positions, they were well placed to provide employment for their students. Having just begun his studies, de la Peña landed a job as an economist in the Office of Economic Studies of the National Railways of Mexico in 1930. Although this research office was short-lived, it conducted pioneering economic studies and served as a model for the establishment of other such agencies. Jesús Silva Herzog, who had just returned from a position as ambassador to the Soviet Union, directed the agency and it was staffed by a number of economists who shaped the profession in Mexico.

The development of socially conscious economics coincided with the presidency of Lázaro Cárdenas. In his November 1934 inaugural address, he argued that "it is fundamental to see the economic problem in its entirety and to observe the connections that link each of its parts with the whole. Only the State has the general interest, and, because of this, only it has the unified vision. State intervention must be greater, more frequent, and deeper."[2] Consequently, Cárdenas enacted policies that sought national development and social reform. These policies included the nationalization of the railroads and the petroleum industry, agrarian reforms encompassing the distribution of approximately 18.8 million hectares of land to more than 800,000 Mexicans, and sweeping labor legislation that invigorated trade unions. During his presidency, Cárdenas traveled throughout the country, meeting with campesinos, workers, and businessmen while articulating a holistic, state-led vision of national development that sought to include all Mexicans.

It is in this context of state planning for national unity and social justice that economists came to play an important role in "mapping" the social and economic landscape. As a student at Mexico's National Economics School, Moisés de la Peña supported his family by working in various government ministries. His work in government agencies, coupled with his university study and his personal experiences farming his family's land, shaped the course of his research. He completed his thesis, "The National Agricultural Problem," in 1936, making him the school's fourth graduate. Published by the Secretary of Agriculture's Institute for Rural Economy, where he had been employed, de la Peña's thesis argued that it was essential that agricultural problems be addressed head-on since the Mexican economy was primarily agricultural and the majority of rural Mexicans lived in poverty. His thesis, replete with statistical tables and maps, was one of the first comprehensive portraits of Mexican agriculture, land tenure, production, and labor conditions. It is here that he first demonstrated the importance of economic study as a prerequisite to creating and implementing policies that would lead to a strong, integrated Mexican economy. In addition to his analysis of agricultural problems, he also exposed the social and economic plight of Mexico's campesinado. This solidarity was expressed in the dedication of his thesis, to "the men of the countryside who struggle defenselessly under difficult conditions to produce a crust of bread that they must share with their exploiters."[3]

Upon graduation, de la Peña was appointed professor of economics at the National School of Economics and he was often in and out of government service in the 1930s. However, unlike many of his contemporaries who became bureaucrats, he dedicated himself to the research and intellectual part of the profession even when in government service. In 1938 he worked for the Banco Nacional de Crédito Agrícola's newly created Department of Economic Studies. During his tenure there, he wrote several articles about agricultural credit policy and conducted an in-depth study of the obstacles to providing credit for cattle raising. He was an active member of the National Union of Economists, where he served as a member of the board of directors for much of the second half of the 1930s, as secretary general from 1937 to 1939, and as a founding editor of the organization's journal, *Revista de Economía*. In addition to his research on the countryside, he carried out several studies on the nation's transportation sector and industry. In these studies, he supported a government policy that led to integrated national development and increased economic efficiency. These productivity gains, he argued, would then be passed on to workers. He paid significant attention to workers' wages, often untangling the complex wage schemes in different industries. As he argued for greater rationalization of particular industries, he was critical of corrupt union leaders who worked for the interests of business. Instead, he hoped to see a fair relationship between workers and employers that would lead to greater efficiency and increase the development of a class-conscious proletariat.

THE DECLINE OF SOCIAL ECONOMICS AND DE LA PEÑA'S RETREAT TO REGIONAL MEXICO, 1940S AND 1950S

By the late 1930s and early 1940s the Mexican government began to reorient its national priorities. As the social reform and national development strategy of the first half of the Cárdenas presidency was replaced by "trickle-down" industrialization with greater emphasis given to exports, the dynamism of public agencies and their reformist nature waned. During the 1940s, Mexico actively sought closer economic ties with the United States. Historian Stephen Niblo has shown how Mexico adopted the system of national accounting that was advocated by the United States such that "the country dropped concern with economic justice in favor of advocating policies to increase production."[4] As measurements used by social economics, such as land concentration and percent of foreign ownership, were eliminated, critical economists found themselves further marginalized and were often forced to accept the measurements and categories that emphasized production vis-à-vis consumption and distribution.

This political shift in the 1940s had a profound effect on the economics profession in Mexico. In 1941 the National Economics School redesigned its curriculum to deemphasize Marxist analysis and increased the technical aspects of the curriculum. Additional revisions of the curriculum in 1946 and 1951 effectively marginalized social economics. This growing emphasis on technical analysis led to improvements in the expertise and respectability that de la Peña felt were lacking before. Nevertheless, these skills were used to increase profits for rich industrialists and not to alleviate poverty, inequality, and exploitation.

For Lic. de la Peña, an important signal of this shift was the rejection of his research plan for an integrated transportation policy to be included in the government's second six-year plan, for 1940 to 1946. A member of the economic team commissioned to develop portions of the economic plan for the Manuel Avila Camacho administration, his carefully elaborated proposal was spurned by party leaders, who felt it was too costly and ambitious. Lic. de la Peña responded to this shift by withdrawing from work within government agencies and focusing his attention on studying the Mexican countryside to find ways of integrating the rural poor so that they, too, could benefit from economic growth.

Between 1941 and 1951, governors commissioned Lic. de la Peña to conduct regional studies of Campeche, Baja California, Zacatecas, Chihuahua, Guerrero, Veracruz, Chiapas, and Oaxaca. These eight states were geographically vast and diverse and had few roads. Many of these governors used the studies to help understand the major problems that their states faced. Others sought to bring remote areas under central control. Cultural critic Carlos Monsiváis has characterized the 1940s as years "of the country's institutional domestication—with governors whose greatest merit was absolute ignorance of the state they headed, and congressmen and senators served as occasional ambassadors from the center to the states."[5] Hence, Lic. de la Peña's studies served as guidebooks to the states and their people to inform policy makers and help them in setting development priorities.

For these studies, de la Peña assembled a research team of economists, geologic engineers, and ethnologists. The researchers traveled on foot and horseback to survey different regions in each state. The studies described each state in significant depth, underscoring the regional variation, climate, terrain, land use, and the agricultural potential of the land. Aside from the physical conditions, the studies analyzed the social terrain by documenting the states' population structures, material conditions, and living standards. The teams documented various labor arrangements and collected wage data, revealing the heterogeneity of Mexican life in ways that few Mexico City policy makers understood.

While a variety of regional studies were conducted by government agencies during the late 1930s and 1940s, few were as comprehensive and well researched as those of Lic. Moisés de la Peña. He believed that fieldwork had to be carried out and that one could not rely merely on official statistics, which he felt were unreliable and did not accurately demonstrate the nature of Mexican life. He explained that there was a great "need for Mexico to know itself: to discover how it is, to identify and underscore its problems, and to study them based on what was actually occurring in order to become familiar with what is and with what can be done, so that it will be possible to adopt measures that can help overcome the obstacles that retard national development in both the social and economic realm."[6]

The major premise underlying these studies was to integrate heterogeneous and often impoverished regions into the folds of the nation-state. These studies illustrated that each region, even within states, had its own unique problems and history that had to be taken into consideration by policy makers. This demanded that in-depth studies be conducted as a prerequisite to policy implementation. De la Peña argued that "it is an error to pretend to resolve economic problems with only one formula applied to the entire country. . . . The educational problems of Sonora can not be appropriately and advantageously solved with the same systems and procedures as those implemented in Veracruz or in Oaxaca."[7]

In each of the regional studies, Lic. de la Peña made several policy recommendations intended to help improve the state's economic development and the living conditions of Mexico's rural poor. These recommendations included increased government investment to improve communications and transportation as well as to develop irrigation works and to expand the nation's electrical capacity. In addition, there were several suggestions to increase the standard of living for the rural poor. These often included encouraging government banks to use credit in ways that would improve technology so that campesinos could increase productivity, and urging state and federal officials to encourage rural population to raise cattle and other animals to supplement their income. His suggestions were specific, demanded serious reprioritization of state and federal resources, and were designed to use federal policy to radically transform the Mexican economy by integrating all areas into the national market.

For Moisés de la Peña, Mexico's economic problems were fairly clear: Mexico was a regionally diverse and complex society that needed to operate as a unified capitalist country. This meant that radical integration of the regions had to occur. This had to take place first by thorough study and then through massive government intervention. It was only through a carefully laid out plan that a coherent economic development policy could be implemented that would help alleviate Mexican poverty. In addition to detailed analysis of the regions, he often wrote articles and studies on specific themes, such as the need for an integrated and rational transportation and freight rate policy and the need to integrate the indigenous population into the nation. For him, these questions were intimately linked and addressing them would help transform Mexico from a semicolonial economy into a modern capitalist nation, which might then set the stage for greater social and political justice.

A number of actions could be taken by politicians to integrate the nation's diverse regions. Lic. de la Peña advocated for the creation of a transportation policy that would mesh rail policy with road construction to facilitate the flow of goods and peoples throughout the country. The construction of rural roads was another major issue that de la Peña had long championed. Since the 1930s he had argued that new highway building programs were misguided and poorly planned. According to de la Peña, many of these lines paralleled existing railway lines, which were themselves planned to meet the needs of the foreign railroad companies who built them during the Porfiriato. Given the fact that much of the country was without roads, such transportation duplication was unjustified. He also sharply criticized freight rate policy on the railroads for explicitly favoring exports over internal trade. He was among the first economists to analyze freight rates systematically, demonstrating that powerful mining companies received low rates for transporting minerals while the rates for shipping corn and beans remained comparatively higher. He felt that setting uniform rates would help the development of a more uniform market price, which could then lead toward competition by region and a growing degree of regional specialization.

De la Peña also argued that agricultural credit and pricing policies could be utilized to foster an integrated national market. However, he was openly critical about how these policies had gone awry. In a November 1943 article, "The Failure of Agricultural Credit in Mexico," de la Peña argued that Mexico's agricultural credit policy, through its two main banks, lost considerable amounts of money and had not had much success in aiding poor farmers and campesinos. The problem did not lie with the farmers, he demonstrated, but resulted instead from administrative ineptitude, growing bureaucratization and centralization, and the manipulation of credit policy by politicians.

For Lic. de la Peña, a crucial element in creating a modern economy would be a concentrated effort to include indigenous populations in the nation-state. This subject pervades each of his regional studies and even when he wrote about states without large indigenous populations, such as Chihuahua, he spent significant amounts of space explaining their material conditions and exploring solutions to their poverty.

The "Indian question" was of widespread intellectual concern during this period. Since national identity was fundamental to the revolutionary project, elites could no longer ignore Mexico's numerous indigenous communities. Postrevolutionary governments financed archeological projects to "recover" the greatness of Aztec civilizations and developed a national identity based on Mexican *mestizaje*. More problematic to Mexican elites, however, was the fate of Mexico's present-day indigenous people, who amounted to at least 15 percent of the total population. Native Americans were looked down on as relics of a bygone era, who needed to be assimilated into the national culture. Spurred by the studies of anthropologist Manuel Gamio and educator José Vasconcelos, anthropologists began to study indigenous communities, arguing that through assimilation, indigenous Mexicans would be able to escape their historic colonization and exploitation. While many anthropologists initially exalted indigenous life and even romanticized their isolation, by the 1940s many were allied with the state in attempting to culturally transform Mexico into a mestizo nation.

Drawing on his numerous regional studies, Lic. de la Peña directly weighed in on the "Indian problem." In his 1945 pamphlet entitled *The*

Mexicanization of the Indian: An Economic Problem, he dismissed the idea that Indians were biologically and culturally distinct and instead argued that indigenous people were remnants of a precapitalist society representative of Mexico's semifeudal economy. He linked indigenous poverty to the relative isolation of many communities. Indigenous communities were excluded from the nation and, therefore, "each person produces for his personal consumption, without buying or selling, division of labor and production efficiencies are ignored, and therefore poverty is generalized and cultural evolution does not occur."[8] To address this situation, he advocated in-depth study of the obstacles to the economic integration he saw as necessary. While he recognized the importance of rural schooling and efforts to culturally assimilate indigenous Mexicans, such approaches were limited because they assumed that acculturation resulted in economic integration. Instead, he argued for an understanding of colonialism and its legacy and its regional variation. He was openly critical of *indigenistas* who called for indigenous populations to be left alone and who celebrated their isolation but did not confront the reality of colonialism and its impact. De la Peña demonstrated that the more geographically isolated indigenous people were, the more likely they were to be exploited by mestizos.

Since he identified the problem as the lack of economic integration, de la Peña argued that attempts to transform this situation must be based on detailed studies of the economy and living conditions in different regions. He calculated the relative isolation of indigenous peoples, demonstrating their lack of participation in the national economy. For Chiapas he showed that "on average, the most backward Indian, who lives a primitive and self-sufficient life, injects into the region's commercial wealth approximately $.01 pesos a day per person, and Indians in more commercial zones contribute $.18 per person, while Mestizos contribute approximately $1.50 pesos per person."[9] Because of the high percentage of indigenous people in the state, he argued that the Mexicanization process was an urgent task for Chiapas.

The social economist was concerned with finding ways to integrate indigenous people into the economy and to improve their standard of living. He criticized programs that encouraged rural people to organize into cooperatives to make and sell crafts. These, he felt, further isolated communities from the national market and kept them involved in the production of crafts that few people wanted and that were not economically viable. He argued that "without any technical study they [policy makers] tried to organize hat cooperatives among the Mixtecas like they did in the Mezquital region with wool and in Chihuahua among woodworking Indians; but such attempts are counter productive because it is absurd to try to make cooperatives out of these poor people when production cooperatives are a failure even in developed regions."[10] Instead, de la Peña suggested that governments needed to make significant investments in the regions to upgrade technology so that indigenous communities could be beneficiaries of modern technology. Aggressive government intervention could solve the problem, but officials did not accord it high priority. Urban-based officials were quick to allocate funds for building theaters and highways as symbols of "progress" while the majority of Mexicans continued to live in misery. He concluded that government officials were not interested in eradicating poverty.

De la Peña's approach to the integration of indigenous populations reflected much of his work as a social economist. Although he was driven by humanitarian impulse, like most policy makers and scholars of the day, he did not contemplate including indigenous populations in the discussion of their living situation. He assumed that implementing modern policies that unified the nation and improved individual opportunities was the most socially just and rational policy. His approach demonstrated that Mexico was indeed a nation of variegated regions that could be unified only after systematic study and massive government reform efforts. The question that began to preoccupy Lic. de la Peña was whether politicians and government officials were actually committed to transforming Mexico.

CLASHING VISIONS: THE REVOLUTIONARY ECONOMIST IN THE AGE OF THE ECONOMIC MIRACLE

Moisés de la Peña's economic analysis reflected the Cardenista developmentalist wing of the revolution. As an intellectual who was committed to connecting fieldwork to policy formation, he pushed the boundaries of social sciences and economic analysis. He attempted to connect his research and use it as the basis of real revolutionary reforms. Yet he was perpetually frustrated in his efforts to contribute to the transformation of Mexican society. Throughout the 1940s and 1950s political and social calls for revolutionary change were muted as the Mexican government sought rapid capitalist expansion.

Lic. de la Peña's dismay and frustration reflected the shifting priorities of Mexico's governing elite during the 1940s. By the late 1930s, there was a shift away from the rural development and social justice programs of the early Cárdenas years to an emphasis on urban modernization. Government policy, while still alluding to the goals of eradicating poverty, reduced funding for many programs and fostered a climate of bureaucratic inertia and corruption that made reform difficult. National leaders extolled the urban and the modern. Hence, the countryside and campesinos again became marginalized by policy makers as large-scale capitalist agriculture was reemphasized. By the 1940s, Mexico's brief experiment with radical social reform was abandoned and the ascension to the presidency of Miguel Alemán marked a swing to the right.

Increasingly, Lic. de la Peña became combative as his pointed and often critical yet well-documented studies went unheeded. A firm believer in the importance of study and state planning, he saw firsthand how government officials were motivated by their own political aggrandizement and implemented policy without significant forethought. In addition, he became increasingly critical of state officials who were more concerned with beautifying cities and increasing services for the urban middle class. He openly characterized these projects as "an insult to the poor!"

When his policy recommendations went ignored, the economist was quick to berate public officials, publicly and with biting words. On more than one occasion, state governors neglected to publish his studies and de la Peña had to scramble to find a publisher. Sections of the reports always found some quick outlet in one of Mexico's economics journals, and the *Revista de Economía* ultimately printed those studies that governors failed to. Nevertheless, de la Peña sharply and publicly criticized governors who delayed publication. For example, in the preface to *Zacatecas económico* (1948), he observed that research for the current volume, as well as another on Chihuahua, had been completed as much as five years earlier, but "both unfortunately, due to circumstances beyond our control, were not published by the governors and instead were saved by the *Revista de Economia. . . .*" De la Peña added, "*Chihuahua económico* was finally in press although three years behind schedule."[11] Apparently such public pressure had some effect, because the governor of Chihuahua took back control of the volume and issued it later that year with a long preface recounting the accomplishments of his administration. In the preface, an aide to the governor argued that it "is evident that many of the most important works that were recommended are in the planning stage or in progress. More than five years of care and honest use of funds by the government in Chihuahua have yielded significant results that are worthy of consideration."[12] State officials also published an eight-page budgetary plan as proof of the government's commitment to addressing the state's social and economic problems. De la Peña, for his part, publicly lauded officials, such as the governor of Campeche, if they published his study soon after it was completed and if they began to implement some recommendations.

De la Peña interpreted delays in publication and the ignoring of his recommendations as symptomatic of a general disrespect for the economics profession and of the growing bureaucratization of government agencies. In a 1942 essay, "The Economists: The Technicians and the Spontaneous Ones," de la Peña took aim at politicians who consulted lawyers about legal matters but rarely listened to economists on economic matters. He argued that this was a grave error made by politicians, many of whom were generals with little formal training in economics, which would further delay the nation's economic development. Because he believed that economic development was Mexico's most pressing issue, he was particularly disturbed by policy makers' lack of systematic planning and ignorance of economic analysis. He pointed to a number of examples of poor policy implementation that resulted from the lack of detailed economic study. For example, he highlighted cases in which the government, without sufficient knowledge of the market, set price controls for basic food items in which the production cost was higher than the maximum sale price set by the government. De la Peña found that such errors were common and hurt both producers and consumers, thereby delaying Mexico's market development. The government, de la Peña repeatedly argued, could solve many of the nation's economic problems, but he concluded that officials lacked the political will. The isolated and impoverished conditions of the Tarahumara peoples in the mountains of Chihuahua could be improved if the government wanted to do so, but "the government of Chihuahua has crossed its arms and decided to do nothing. If we look at the millions of pesos it spends on beautifying the cities of Chihuahua, Juárez, and Parral, the most costly venture that state has embarked on, they do not spend any money worth mentioning on the Tarahumara problem."[13]

By the 1950s the "economist on horseback" became increasingly marginalized. As politicians poured resources into urban infrastructure and encouraged large-scale industrialization, the countryside once again fell into neglect. Economic growth would characterize much of the 1940s to the 1970s; however, it would lead to the exacerbation of inequality. The utopian character of the Cárdenas years and the idealism that it spawned had been tamed and reshaped so that the army of professionals had become government bureaucrats. In this transformation, Lic. de la Peña remained a defiant researcher who believed that social justice was possible and that Mexico, like other revolutionary societies, had to engage in self-criticism to put the nation back on the path to economic development for all. It would not be until the late 1960s and the 1970s that academic economists again turned a critical eye toward the unequal economic policies that the Mexican elite mapped out in the name of revolution.

NOTES

1. Alan Knight, *The Mexican Revolution*, 2 vols. (Cambridge: Cambridge University Press, 1986), 1:2.

2. Cited in Enrique C. Ochoa, *Feeding Mexico: The Political Uses of Food Since 1910* (Wilmington, DE: Scholarly Resources, 2000), 41.

3. Moisés T. de la Peña, *El problema agrícola nacional* (México, 1936), 1.

4. Stephen R. Niblo, *War, Diplomacy, and Development: The United States and Mexico, 1938–1954* (Wilmington, DE: Scholarly Resources, 1995), 17.

5. Carlos Monsiváis, " 'Just Over That Hill': Notes on Centralism and Regional Cultures," in *Mexico's Regions: Comparative History and Development*, ed. Eric Van Young (La Jolla: Center for U.S.-Mexican Studies, UCSD, 1992), 247–54.

6. Moisés T. de la Peña, *Zacatecas económico* (México, 1948), 8.

7. From "Campeche económico," as cited in "Notas Bibliográficas" in *Revista de Economía* (Febrero 20 de 1942), 38.

8. Moisés T. de la Peña, *La mexicanización del indio: Un problema económico* (México: *Revista de Economía*, 1945), 5–6.

9. Moisés T. de la Peña, *Chiapas económico*, 4:1255.

10. De la Peña, *La mexicanización del indio*, 26–27.

11. De la Peña, *Zacatecas económico*, 9.

12. Moisés T. de la Peña, *Chihuahua económico* (México, 1948), prologue.

13. Moisés T. de la Peña, "Ensayo económico y social sobre el pueblo Tarahumara," *Investigación Económico* 4, no. 4 (1944): 398.

SUGGESTED READINGS

Babb, Sarah L. *Managing Mexico: Economists from Nationalism to Neoliberalism.* Princeton, NJ: Princeton University Press, 2001.

Bantjes, Adrian. *As if Jesus Walked on Earth: Cardenismo, Sonora, and the Mexican Revolution.* Wilmington, DE: Scholarly Resources, 1998.

Bonfil Batalla, Guillermo. *México Profundo: Reclaiming a Civilization.* Trans. Philip A. Dennis. Austin: University of Texas Press, 1996.

Gledhill, John. *Casi Nada: A Study of Agrarian Reform in the Homeland of Cardenismo.* Albany: State University of New York, 1991.

Hamilton, Nora. *The Limits of State Autonomy: Post-Revolutionary Mexico.* Princeton, NJ: Princeton University Press, 1982.

Niblo, Stephen R. *War, Diplomacy, and Development: The United States and Mexico, 1938–1954.* Wilmington, DE: Scholarly Resources, 1995.

Ochoa, Enrique C. *Feeding Mexico: The Political Uses of Food Since 1910.* Wilmington, DE: Scholarly Resources, 2000.

Vaughan, Mary Kay. *Cultural Politics in Revolution: Teachers, Peasants, and Schools in Mexico, 1930–1940.* Tucson: University of Arizona Press, 1997.

PART IV

MEXICANS IN THE GLOBAL VILLAGE, 1940 TO THE PRESENT

Mexico's entry into World War II, after the sinking of two oil tankers by German U-boats in 1942, ushered in a new era of globalization that continued to gain momentum for the remainder of the century. Although Mexican pilots of the 201st Squadron served in combat in the Pacific, the country made its primary contribution to the Allied cause through economic means, particularly by coordinating industrial and agricultural production with the United States, a step on the path to the North American Free Trade Agreement (NAFTA). Moreover, the bracero program sent Mexican workers to the United States to fill in for men who had volunteered for service and thereby established patterns of migration that continued informally after the program ended in 1964. Finally, the mobilization for hemispheric defense allowed civilian politicians to replace revolutionary veterans, helping to ensure that Mexico never suffered the fate of the military dictatorships that plagued many other Latin American countries.

The economic boom of the wartime years continued through the 1960s, giving Mexico the appearance of an economic "miracle." Motivated by high protective tariffs, both Mexican and multinational corporations invested heavily in industry, while agricultural improvements of the Green Revolution allowed the country to achieve self-sufficiency in basic grains at least temporarily despite a rapidly growing population. The ruling party also sought to build social consensus around the idea of an "institutional revolution" that represented all sectors of society, including labor unions and agrarian leagues formed during the 1920s, as well as the rapidly growing urban middle class. The mass media also contributed to this sense of unity by creating national audiences for celebrities such as Agustín Lara and María Félix (Chapter 12). Large-scale migration, tourism, and economic integration also helped to promote this national identity by allowing middle-class Mexicans to experience the diverse regional cultures, for example, by sampling their cooking specialties (Chapter 13).

Yet for many poor people in the countryside, as well as for urban workers, the benefits of this supposed miracle were illusory. Corrupt union officials cooperated with business owners to hold down wages despite the rapidly rising cost of living, and workers who followed an independent course to demand better pay, such as the railroad strikers of 1959, were brutally repressed. At the same time, the process of agrarian reform came to a virtual standstill although farming families needed more land to keep up with population growth. Unable to earn a living in the countryside, millions of people migrated to the cities, depressing factory wages still further.

The crisis of 1968 destroyed faith in the Mexican miracle just as it seemed to be at the point of fruition. The scheduling of the Olympic Games in Mexico, the first time they had been held in a developing country, focused international attention on the country's progress. As a result, when student protests against police brutality that summer began to cast doubts on the benevolent rule of the official party, the government responded with draconian measures. On October 2, the army massacred hundreds of peaceful demonstrators in the Plaza of Tlatelolco, and thousands more were hospitalized and imprisoned. Authoritarian measures had been used before against workers and peasants, but as middle-class families lost their children, any lingering doubts about the benefits of the single-party state vanished. The international student movement, which had already been embraced by many young Mexicans as an alternative to the stifling official culture of the PRI, had a brief renaissance a few years later at Avándaro, an open-air rock concert modeled on Woodstock, but after that the counterculture was forced underground in working-class neighborhoods (Chapter 14).

The slaughter at Tlatelolco signaled the beginning of a downward economic spiral that lasted for more than two decades. The "trickle-down" policies followed since the 1940s had not only deprived a generation of workers of adequate incomes but also failed to deliver a solid industrial foundation. The peso began to fall in the early 1970s, then recovered briefly with the discovery of petroleum reserves, before plummeting during the oil glut of the 1980s. The currency bottomed out at a rate of 3,000 to the dollar, while Mexico threatened default on its foreign debt of more than $100 billion. With nearly 40 percent of the population malnourished as a result of the economic crisis, opposition parties made rapid progress against the PRI. The conservative National Action Party (PAN) won local elections throughout the north, and in 1988, Cuauhtémoc Cárdenas, son of the reformist president, is widely believed to have won the presidential election, although the ruling party declared the victory of its own candidate after a weeklong delay in the vote counting.

Although the troubles continued into the 1990s, there were also grounds for optimism in the new millennium. The implementation of NAFTA, on New Years' Day 1994, coincided with the outbreak of the Zapatista rebellion in Chiapas. Meanwhile, Mexican drug lords began wrestling control of the cocaine traffic from Colombian cartels, at a high cost in corruption and violence, particularly along the U.S. border. Nevertheless, Mexico also began gaining international recognition for the quality of its cultural exports, ranging from the hit films *Amores Perros* (2000) and *Y tu mamá también* (2001) to top-shelf tequilas (Chapter 15). Moreover, decades of work by opposition parties were finally rewarded in 2000, when the PRI acknowledged the presidential election of PAN candidate Vicente Fox. Although the populist leader's program soon bogged down in the legislature, his victory opened a new political era for Mexico.

CHAPTER TWELVE

María Félix and Agustín Lara

A Public Romance

Andrew G. Wood

However convenient the metro may be, users soon learn to be wary of station names. The former Puerto Aéreo station, on the pink line, now bears the added abbreviation "Blvr." Pto. Aéreo, because so many tourists found themselves stranded in the middle of a busy highway rather than at the airport, which is actually accessible at Terminal Aérea, on the yellow line. Similarly, the green-line stop Coyoacán leads not to the plush southern suburb but rather to a shopping mall. Thanks to its seclusion, the former pre-Hispanic town of the Coyotes retains much of the atmosphere of the 1940s, when it was an artists' colony and the center of the burgeoning Mexican film industry.

*In contrast to the quaint charm of Coyoacán, mass media such as radio and movies have become both big business and important channels for projecting images of modernity and national identity. In Mexico as elsewhere, these cultural industries developed from existing forms of popular entertainment such as street theater (*carpas*) and folk songs (*corridos*). The subject matter for these local traditions included both a nostalgic view of the rural past and a concern for the modern problems of urban life. The transition from a rural to a predominantly urban society at mid-century ran parallel with the career trajectory of two prominent celebrities, María Félix and Agustín Lara.*

The beautiful actress Félix sometimes appeared onscreen dressed as a china poblana, *a woman of the people wearing folkloric national costume. Other roles, whether teacher, belly dancer, cabaret singer, brothel madam, or Roman empress, nearly always projected her pioneering status as a modern Mexican through characterizations that set her as a fiercely independent woman in competition with members of the opposite sex. For his part, the popular musician Lara generally turned his back on the rural past and cultivated a cosmopolitan image through compositions (many of them boleros) that dramatized the shadowy world of Mexico City nightlife. Singing about the often tragic tales of blind men, thieves, and that quintessential victim of urbanization, the fallen woman, Lara's melodramatic chronicling of broken hearts stood in contrast to more traditional musical subjects. Thus, for a short time, the celebrated relationship of these two pioneers symbolically bound together two powerful agents of modernity in Mexican society, just as the national government—in conjunction with the highly regulated mass media—endeavored to unify the nation and establish Mexico as an industrial power in the hemisphere.*

Mexican cinema generally sought to provide models for proper behavior, but the public images of both Félix and Lara offered an alternative take on traditional gender roles. Film roles tended to compress women into two opposing archetypes, the saint and the whore, yet as historian Julia Tuñón has shown, actresses often escaped the simplistic dualism implied by this formula. María Félix, in particular, created a singular persona as a woman who defined her own fate. Although often doomed in the melodramas common to Mexican cinema, her characters gave women an attractive alternative to more traditional feminine roles. Agustín Lara, meanwhile, challenged the standard macho image of Mexican masculinity by articulating a bohemian, deeply romantic personality. Because of the controversial public image cultivated by each of these popular figures, their courtship and short-lived marriage in the mid-1940s attracted the attention of paparazzi and film studio executives as well as much of Mexican society.

This essay briefly describes the careers of Lara and Félix leading up to their public romance, which began with an initial courtship in early 1943, saw the two marry in December 1945, and then divorce less than two years later. The author briefly chronicles the careers of both Félix and Lara while inviting readers to consider how the cultivation of their celebrity status helped to promote both the entertainment industry and, by extension, Mexico's transition to modernity during the mid-twentieth century.

Andrew G. Wood earned his doctorate at the University of California, Davis, and is now assistant professor of history at the University of Tulsa. His first book, Revolution in the Street: Women, Workers, and Urban Protest in Veracruz, 1870–1927 *(2001), won the Michael C. Meyer prize and the Thomas F. McGann award. Continuing his work on urban popular culture, he is completing a biography of Agustín Lara while also conducting research on the celebration of Carnival in Mexico.*

*W*ith the development of film and radio during the early twentieth century, several Mexican entertainers established international reputations in a variety of artistic endeavors. Among the most popular was composer of romantic song Agustín Lara, who toured extensively throughout the Americas and Europe. When Lara began a relationship with the attractive young film star María Félix (known as "the most beautiful woman in Mexico") during the early 1940s, the celebrity couple attracted a tremendous amount of public interest. Hounded by paparazzi, speculated about in gossip columns, and toasted at countless bars and banquets, their high-profile combination of personal style and star power effectively promoted not only their own individual careers but also the entertainment industry. In some immeasurable yet important way, through an alluring celebrity discourse that they themselves helped pioneer, the two played a significant role in facilitating Mexico's postrevolutionary transition to a modern, urban-based society.

Before Lara died in late 1970 he had penned hundreds of songs, participated in the making of several movies, performed countless shows, and become renowned internationally as Mexico's "musician-poet." Resplendent when seated at his piano and never far from a pack of El Buen Tono #13 cigarettes and a snifter of brandy, Lara's earliest public reputation was that of a dandy during the Jazz Age of the 1920s. Ever the romantic to his admirers who saw past his exceedingly thin, less than handsome appearance (he was nicknamed *el flaco de oro*, "Gilded slim"), he effectively played the role of the cosmopolitan, bohemian, quintessentially Spanish gentleman both on stage and off. Adopting the tropical state of Veracruz as his "native" home, Lara continually reinvented himself, becoming a legendary ladies' man and eventually attaining the status of a national icon ("as Mexican as epazote or tequila"). A groundbreaking figure at a critical time in Mexican history, Lara was described by Carlos Monsiváis as one who "constitutes an approximate summing-up of what happens when an isolated culture breaks out into the world."

Equally magnificent in Mexico's cultural pantheon was Félix who, before her death at the age of eighty-seven in the spring of 2002, had acted in forty-seven films (made not only in Mexico but in Spain, Italy, France, and Argentina) while forever establishing herself (along with Dolores del Río) as the "Supreme Goddess" of Spanish-language cinema. Equally conscious of the importance of public image was Félix, who quickly distinguished herself from other female stars by capitalizing on media characterizations of her as an irresistibly attractive, fiercely independent woman. In the words of Mexico's great poet Octavio Paz, "María Félix [was] a woman—such a woman—with the audacity to defy the ideas machos have constructed of what a woman should be. She's free like the wind, she disperses the clouds, or illuminates them with the lightning flash of her gaze." Powerfully, Lara and Félix pioneered the construction of celebrity identity in Mexico. With the help of a national entertainment industry infrastructure made up of publicists, photographers, and promoters, their brief union during the mid-1940s invited Mexicans (and countless others throughout the Spanish-speaking world) to identify with the "modern love" the couple engendered and thus, in some small way, vicariously live the glamorous life through them.

BEGINNING WITH THE BORDELLO

By the time Agustín Lara began courting María Félix in the spring of 1943 his reputation as a sentimental crooner was well established throughout the Spanish-speaking world. Similar to other popular American musicians with humble beginnings (such as jazzman Louis Armstrong and tango singer Carlos Gardel), Lara's road to superstardom had required equal parts creativity, resourcefulness, and persistence. During his formative years the young musician gradually moved from playing in downtown bordellos, dance academies, and cafés before emerging as a regular performer in more reputable nightclubs and theaters. All the while, Lara carefully crafted a growing repertoire of popular songs and a corresponding public image as a modern romantic.

Born in Tlatlauquitepec, Puebla, in October 1897 and brought to Mexico City as an infant, Lara came of age during a tumultuous era. After receiving some musical training during his early years, at the age of twelve Agustín made his way to the rough La Lagunilla district of the capital on the eve of the Revolution. Determined to establish his independence in whatever capacity he could, Lara found work as the house musician in a bordello, where he played what he could for the mix of politicians, entrepreneurs, artists, intellectuals, and military men who frequented the establishment. Witness to all kinds of personal intrigues, the young artist provided regular entertainment until the outbreak of civil war in the capital during early February 1913 (the Ten Tragic Days) temporarily closed down the business. Shortly thereafter, his father shipped him off to military school.

By the time he was nineteen, Lara had again returned to the Mexico City entertainment scene, where he played piano in various evening establishments including a bordello located at 61 Libertad in the Santa María la Redonda neighborhood. One fateful night, according to legend, Lara somehow crossed one of the prostitutes, who slashed his face with a broken bottle and scarred him for life. Dejected, he traveled to the city of Puebla and ended up working under dubious circumstances for two years in an assortment of seedy bars.

Once he had returned to the capital, Lara took a job in a dance academy on Tacuba Street where he played for sometimes eight or nine hours per session. Then, after he worked briefly in the Agua Azul cabaret, a tip from an old friend introduced him to the Bruschetta family, who owned a little spot called the Café Salambó located only a few blocks west of the Zócalo. At the Salambó he enjoyed a good-sounding piano and the Italian family's warm hospitality. Before long, Agustín began what would be a ten-year relationship with the attractive Angelina Bruschetta.

During this formative period in the late 1920s, the ambitious young artist used his abilities to interpret waltzes, fox-trots, tangos, Cuban *danzones*, blues, jazz, and other popular song forms. Soon, he was writing his own compositions. About the same time, Lara teamed up with singer Juan Arvizu and the two began making the rounds of the many new theaters, cabarets, and nightclubs that comprised Mexico City's growing entertainment district. Also meeting future sidekick and lyricist Rodolfo "El Chamaco" Sandoval as well as impresario Raúl G. Rodríguez ("Raulito"), the young musician used his considerable talent and personal charm (some compare him at this time to the film star Rudolph Valentino) to create critical career opportunities. In fact, shortly after befriending Raulito, the two arranged to have Lara's composition "Imposible" recorded in New York.

In late 1928, Arvizu introduced Agustín to a Mexico City chanteuse named Maruca Pérez. Almost immediately, she took a liking to Lara's music and asked him to perform with her. After playing a few clubs in the capital, the duo then teamed up with singer Ana María Fernández and traveled to the eastern cities of Jalapa and Veracruz. After several successful shows in the provinces, Lara was back in the capital. By early 1930 he was working at two of the city's most popular theaters—the Lírico and the Principal.

Along with an assortment of singers and dancers, Agustín performed many of his own compositions in a musical review at the Lírico titled "Cachitos de México." With the show enjoying a run of over a hundred performances, the emerging artist gained valuable experience, exposure, and legitimacy. Soon a promoter named Dagoberto Campos contracted him to perform at the Iris Theater. There, Lara worked with a number of popular Mexico City singers including Sofía Alvarez, Lucha Guzmán "Tabu," Beatriz Ramos, Margarita "la Mayata" Carbajal, and eventually, one of his best-known interpreters, the incomparable singer María Antonia del Carmen Peregrino de Cházaro (also known as Toña la Negra) from the port of Veracruz.

Riding high on his growing artistic and commercial success, Agustín Lara penned several songs during this period, including one of his most famous boleros, "Aventurera," which glorified prostitution with the lyrics, "Sell your love expensively, Adventuress." Performing in the Politeama Theater and soon on Mexico City's powerful XEW radio station ("The Voice of Latin America from Mexico," established in September 1930) each week, the popular composer could be heard throughout Greater Mexico (including portions of Central America and the U.S. Southwest) and as far away as Havana, Cuba. From New York to Buenos Aires, nearly everyone in the Spanish-speaking world sang his songs while journalists wrote about him in glowing terms and almost always included Agustín in illustrated magazine features on various "radio stars." Soon, Lara began writing music for Mexico's growing film industry as well.

One of the first sound films produced in the country, *Santa* (1931), featured both a *danzón* and a fox-trot written by the popular composer. Adapted from a turn-of-the-century novel by Federico Gamboa, the screenplay depicted a young woman who was seduced and forced into a life of prostitution. Like the many "fallen" women who would follow her in what would become by the 1940s an entire cinematic genre dubbed *cabareteras*, *Santa* offered a highly melodramatic yet nonetheless important commentary on the plight of Mexico's urban middle and working class. Essentially a cautionary tale for the thousands who made their way to the "big city," the film made visible the social anxiety engendered in Mexico's unique transformation into a modern, industrial nation during the early twentieth century. As he passionately identified with *Santa* in his lyrics, the composer's earliest film collaboration successfully contributed to his growing public image as one of Mexico's most promising young stars.

Yet during these formative years Lara established a reputation as a different kind of leading Mexican man. With a deep facial scar further compromising an already less than ordinary appearance, it was not only his bohemian lifestyle (complete with cigarettes, brandy, and rumored marijuana and cocaine use "for inspiration") but also his self-proclaimed obsession with romance that appealed to audiences. Thought to be the main protagonist in many of his songs, Agustín often sang of his longing for a female muse—whether she be his own mother or aunt, a movie star, a cabaret dancer, or a misunderstood prostitute with a heart of gold. Central to his image as a romantic gentleman was the fact that his fans saw Lara as a visionary who could appreciate the inner beauty present in ordinary people. Observers suggest that, having constructed an alternative masculine identity, Agustín was generally not seen as a rival but more as a brother or uncle figure by other Mexican men. Thus, given the special role he created for himself, Lara provided an escape from the drudgery of everyday life for thousands across Mexico by articulating an alternative fantasy world of love and passion.

Throughout the 1940s many waxed poetic about the musician-poet and claimed him as a national treasure. In an issue of a popular illustrated magazine at the time, one commentator wrote that the artist had forged a new musical style that combined "the heat of the tropics and the sentimentality of love." The same interviewer also described how he was surprised to learn that "Lara does not have theories or systems for inspiration." Instead, the musician-poet simply waited patiently to be visited by his Muse. Thus, while Mexico's celebrated popular composer busied himself during the 1930s by producing what seemed like one hit song after another, it was on a fateful day in the spring of 1943 that he met his match in film star María Félix. An ensuing relationship with the young beauty generated the same level of frenzied attention throughout the Spanish-speaking world that the famed union between Marilyn Monroe and Joe DiMaggio later produced in the United States.

FROM SONORA TO SUPERSTARDOM

María de los Ángeles Félix Güereña was born in the town of Álamos, Sonora, on May 4, 1914. Her father, Bernardo Félix, was a merchant while her mother, Josefina Güereña, came from a deeply Catholic family of Spanish descent. In the early 1920s, María moved with her family to Guadalajara after President Álvaro Obregón offered her father a job there. Blossoming into an attractive young woman, she was introduced to the practice of yoga, learned to dance, and enjoyed reading.

In early 1930, students in Guadalajara chose Félix to be University Carnival Queen. Shortly thereafter, María met Enrique Álvarez at a costume ball. Working as a representative of the Max Factor cosmetic company, Álvarez initiated their courtship with a home demonstration and eventually proposed marriage. Eager to free herself from her parents' supervision, Félix consented and the two teenagers were married in a small ceremony on January 10, 1931. Although unhappy with the relationship nearly from the start, María nonetheless gave birth on April 6, 1934, to a baby boy the couple named Enrique (he died in 1996). A short while later, she separated from Álvarez and returned with her infant son to Álamos, and the two soon moved to Mexico City.

After establishing a modest residence in the capital, Félix happened one day to meet engineer Fernando Palacios, who soon introduced her to members of the Mexican artistic community. At the invitation of the filmmaking Calderón brothers, María traveled to Los Angeles in 1940, where she adorned a Mexican float in a Mexican Independence parade and later was taken to Hollywood. After meeting actors Robert Taylor and Walter Pidgeon, the young Mexican actress lunched with famed director Cecil B. DeMille.

Soon back in Mexico City, Félix found only occasional work during the early 1940s until she landed a part in the 1942 film *El peñón de las ánimas* (The rock of the spirits), directed by Miguel Zacarías and costarring Jorge Negrete, one of the leading men in Mexican cinema, whose macho image defined traditional Mexican masculinity at the time. (In 1952 the actress would marry Negrete, who died two years later.) Although still very much a novice, Félix learned quickly under her director's tutelage while attempting to apply what little she had absorbed in Hollywood to negotiate for her salary, costume, and an assortment of other details. Negrete, who was already well established in the industry and had hoped to costar with the better-known Gloria Marín, missed no opportunity to put the young actress in her place. Through several difficult weeks their clash of wills on the set helped make the film a romantic hit despite the disparaging things critics have had to say about it then and since. Based on that success, María began work on another project the same year titled *María Eugenia*. During the filming, Félix caused quite a stir when she appeared in a white bathing suit for a beach scene and allegedly sketched the word "Amor" (love) in the sand. As photographers maneuvered for a glimpse of the young beauty, María apparently obliged them with the occasional "candid" shot that soon was made available to eager admirers across Mexico. Following this now legendary event, the entertainment press began promoting Félix as a leading lady. Yet despite her alluring appearance and maturing dramatic talent, she would not fully distinguish herself as a creative force until the success of her 1943 film, *Doña Bárbara*, based on the novel by Venezuelan Rómulo Gallegos.

In this film the actress assumed the character of an aggressive, sometimes ruthless woman who presides over an extensive ranch she has essentially stolen from the family of a handsome young doctor named Santos Luzardo (Julián Soler). At the beginning of the film we learn that, as a young girl, Doña Bárbara had been raped by sailors when she was traveling on the Orinoco River. Embittered by this tragedy, she later abandoned a daughter, Marisela (María Elena Marqués), whom she bore with a former lover, as well as nearly all vestiges of traditional womanhood. As the drama unfolds, Doña Bárbara acts out a highly conflicted gender identity that rejects the attention of men so as to preserve her status as a powerful landowner. Appropriating a masculine behavior toward this end, she dons the local frontier-style clothing, smokes cigarettes, and rides her horse like a man would.

As film historian Joanne Hershfield has argued, the film is ultimately about maintaining traditional family values through the articulation of clear, heterosexual gender roles. Watching the narrative of *Doña Bárbara* unfold, the audience quickly realizes the unique "reversal" being played out and is thereby warned about the "dangers" of blurring sexual identity. As we see María Félix portray a "manly" woman eventually in competition with her own daughter (for the attention of Santos Luzardo), the cautionary message is clear. As a predominantly Catholic audience observes this "terrible" woman resorting to witchcraft in the hope of getting what she wants, Doña Bárbara is made out to be an archetypal devouring woman (*la devoradora*) who is surely doomed. In the end, the film does not fail to draw the moral regarding not only the negative effects of greed and manipulation but also the allegedly dire consequences of crossing traditional gender boundaries.

After its release, *Doña Bárbara* garnered unprecedented box office receipts as well as significant praise for director Fernando de Fuentes and his female star. Enamored with her magnetic appearance and powerful persona, fans referred to Félix simply as *La Doña* and her unique celebrity status began to grow. Building on this success, Fernando de Fuentes cast the actress in a similar "man-eating" role in *La mujer sin alma* (Woman without a heart, 1943). In this film, María further added to her reputation by playing a variety of strong, if not outright femme fatale, characters. Other films of this period include *La china poblana* (1943), *La monja alférez* (The ensign nun, 1944), *Amok* (1944), *El monje blanco* (The white nun, 1945), *Vértigo* (1945), *La devoradora* (The devourer, 1946), *La mujer de todos* (Everyone's woman, 1946), and probably Félix's most critically acclaimed performance, *Enamorada* (In love, 1946). In these performances, Félix effectively combined an undeniable physical charm with her ever-growing reputation as an independent, characteristically modern woman.

About the same time she was establishing herself as Mexico's leading female film star, María Félix further attracted public attention when she began a relationship with the considerably older and less attractive Agustín Lara. For the short time they spent together during the mid-1940s, paparazzi captured this celebrity odd couple as they made regular appearances in restaurants, nightclubs, cabarets, movie sets, at the bullfights on Sunday, and at a host of other locations. All the furious attention helped generate important publicity not only for their individual careers but for the growing Mexican entertainment industry at large.

BEAUTY AND THE BOHEMIAN

While beginning work on *La china poblana* in early 1943, María Félix met Agustín Lara one night through a mutual friend. Soon courting the attractive young actress, Lara showered Félix with a number of gifts while introducing her to Mexico's cultural elite. During their initial courtship, the couple attracted the attention of the press, who at first accused María of publicity-seeking. Countering these charges by claiming that she had maintained a special fondness for the debonair radio star for years, Félix would later testify that "Agustín was *muy sexy* [and possessed] the most exciting voice in the world." Given the pairing of Mexico's most beloved bohemian crooner with one of its favorite young film stars, it was not long before the two had become a "hot item" on the celebrity circuit.

As word spread, Félix and Lara could be seen together attending theater openings, dining in upscale restaurants, and visiting celebrity homes. Sunday afternoons were often spent at the bullfights. Thus, by late 1943, society columns in illustrated magazines such as *Revista de Revistas*, *Cinema Reporter*, *Cinelandia*, *México Cinema*, and others offered reports of Félix and Lara out on the town. Journalists often hounded the two as an adoring Mexican public yearned for news and photographs of the celebrity couple. About the same time, Lara and Félix both worked on the film *Amok*, for which Agustín provided the main theme and a few songs and recorded the background music. Ever the romantic, Lara was said to have treated Félix with great care and soon began writing new songs that were inspired by his young love.

When Lara fell ill during the spring of 1945, Félix was closely watched as she regularly visited her beloved boyfriend in the hospital. An interview that year displayed the two celebrities as sophisticated modern lovers drinking cocktails and listening to freshly minted bolero recordings. With the Mexican public proudly regarding Lara and Félix as one of the great romantic couples of all time, publicity photos, interviews, and gossip columns consistently kept them in the spotlight. When asked, the young actress repeatedly testified to reporters about her happiness with the older Lara. When the musician-poet regained his health, the two—who had been living together for nearly two years—were married in a small civil ceremony at their home on Christmas Eve, 1945, with a host of celebrity friends in attendance.

WE'LL ALWAYS HAVE MARÍA BONITA

On their honeymoon in Acapulco, Lara penned his famous "María Bonita" (Pretty Maria), in which he affectionately declares, "I've had many loves, but none so fine, so honorable as this." With news of their nuptials causing another tremendous wave of public adoration ("the wedding of the century"), members of the press were soon invited to capture Félix and Lara celebrating at home with an assortment of movie star friends in late August 1946. The following year, María's film *La diosa arrodillada* (The kneeling goddess) featured another of Lara's songs.

Amid all the fanfare, however, difficulties between Félix and Lara developed and soon became a matter of public speculation. In the December 1946 issue of *México Cinema*, for example, curiosity about their private life produced a horoscope-like article titled "The Destiny of María Félix" that characterized her as a strong woman who—not unlike her on-screen reputation—could be impetuous, erratic, and even violent. Her love life, according to the magazine, was subject to frequent changes.

With this and other examples of public scrutiny, word spread that certain male admirers had been showering María with expensive gifts. At one point, rumors circulated regarding an affair between the actress and a high-ranking military man.

Given María's reputation as "the most beautiful woman in Mexican Cinema," her decidedly less attractive partner was increasingly viewed as an insecure husband given to fits of jealous rage. Mocked by the press, Lara soon became the butt of jokes and cartoons. As before, many wondered how someone so ugly could command the attention of such a beautiful young woman. In response, Lara continued to cultivate his image as a romantic gentleman but also skillfully played off rumors of uncontrollable jealousy and marital tension by writing songs such as "Humo en los ojos" (Smoke in the eyes), "Noche de ronda" (Night games), and "Cuando vuelvas" (When you return) that spoke not only of his love for his wife but also of his growing insecurity. With the public transfixed on the couple's every move, the songs were not surprisingly big hits for the popular composer.

Despite the turmoil, Félix and Lara managed to remain together. Yet when María's love scenes with actor Pedro Armendáriz were seen in the 1946 film directed by Emilio Fernández, *Enamorada*, the couple again faced a difficult challenge to their already fragile bond. Apparently, even María's father, Bernardo, complained that he felt ashamed and embarrassed by his daughter's recent on-screen roles after seeing the film. These comments aside, *Enamorada* also attracted criticism from conservatives associated with the Catholic Partido de Acción Nacional, who felt strongly that traditional values had been compromised. The controversy not only helped stimulate debates in the national press but also promoted the legendary status of Lara and Félix as well as sales at the box office.

Still, the fact that Agustín performed nearly every night while Félix worked during the day on a new project titled *Río Escondido* (Hidden river, 1947, also directed by Emilio Fernández) helped the couple avoid a face-to-face confrontation. Before long, however, new rumors spread as Félix was pictured at various celebrity nightspots with a number of male friends associated with the movie industry.

Eventually, pent-up resentment, paranoia, and public pressure peaked when Lara confronted Félix about several gifts sent by an adoring fan. In response, María retaliated by claiming defiantly that Agustín was having an affair with a young dancer. Making a public spectacle of her own insecurity, Félix had some of Lara's clothing taken from his closet and thrown onstage just as he was about to perform at the Arbeu Theater one night. When news of this and other heated confrontations hit the streets (there were also rumors that Lara pointed a pistol at Félix one night during an argument), everyone in Mexico knew that the celebrity marriage was all but over. Soon thereafter, newspaper reports indicated that Félix and Lara had separated. When questioned by reporters, María confirmed the breakup but expressed no interest in discussing the matter publicly.

Official word of their divorce came in late October 1947, just as Félix announced plans to leave for Los Angeles, California. A short while later the actress flew to Spain to begin working on a new project in which she assumed the role of a Latin belly dancer for the film *Mare Nostrum*. Having lost what may have proved to be his most awe-inspiring muse, Lara temporarily retreated from public view to regain his composure and begin work on a number of new compositions.

CONCLUSION

In Mexico during the 1940s, images of María Félix graced the silver screen while the music of Agustín Lara filled the air with sweet bolero sounds. Each attractive in their different roles as *la doña* and *el flaco* (beauty and bohemian), the two artists enjoyed considerable attention from an adoring public seeking to make sense of their own lives in an era of rapid social change. When the two began their relationship in 1943, boosters effectively used the celebrity couple to promote the entertainment industry (and its various commercial affiliates) both in and outside of Mexico. As scholars have noted in discussing the history of tourism in Mexico, there is little doubt that María Félix and Agustín Lara also helped sell a new image of Mexico in the 1940s, one no longer based on a romanticized, traditional culture but rather on an urbanizing nation rapidly taking on a new, modern, cosmopolitan character. Though they were together for only a short time, their public romance helped mediate the anxiety of the time by serving as a critical distraction for audiences. Still today, many with memories from Mexico's "Golden Age" feel the same emotional thrill they did years ago when hearing the opening bars of the song "María Bonita."

SUGGESTED READINGS

Abaroa Martínez, Gabriel. *El Flaco de Oro*. Mexico City: Grupo Editorial Planeta, 1993.

De los Reyes, Aurelio. *Cine y sociedad en México: Bajo el cielo de México, 1920–1924*. Mexico City: UNAM, 1993.

Félix, María. *Todas mis guerras*. Mexico City: Clío Editions, 1993.

Hershfield, Joanne. *Mexican Cinema, Mexican Woman, 1940–1950*. Tucson: University of Arizona Press, 1996.

Joseph, Gilbert, Anne Rubenstein, and Eric Zolov, eds. *Fragments of a Golden Age: The Politics of Culture in Mexico Since 1940*. Durham: Duke University Press, 2001.

López, Ana M. "Tears and Desire: Women and Melodrama in the 'Old' Mexican Cinema." In *Mediating Two Worlds: Cinematic Encounters in the Americas*, ed. John King, Ana M. López, and Manuel Alvarado. London: British Film Institute, 1993.

Paranaguá, Antonio, ed. *Mexican Cinema*. Translated by Ana M. López. London and Mexico City: British Film Institute/Instituto Mexicano de Cinematografía (IMCINE), 1995.

Taibo, Paco Ignacio. *La Doña*. Mexico City: Grupo Editorial Planeta 1985.

Tuñón, Julia. *Mujeres de luz y sombra: La construcción de una imagen, 1939–1952*. Mexico City: Colegio de México/Instituto Mexicano de Cinematografía, 1998.

CHAPTER THIRTEEN

Josefina Velázquez de León

Apostle of the Enchilada

Jeffrey M. Pilcher

 *Isabel la Católica, the pious queen who sent Columbus on his mission of exploration, is still remembered in Mexico City with a stop on the pink metro line. Just outside the subway station, on the northeast corner of the street, is the Claustro de Sor Juana, the convent where another famous and devout woman from Mexican history, the great seventeenth-century poet and precursor to modern feminism, spent much of her life. In her famous "Respuesta a Sor Filotea," written in 1690, Juana Inés de la Cruz refuted the stereotype of women as ignorant by describing the natural laws of chemistry revealed through the act of frying eggs. She concluded: "[H]ad Aristotle cooked, how much more he would have written." Appropriately, the Claustro de Sor Juana is now the home of Mexico's premier culinary academy, where men and women alike train for positions in top restaurants and hotels. Moreover, the Claustro stands just a few blocks from the former site of another historic cooking school, the Academia de Cocina Veláquez de León, where an earlier generation learned the secrets of Mexican cuisine.*

Josefina Velázquez de León built a successful business as a cooking teacher and publisher by providing stability in a time of social disruption. Economic modernization and urbanization were upsetting the traditional patterns of Mexican life, but at the same time opening new opportunities. As migrants from all over the republic converged on Mexico City, it became possible to imagine a national community through the diverse regional foods. In helping to construct such a domestic nationalism, Velázquez de León relied heavily on her Catholic upbringing, thereby ignoring more secular versions of nationalism advanced by the ruling party. Moreover, she maintained connections with the past by reviving and reinventing traditional dishes that had held communities together in previous times.

Jeffrey M. Pilcher, the editor of this volume, began his study of Mexican culinary history with the prize-winning book, ¡Que vivan los tamales! Food and the Making of Mexican Identity *(1998).*

Cuisine provides one of the most basic components of human identity. Children take one of their first steps into Mexican culture by learning to eat chile peppers—a rite of passage that often precedes both speaking the Spanish language and cheering at the World Cup. Nevertheless, before food could become a source of national identity, Mexicans had to find a common ground on which to unify their enormously diverse regional cuisines. Even those ingredients used throughout the republic, such as chiles and frijoles, differed significantly from one state to the next; and until the twentieth century, most people had tasted only the local specialties of their own region. But as internal migration, economic development, and the mass media brought Mexicans closer together, women began to experiment with new ingredients, exchange recipes, and combine these regional cooking styles into a unified national cuisine. Josefina Velázquez de León, the foremost advocate of culinary nationalism, wrote more than 150 cookbooks revealing the mysterious nuances of regional cuisines and exalting lower-class dishes such as enchiladas as symbols of national identity.

Patriotism came naturally to doña Josefina, daughter of one of Mexico's most illustrious families. She traced her ancestry back to Diego Velázquez, whose *Instrucciones a Cortés* (1518) authorized the Spanish conquest of Mexico, and to Joaquín de Velázquez Cárdenas de León, who prepared the *Ordenanzas de Minería* (1778) to promote and regulate New Spain's mining industry. The family maintained its eminence through the nineteenth century, while appearing in some of the less fortunate episodes of national history. Josefina's great-great-grandfather, Juan Luis Velázquez de León, served as a captain under the Emperor Iturbide, while her great-grandfather, Joaquín, led the commission offering a Mexican crown to Maximilian of Austria. Moreover, as Minister of Development under Antonio López de Santa Anna in 1853, Joaquín had signed the Gadsden Purchase ceding southern Arizona and New Mexico to the United States.

Josefina's mother, María Peón Valdez, grew up in a socially prominent family from Guadalajara. She was living with her sister on the Hacienda de Pabellón, on the border between Zacatecas and Aguascalientes, when two Velázquez de León brothers came courting. The two couples married and then sold the ranch and purchased another, Los Cuartos, in Aguascalientes, where Josefina was born in 1899. Three sisters followed, the youngest, María Luisa, in 1905, after the family had moved to a home on the fashionable southwest side of Mexico City.

There the girls were educated in the domestic skills appropriate to elite women, who were supposed to devote their lives to serving their husbands and children. María Peón had tastefully decorated the two-story house with expensive French furniture, providing the young girls an object lesson in gracious living. And at a time when presidential banquets featured European haute cuisine, she taught them the demanding techniques of French cooking. Their education also emphasized penmanship and drawing, the better to prepare and answer the formal invitations that opened the doors of high society. Embroidery offered another acceptable outlet for the young girls' budding artistic talents. Most important of all, María Peón taught her children respect for the rituals of the Catholic Church.

But the girls also received a more practical education after the Revolution of 1910 toppled the government of Porfirio Díaz. Residents of Mexico City continued their daily routines with little interruption until 1915, known as "the year of the hunger" (*el año del hambre*). As the followers of Emiliano Zapata and Venustiano Carranza fought for control of the nation's capital, even wealthy Mexicans grew thin. The Velázquez de León family survived the decade of fighting, but the difficult times made a deep impression on the teenage Josefina. Throughout her life she emphasized the need for hard work and economy in the kitchen to assure the family's well-being.

A photograph from the 1920s shows her as a pretty young woman in the currently fashionable flapper style, complete with bobbed haircut, pearl necklace, dark lipstick, and sleeveless gown. Yet beneath the painted shadow, her eyes reveal a somber look quite foreign to the cabaret nightlife of San Juan de Letrán. Certainly her strict Catholic upbringing condemned such frivolous dissipation. The solemn eyes may also have reflected her concern about the loss of the family ranch to agrarian reformers late in the decade. Finally, this period in her life was beset by personal tragedy. Even as Josefina approached thirty, an almost certain mark of a spinster, her family worried about her decision to marry Joaquín González, a businessman twenty years her senior. Her mother objected that he was an unhealthy man, that the marriage was doomed to grief; but her most disapproving sighs could not dissuade Josefina. González then proved the old lady right, outliving the wedding by just eleven unhappy months.

As a widow, Josefina gained a privileged position among Mexican women, free from the authority of both parents and husband. Although women had gained the legal right to live alone, social customs still dictated the subjugation of daughters and wives. Whether freedom was the goal of this strong-willed young woman we can only guess, but she took over her dead husband's business immediately while still wearing the black mantle of mourning. She did not enjoy the merchant life, however, and soon sold her interest to González's partners. Then she fell back on her childhood education and began teaching cooking classes to support her family, left with no other source of income after the expropriation of their hacienda as a result of agrarian reform. By 1935 she had remodeled the entire downstairs of the family house on Abraham González Street and gained the sponsorship of a domestic appliance manufacturer.

News of the excellent classes offered at the "Caldroth Stoves" Cooking Academy spread quickly through Mexico City's ever-widening social circles. Imposing matrons and aspiring brides flocked to learn some elaborate new dish from the classical European repertoire or simply to improve a traditional Mexican favorite such as *sopa de fideos* (noodle soup). Mothers of young children took special note of Josefina's impressive cake decorations using sugar sculptures of the latest Hollywood icons like Snow White and the Seven Dwarfs and Popeye the Sailor Man. At first, the school offered banquet facilities for communion breakfasts and wedding dinners, but Josefina found catering to be more trouble than it was worth and later reserved the salon for special occasions such as her niece's wedding.

Josefina used her cooking school as the foundation for a virtual publishing empire. She began by submitting articles to women's magazines such as *Mignon*, which had featured a picture of a "mosque" cake with seven levels and a domed ceiling made in honor of the Spanish consul's silver anniversary. Josefina knew she could match that, and sent in a photo of a cake decorated to resemble the pastoral scenes common in Mexican homes at Christmas. The cake appeared in the December 1938 issue and adorned the first of what would be a regular column by Josefina that lasted for more than two decades. In the late 1930s, Josefina published her first book, *Manual práctico de cocina y repostería* (Practical Manual of Cooking and Pastry), an instant classic that went through five editions. In 1954 it was named by the editors of *Restaurante* magazine as one of the most important cookbooks in Mexico. Her other early works included *Los 30 menus* and *La cocina económica*. By the mid-1940s, she had established her own press, Ediciones J. Velázquez de León, which ultimately offered more than 140 separate titles.

The growth of mass media in the postwar era allowed Josefina to extend her circle of students still further. In February 1946 she took to the radiowaves of station XEW for a daily program, *La flojera en la cocina* (Laziness in the Kitchen). Laziness, she explained in a promotional interview with the Mexico City daily *Excelsior*, had reached epidemic proportions among women who had grown tired of the repetitive daily obligation of cooking. But with modern appliances and packaged foods—such as the concentrated tomato puree offered by the sponsors, Empacadoras Calidad (Quality Packing Company)—plus the expert advice of Josefina herself, Mexican women could prepare delicious meals every day with little effort and keep their men from straying. Josefina soon developed a number of other cooking programs for the Mexico

City radio stations XEQ, XEK, and XEJP, and in 1947 she compiled the diverse recipes into a book entitled *La cocina en el aire* (Cooking on the Air).

The popularity of her radio broadcasts inspired Josefina to develop a television show in the early 1950s called *El Menu de la Semana* (The Menu of the Week). This was before the time when programmers demanded fashion-model thinness of all female television personalities, for she had already acquired a substantial girth, which loomed all the larger under a beehive hairdo. Nevertheless, if the small screen seemed inappropriate to her frame, it did allow her to indulge her fancy for baroque decoration. She led viewers step by step through the creation of geometric gardens of meat loaf, shimmering arctic landscapes of gelatin, and bizarre sea creatures encrusted with canapé. These programs also provided a series of *Tele-cocina* booklets to add to her nascent publishing empire.

The early works of Josefina, and indeed the vast majority of Mexican cookbooks published before 1946, had concentrated on international cuisine and largely ignored national dishes made of corn because of the stigma of their lower-class, Native American origins. Mariano Galván Rivera's *Diccionario de Cocina* (1845) explicitly questioned the morals of any family that served tamales, the food of the "lower orders." Other works relegated enchiladas and tamales to a section entitled "*almuerzos ligeros*" (light brunches). The nineteenth-century's finest collection of the national cuisine, *La cocinera poblana* (The Puebla Cook), was assembled in 1877 by a Spanish immigrant, Narciso Bassols. The author of the 1896 volume, *Cocina michoacana* (Michoacán Cooking), Vicenta Torres de Rubio, boldly included recipes for a few "secrets of the indigenous classes"—*pozole* (hominy stew), *gorditas* (corn fritters), and *carnero al pastor* (shepherd's mutton)—but out of deference to her elite audience, she carefully set them apart with the label "*indigenista.*"

Strong regional rivalries likewise impeded the development of a national cuisine. The anonymous author of *El cocinero mexicano* (The Mexican Chef) noted with dismay in 1831 that patriotic *jarochos* considered the tiny black frijoles of Veracruz superior to all others and when forced to live in exile in Mexico City they willingly paid exorbitant sums to import them. Francisco J. Santamaría, in his dictionary *Americanismo y barbarismo* (1921), waxed nostalgically about his *patria chica* Tabasco's tamales, which supposedly contained the finest dough and fillings, far superior to those of central Mexico. And the nationalist manifesto *Forjando patria* (1916) related Manuel Gamio's experience of ordering an imported beer in Mérida and receiving a Dos Equis from Orizaba. The waiter explained it was the only foreign beer available; if Gamio wanted a domestic he could have a Yucatecan brand.

As a result of regional chauvinism and class distinction, nineteenth-century cookbooks covered only a limited sample of Mexico's local cuisines. Readers could find the seafoods of Veracruz and Campeche, the *moles* of Puebla and Oaxaca, and the roasted meats of Monterrey and Guadalajara, and little more. In the case of Oaxaca, sometimes called "the land of seven *moles*," cookbooks featured the black version, filled with spices like Puebla's famed dish, but ignored the more indigenous green, perfumed with the incomparable anise-like fragrance of *hoja santa*. By centering the national cuisine on areas of Spanish settlement, authors ignored a gastronomic geography dating back to pre-Hispanic times. The Huasteca, for example, split between San Luis Potosí, Tamaulipas, and Veracruz, although never mentioned in cookbooks, was renowned within the Aztec Empire for its sophisticated cuisine, including the fabled *zacahuil* tamal. Along the Pacific Coast, the hominy stew *pozole* assumed countless forms, yet because of its indigenous associations, it was excluded from elite cooking manuals.

But following the Revolution of 1910, cultural convergence became an essential element of the central government's nationalist program. Josefina Velázquez de León dedicated much of her career to overcoming the regional and ethnic chauvinism that impeded the formation of a Mexican national cuisine. Her classic 1946 work, *Platillos regionales de la República mexicana* (Regional Dishes of the Mexican Republic), collected for the first time the country's diverse cuisines in a single volume. The preface declared with nationalist pride that highly skilled Mexican cooks of the past had created some of the world's finest dishes, notable for their exceptional taste, distinctive condiments, and refined nature. Motivated by her zeal as a Mexican woman, Josefina wished to introduce her students to the culinary customs of each region of the Republic. The culinary arts, she believed, could contribute as much as music or painting to Mexico's national integration.

This was a lofty claim indeed, for the artistic renaissance of the postrevolutionary era had helped forge a national consensus that assured political stability and economic growth for three decades beginning in the late 1930s. At this time such cultural icons as mariachi music, *charro* horsemen, and *china poblana* beauties were exalted as representations of *lo mexicano*. The murals of Diego Rivera, the symphonies of Carlos Chávez, and the films of Emilio "El Indio" Fernández likewise brought life to the ideology of *indigenismo*, which rejected the exaggerated nineteenth-century adulation of Europe and recognized the significant Native American contributions to Mexican culture. Doña Josefina proclaimed tamales and other pre-Hispanic dishes to be a source of pride for Mexican cuisine. The goal of this somewhat misleadingly named ideology was not a return to the indigenous past, but rather the incorporation with dignity of Mexico's Indians into a unified mestizo cosmic race. All Mexicans could then be represented by the supposedly inclusive politics of the official political party, known after 1946 as the Institutional Revolutionary Party (PRI), and theoretically share in the 6 percent annual economic growth produced by the seeming miracle of industrialization.

Modernization certainly transformed the Mexican kitchen in the twentieth century. The most difficult task of Mexican cooking, preparing tortillas, was mechanized first through the development of *nixtamal* mills that replaced laborious daily hand grinding of corn; and in the 1950s fully automated tortilla machines achieved commercial success. Middle-class housewives in the postwar era purchased electric blenders for grinding *mole* and pressure cookers for frijoles. Josefina experimented with all the latest technical advances, both to ease the domestic chores of her students and as a valuable source of sponsorship. Her cookbooks endorsed brand-name kitchen appliances, disinfectant drops, canned foods, and monosodium glutamate, and these same products were prominently displayed for sale at the Academia de Cocina Velázquez de León (Velázquez de León Cooking Academy).

Postrevolutionary highway building and economic integration also helped bring together the national cuisine. Improved transportation made specialized regional ingredients such as *hoja santa*, the distinctive herb used in Oaxaca's green *mole*, available to shoppers in the nation's capital. Once again, Josefina was determined to lead the way; she purchased an automobile, hired a chauffeur, and set off with her loyal servant and traveling companion Luisa. Together they gave cooking classes to women throughout Mexico, usually to benefit local Catholic charities. At the same time they collected local recipes, which provided the material for a series of regional cookbooks ultimately covering more than half the states in the republic. Josefina also dedicated new creations to her students; for example, in San Luis Potosí she fashioned a "national flag" of pork loin, dressed in green avocado, white cream, and red chipotles, and served with an imitation "maguey cactus" of duchess potatoes.

These books published in the 1950s continued to pursue the goal stated in 1946 in *Platillos regionales* of forging a national community in the kitchen. Women could exchange recipes with their counterparts throughout the country and combine them with local favorites to form intriguing new national menus. Josefina suggested juxtaposing the fish in caper sauce of coastal Veracruz with prickly pears and wine from the arid highlands. Another menu paired *norteño* beef *menudo* (tripe stew) with a tropical coconut and pineapple dessert. The national cuisine was even open to foreign immigration; Josefina personally granted citizenship to enchiladas "Italia Mexico" made of sardines, potatoes, and

Parmesan cheese—a lesser-known cousin of the Swiss enchiladas doused in cream and cheese. Experiments such as these expanded the possibilities of *lo mexicano* and helped to break down geographical and ethnic barriers to national unity.

Nevertheless, the construction of a national cuisine also reduced complex regional cooking styles to a few stereotyped dishes, which often misrepresented the foods eaten in those areas. Even the thickest volume could contain only a fraction of the total number of Mexican dishes, and conscientious efforts were needed to avoid losing precious recipes. Even an author as sensitive as Josefina adapted traditional village recipes to the needs of urban cooks. For the *zacahuil*, the giant Huastecan tamal cooked in a pit and capable of feeding an entire community, she instructed readers to use a scanty three kilograms of maize and to bake it in the oven. Yet the very attempt to recreate village foods in an urban setting reflected the rapid changes overtaking Mexican society as a result of industrialization and urbanization.

Women sought to build a sense of community in the rapidly growing and increasingly anonymous cities by sharing with neighbors traditional dishes such as *moles*, which were associated with family rituals and village festivals. In a volume on *Cocina oaxaqueña* (Oaxacan Cooking), for example, Josefina emphasized the authenticity of her recipe for Oaxaca's black *mole*, which she labeled the *"legítimo mole negro antiguo."* She also published a regular column in *Restaurante* magazine of venerable Mexican recipes. Her 1950 work, *Cómo cocinar en los aparatos modernos* (How to Cook with Modern Appliances), made special efforts to create links with the past by juxtaposing modern housewives with stereotypes of historical figures. The book's illustrations showed fashionable women effortlessly using blenders and pressure cookers to make tamales with peasant girls, *pulques* with maguey planters, and sweets with colonial nuns.

The religious associations attached to the national cuisine distinguished this female vision of the national identity from the more secular versions of government propagandists and male intellectuals. Many politicians had worried that if women gained the vote, which they finally did for national elections in 1954, this would increase support for conservative parties and the Church. While the PRI continued to sweep elections for another four decades, many women did assign less importance to traditional liberal leaders such as Father Hidalgo or Benito Juárez. The heroes of the national cuisine were instead the legendary seventeenth-century nuns credited with inventing *mole poblano*, the Emperor Agustín Iturbide who reputedly inspired the creation of the tricolor *chiles en nogada* (stuffed green chiles in white walnut sauce garnished with red pomegranate seeds) to match the national flag, and the ill-fated Maximilian and Carlota supposedly responsible for introducing French cooking to

Mexico. Josefina shared this conservative, religious ideal of the nation, and even made votive offerings that the recipes in her cookbooks would be understood and faithfully interpreted by her fellow cooks. The proceeds from her traveling cooking classes often went to support Catholic charities, and in her own kitchen she hung an image of her patron, Saint Eduviges.

Josefina's Christian benevolence thus extended to the masses of people excluded from the economic "miracle" of the postwar era. Having personally suffered hunger in her teenage years as a result of revolutionary fighting, Josefina had learned to prepare satisfying meals from the most meager raw materials. She adopted the motto *"saber cocinar es base de economía"* (knowing how to cook is the basis of economy), and published inexpensive cookbooks such as *Cómo cocinar en tiempos de carestía* (How to Cook in Hard Times). Her volume *Cómo aprovechar los sobrantes de la comida* (How to Use Leftover Food) would make the most frugal campesina proud, with recipes for onion stalks, radish leaves, and pea pods. Another work, *La cocina como negocio: Cómo establecer un negocio lucrativo en la Cocina del Hogar* (Cooking as a Business: How to Establish a Lucrative Business in the Kitchen of Your Home), encouraged women to supplement their family income with homemade sausage, cheese, bread, liquors, and gelatin.

Josefina's personal example helped overcome the prejudice that respectable women tarnished themselves by entering the money economy. She devised countless techniques for expanding her business, offering coupons for free classes, obtaining sponsorship from manufacturers, publishing her own works, and preparing radio and television programs. To accommodate her numerous students, she rented a house downtown on Simón Bolívar Street, a block west of Isabel la Católica, and brought in her younger sisters Guadalupe and María Luisa to assist with the classes. She personally worked an exhausting schedule, teaching classes in the morning and evening, experimenting with recipes in the afternoon, and writing and illustrating books well into the night. Although she did not return home until ten or eleven at night, she invariably made it to work the next morning by nine.

She took enormous satisfaction from her wide circle of friends and from the accomplishments of her work. She earned the respect of the gastronomic luminaries of the 1950s, a golden age of fine dining in Mexico City, when the original recipes of nouvelle Mexican cuisine were created, the *carne asada a la tampiqueña* (grilled steak Tampico style) of the flamboyant restaurateur José Inés Loredo, and the *crepas de cuitlacoche* (crêpes with corn fungus in bechamel sauce) of gourmet Jaime Saldívar. Because Josefina had no children of her own, her students organized a party each year on her saint's day, decorating the academy and preparing the Mexican equivalent of birthday cake. Working with her sisters and feeding their children provided her another source of pleasure.

But by the 1960s her formerly boundless energy had begun to wane. She no longer contributed recipes to women's magazines, and increasingly experimented with foods for the sick and aged. Her last book, *Cocina para enfermos* (Cooking for the Ill), published in 1968, contained special diets for the overweight, the anemic, and diabetics, reflecting not only her own declining health, but also the harmful effects of modernization on the national diet. Surveys conducted by the National Institute of Nutrition in that period showed that Mexicans were falling victim to the dietary diseases of the rich world without escaping the nutritional deficiencies of the poor world. Excessive consumption of sugar, salt, and fat in snack foods and soft drinks contributed to an alarming spread of diabetes, hypoglycemia, hypertension, arteriosclerosis, heart disease, and various forms of cancer. These diseases seemed all the more tragic given the continuing prevalence of serious malnutrition, particularly among children. Indeed, many Mexicans suffered from both obesity and anemia at the same time.

Despite her rapidly failing health, in the summer of 1968, Josefina accepted the invitation of a Catholic charity to give a three-day cooking seminar in the city of Veracruz. While in the capital of *jarocho* cooking, she fell ill and had to return to Mexico City. On September 19, 1968, at the age of 69, Josefina Velázquez de León passed away. Her sisters attempted to carry on the business, but without her guidance and energy, they eventually closed the school and sold the rights to her books. The ground floor of the family house on Abraham González Street, where doña Josefina had opened her first cooking academy, was rented out as an auto parts store.

Another possible explanation for the cooking school's failure was the spread of North American fast food beginning in the 1960s. With the arrival of an Aunt Jemina's restaurant in the Zona Rosa, and later the spread of McDonald's, Denny's, and their national counterpart Vips, middle-class Mexicans increasingly ate hamburgers to the neglect of traditional dishes. Josefina may even have contributed to the infiltration of processed foods from the United States by including in her cookbooks recipes for *hamburguesas*, hotcakes, and the more exotic shrimp with corn flakes. Yet such apocalyptic views of cultural imperialism fail to account for the vitality of Mexican cuisine as expressed both by vendors of *torta-tamales*, who do a thriving business on street corners throughout the Federal District, and by chefs serving nouvelle Mexican dishes that compete with the most refined international cuisines. Moreover, traditional Mexican favorites have gained widespread popularity in the United States, where the sales of salsa recently surpassed the formerly ubiquitous catsup.

Josefina Velázquez de León's work as an apostle of popular cuisine contributed to the development of a genuinely inclusive national identity. European foods had dominated elite tables in the nineteenth century, and her mastery of classical French technique reassured status-conscious women even as she spread the gospel of national dishes such as enchiladas. True, her cookbooks and classes still conveyed conservative, middle-class ideals to women who worried that spending time outside the home threatened the family. Josefina firmly believed in the value of domestic work, and she sought to gain recognition of that value for its aesthetic and economic contributions to the family and the nation. At the same time, by giving women a new appreciation of the richness and diversity of Mexican cuisine, she allowed them a sense of participation in the national community. Culinary patriotism therefore provided not an impediment but a stepping-stone to direct political action for future generations of Mexican women.

SUGGESTED READINGS

Avila Hernández, Dolores, et al. *Atlas cultural de México: Gastronomía*. México, DF: Secretaría de Educación Pública/Instituto Nacional de Antropología e Historia/Editorial Planeta, 1988.

Belasco, Warren, and Philip Scranton, eds. *Food Nations: Selling Taste in Consumer Societies*. New York: Routledge, 2001.

Chávez, Adolfo, et al. *La nutrición en México y la transición epidemiológica*. México, DF: Instituto Nacional de la Nutrición "Salvador Zubirán," 1993.

Esquivel, Laura. *Like Water for Chocolate: A Novel in Monthly Installments with Recipes, Romances, and Home Remedies*. Translated by Carol Christensen and Thomas Christensen. New York: Doubleday, 1992.

Lomnitz, Larissa Adler, and Marisol Pérez-Lizaur. *A Mexican Elite Family, 1820–1980: Kinship, Class, and Culture*. Translated by Cinna Lomnitz. Princeton: Princeton University Press, 1987.

Novo, Salvador. *Cocina mexicana o Historia Gastronómica de la Ciudad de México*. México, DF: Editorial Porrúa, 1967.

Pilcher, Jeffrey M. *¡Que vivan los tamales! Food and the Making of Mexican Identity*. Albuquerque: University of New Mexico Press, 1998.

Theophano, Janet. *Eat My Words: Reading Women's Lives through the Cookbooks They Wrote*. New York: Palgrave, 2002.

CHAPTER FOURTEEN

Armando Nava and Los Dug Dug's

Rock Musicians

Eric Zolov

One location where virtually all metro users, both foreigners and locals alike, eventually wind up is the Insurgentes Avenue station. Situated inside a traffic circle on the capital's busiest thoroughfare, it offers easy access to the hotels, boutiques, sports bars, and Internet cafés of the Zona Rosa tourist district. The culture there is mostly imported—except for the shops crowded with folkloric handicrafts for export—and one constantly encounters local versions of everything from long-haired musicians covering the Beatles to Goths complete with pancake makeup. Although some might dismiss them as the victims of globalization, their imitation of pop culture trends from the United States and western Europe could actually function as a political statement. Mexico's authoritarian government went to great effort constructing a monolithic national identity based on the revolutionary heroes Emiliano Zapata and Pancho Villa as well as popular culture icons such as María Félix and Agustín Lara (see Chapter 12). As a result, the youth protest movement of the 1950s and 1960s, with its throbbing rock 'n' roll beat, had great appeal to Mexican students seeking to escape the oppressive conformity of patriarchy, nationalism, and mariachis. Although condemned by both conservative officials and leftist intellectuals for selling out to foreigners, young Mexicans cultivated their own patriotic image as jipitecas, *combining the international hippie movement with the authenticity of pre-Hispanic Aztecs. The life of Armando Nava illustrates the predicament of aspiring musicians, seeking to find a voice of their own while trapped between multinational record labels and the Mexican ruling party.*

 Eric Zolov, an assistant professor of history at Franklin and Marshall University, is the author of Refried Elvis: The Rise of the Mexican Counterculture *(1999). He has also coedited a number of books, the most recent of which is* Fragments of a Golden Age: The Politics of Culture in Mexico Since 1940 *(2001). His current research focuses on diplomatic and cultural relations between the United States and Mexico in the 1960s.*

𝒥n Durango, Durango, where Armando Nava comes from, the young and restless tend to look north to the border rather than south to Mexico City in planning their escape from the provinces. The northern states are proud of their revolutionary traditions—it was in the north, after all, that Madero launched his quixotic campaign to unseat Porfirio Díaz in 1910—but they also share in a historical distrust of the centralizing tendencies of the nation's capital. Mexico City has consumed from the provinces in the form of tax revenues, raw materials, and even cultural symbols but, as far as many northerners are concerned, gives little in return except for political domination. "*Haz patria, mata un chilango*" (Be patriotic, kill a chilango [that is, someone from Mexico City]), is a common *dicho* heard throughout the provinces. The border offers a rich fusion of cultural practices, a break from the confines of traditional Mexico, and especially the allure and adventure of life *al otro lado*.

Armando first went to Tijuana in 1964 when he was eighteen. It was an exciting moment to be young: the Beatles had crossed the Atlantic and with them came a whole new language of the rock revolution, which filtered across the border to mix with the traditional *norteño* sounds of mariarchi and *ranchera*, those staples of northern culture. Armando was already playing in a high school rock 'n' roll band at home and, excited about the prospects of making it big—or at least bigger than in Durango, Durango—he convinced the rest of the band to follow him back to the border. Although he may not have realized it yet, he was indeed going to be a rock star. By 1971, Armando Nava and his group, Los Dug Dug's, came to embody the passions, frustrations, and contradictory aspirations of a generation of youth that became the basis of Mexico's vibrant countercultural movement of the late 1960s, La Onda.

To understand how and why Mexico came to have its own rock counterculture, we need to examine the first shock waves of rock 'n' roll's entry into Mexico in the late 1950s. The United States was already deeply mired in its own debates over juvenile delinquency and the "moral crisis" induced by Elvis Presley, Little Richard, and others when rock 'n' roll first took hold in Mexico. Given that the two countries are neighbors, perhaps it should not be much of a surprise to learn that the rebel icons of America's youth culture had also drifted south across the border. But it was not simply the sharing of borders that allowed this to happen (though in Mexico's case, this clearly facilitated the process). The simple fact that rock 'n' roll was intrinsically linked to mass cultural production—through film, record albums, and the general commodification of youth paraphernalia—meant that, from the start, rock 'n' roll was globally distributed. In other words, while teenagers were bopping to Elvis in America and England, they were doing the same thing (with a local tinge, of course, and with varying degrees of access) in South Africa, Argentina, the Philippines, and even Russia.

One of the principal ways rock 'n' roll culture was introduced into Mexico was via films such as Bill Haley's *Rock Around the Clock* (1957) and Elvis Presley's numerous flicks. In fact, Presley's *King Creole* (1958) sparked a riot at a Mexico City theatre in 1959 and led to a de facto ban on imported youth rebellion films for years to come. Marlon Brando's mockery of authority in *The Wild One* (1953) and James Dean's destructive youth angst in *Rebel without a Cause* (1955) were equally scandalous, though of course immensely popular, especially among middle-class youth who were eager to emulate these foreign icons of rebellion. In the editorial pages of the country's government-dominated press, a mounting fear was expressed that these imported rebel idols were displacing the country's own revolutionary heroes. Youth were allegedly succumbing to *rebeldismo sin causa*, a phrase invented by the press that captured the public's disgust and fear of the wanton challenge to patriarchal authority that the fashion of rebellion seemed to introduce. For a generation that had grown up under the repressive stability and ideological conformity of a single-party state, the outlaw appeal of James Dean was indeed stronger than that of Pancho Villa or Emiliano Zapata, much less of Benito Juárez, former revolutionaries now idled by the rhetoric of a regime whose credibility had substantially diminished.

Brought in on the wings of transnationalism—major record companies such as RCA (which recorded Elvis Presley) distributed these albums through their Mexican subsidiaries—and in the suitcases of upper-class teenagers traveling abroad, rock 'n' roll threatened to subvert the very ideological foundations of the nation itself, at least as far as the most vocal opponents were concerned. Following a public outcry and nationalist backlash against such dangers of "foreign influence," the Mexican legislature passed a sweeping communications bill in 1960 aimed at protecting the *buenas costumbres* (proper family values) of Mexican youth and safeguarding the state's revolutionary project. A high tariff wall was soon thrown up to keep out imports of rock 'n' roll (safeguarding the popularity of traditional Mexican performers in the process), while strict rules of conduct delimited the boundaries of propriety that film producers and distributors would now have to respect to avoid harassment or worse by the authorities. But while some predicted youth had "turned their backs on the rabid 'rock-roll' [*sic*]" for more "sentimental melodies," that was mere wishful thinking.[1] Instead, the movement soon exploded as scores of local bands, now ironically protected by tariff restrictions on imports, filled the gap. The era of Mexican *rocanrol* had begun.

The *rocanrol* of the early 1960s was called the period of the *refritos* (from the verb, *refreir*, to refry). Conjuring up notions of appropriation—the "refashioning" of foreign culture through native ways—Mexican bands took names such as Los Locos del Ritmo, Los Loud Jets, Los Crazy Boys, Los Hooligans, and others to record Spanish-language cover versions of the foreign originals, keeping as true as possible to the original rhythm while cleaning up the lyrics to conform with conservative standards set by the state. In fact, the bands themselves had little control over the lyric content of these "refried" covers, much less of the bands' image. All marketing and recording aspects were tightly controlled by the record companies, which were careful not to be too provocative lest the government find a pretext to respond. For example, Little Richard's lyrics to "Good Golly, Miss Molly" were changed from "Sure likes to ball, and when she's rockin' and a-rollin' can't hear your mamma call" to "Here comes the gal, sure likes to dance and when she's rockin' and a-rollin' she's the queen of the place." Where the original has "I'm going to the corner, gonna buy a diamond ring/Would you pardon me a-kissin' let me ting-a-ling-a-ling" in the final stanza, the version by Los Teen Tops finishes: "Let's go see the priest 'cause I want to get married/It's not that you're good lookin' but you sure know how to dance!"[2] In the Mexican version, the provocativeness of the original, with its implicit challenge to parental control and the celebration of sexual rebellion, was thus contained. At the same time, however, a space for a separate youth identity had nonetheless been forged: this was music to be listened to at full volume and, even if the lyrics no longer offended adults' sensibilities, "knowing how to dance" encoded a new language of youth rebellion through social practice.

Domesticating the lyrics and media representation of *rocanrol* proved to be a winning formula for the cultural industries as well as the bands themselves. By agreeing, in effect, not to exploit the intrinsic challenge to authority that the new youth culture embodied, the mass media were able to promote this movement as a reflection of Mexico's own middle- and upper-class aspirations of keeping pace with the United States, rather than being an imperialist import that threatened to subvert national cultural values. Rock 'n' roll epitomized, after all, the very essence of modernity: speed, youth, technology, consumerism. Fanzines such as *Mexico Canta* and *Notitas Musicales* promoted the new bands while offering gossip and even the English lyrics from their Anglo counterparts, always staying clear of promoting any imagery or editorials that explicitly challenged *buenas costumbres* or parental control. Many bands also found an outlet on television, through American Bandstand–style programs sponsored by the major record companies. And a whole genre of *rocanrol* films became vehicles for promoting the new stars (especially Enrique

Guzmán of Los Teen Tops and César Costa of Los Black Jeans). Although several of these films dealt with themes such as divorce and delinquency, they all ended with the resolution of youths' respect for the values of family and patriarchal authority. By the mid 1960s it appeared that the potentially disruptive rebellion of imported youth culture had been successfully contained via its domestication, conforming to parental concerns while staying within the boundaries of a conservative yet "revolutionary" propriety.

Mexico's first wave of *rocanrol* was a national phenomenon that radiated outward from the capital into the provinces and beyond. Many of these bands, for example, toured throughout Latin America and even the United States, Europe, and Asia. Indeed, though isolated in other ways from the capital, Armando was raised on the sounds of Los Locos del Ritmo, Los Teen Tops, and others. The band he and his friends formed in high school—Los Xippos—in fact played covers of these same *refritos* (covers of covers, in effect). With Armando playing keyboard and rhythm guitar (he later played flute as well), Jorge de la Torre on vocals, Genaro García on bass, and Gustavo Garayzar on lead guitar, they gained a decent reputation for a hometown act. But Durango, Durango, was too provincial for Armando's vision of a rock 'n' roll band and, having already experienced the potential in Tijuana, he convinced Los Xippos to return with him to try to strike it big. En route to the border, Armando also changed the band's name to Los Dug Dug's, a name that reflected the band's origins—Durango, Durango—but also, and perhaps more important, with the inclusion of an apostrophe (nonexistent in Spanish grammar) now conveyed a more "modern" sensibility.

The experience in Tijuana changed the musical direction of the band dramatically. Their first gig was playing at an all-night striptease joint (Fantasitas), where they performed from 7 P.M. to 10 A.M. for a mere $3 per day. The audience was largely composed of U.S. tourists and seamen on leave, who were there to take advantage of the cheap liquor and lack of curfew on the Mexican side of the border. These paying customers did not want to hear Spanish-language *refritos* (what Los Dug Dug's were playing), but rather hits by groups such as the Beach Boys, the Zombies, and especially the Beatles. And they wanted to hear them in English. Los Dug Dug's responded by learning the songs their audiences demanded. To do so, they needed to cross over the border into Southern California where they were able to purchase the new albums (they even managed to play a few gigs in the process). In this way, Los Dug Dug's changed their repertoire by learning to mime the English-language lyrics that none of them truly understood. But it worked. Quickly their reputation grew as a first-rate bar band and they advanced beyond the confines of Fantasitas to Mike's Bar, where they performed a straight rock show playing covers of the latest hits—in English. Armando knew that Mexican youth were dying to hear the songs they now played to perfection. Next stop: *La capital.*

The capital is a magnet—some might say a black hole—for millions seeking better fortunes, most of them rural migrants pushed aside by the very process of modernization that made Mexico City attractive to someone like Armando. For Los Dug Dug's, the capital offered not only the prospect of a recording contract and media exposure but an audience of their peers, primed to hear what the band now had to offer. Middle-class youth were tired of the *rocanrol refritos*, yet had little or no opportunity to hear the originals by groups they were only reading about. Landing in Mexico City in 1966 (replacing two of the original band members along the way), Los Dug Dug's quickly established a following. As Armando recalls, "[T]he market [in Mexico City] was virgin in terms of the music we brought with us. . . . They hadn't heard this music before. For example, we started [our first concert] with the Beatles, 'You've Got to Hide Your Love Away,' and the crowd went nuts. Nobody played those things." Most of the *cafés cantantes*, live music cafés where an earlier generation of *refritos* rock 'n' rollers performed, had been shut down in a repressive crackdown by the capital's law-and-order mayor, Ernesto Uruchurtu, in 1965. But other venues included the more upscale hotels and bars in the posh Zona Rosa district (which catered to foreign tourists) and an outdoor ice-skating rink located near the National University that, perhaps by default, became a key gathering point for the new generation.

Within a short time, Los Dug Dug's attracted the attention of RCA records, which had first introduced Mexican youth to Elvis Presley a decade earlier and now provided the band with an opportunity to record. (Their first LP, however, was not released until 1971.) Soon the band was performing on television and was even featured in two 1967 films: *El Mundo Loco de los Jovenes* (The Wild World of the Young) and the semiunderground cult film, *Cinco de Chocolate y Una de Fresa* (Five of Chocolate and One of Strawberry), which featured the ballad singer Angélica María as a cloistered Catholic-girl-turned-psychedelic-hipster. (The screenplay was cowritten by the young experimental novelist, José Agustín.) Los Dug Dug's were not alone in transforming the sound and performance style of rock in the capital. Other bands, several of which also came from the northern frontier and with backgrounds similar to Los Dug Dug's, also descended on Mexico City. One of those groups, Los Yaki (an anglicized spelling of Los Yaqui, a combative Indian tribe from Mexico's northwest), became known for their energetic performances of songs by the Rolling Stones and the Doors—all in English!

By 1967 a new term had been coined to describe the various phenomena linked to a new youth countercultural sensibility that was everywhere apparent: La Onda. Literally meaning "the wave," La Onda was described at the time by essayist Carlos Monsiváis as "a new spirit, the repudiation of proper morals, the expansion of consciousness, the systematic revision and critique of the values offered by the West as sacred and perfect."[3] Encompassed by La Onda were not only the new sounds of foreign rock (disseminated through mass performance by groups such as Los Dug Dug's and, with greater difficulty, accessed directly from albums brought in from abroad), but the fashion styles, images, and even language of the counterculture exploding in the United States and western Europe. La Onda soon referenced an evolving youth argot whose newly invented phrases (*"Que buena onda,"* for "Cool vibes," and *"Simón"* for "Right on," for example) also formed the basis of a new literary movement, led by such authors as José Agustín, Gustavo Saínz, Parménides García Saldaña, and others. The new values and aesthetics of La Onda— the long hair on men and miniskirts on women, the questioning of authority, the celebration of youth as the vanguard of a social transformation —unsettled many adults, who began to view these changes as dangerous by-products of a modernization process they otherwise embraced.

Indeed, the new consciousness underlying the otherwise stylistic aspects of La Onda culminated in a frontal critique by youth of the patriarchal authoritarianism espoused by the ruling Partido Revolucionario Institucional (PRI). In the summer of 1968, sparked by the example set by youth in Paris, Berkeley, New York, Prague, and other cities around the world, Mexican students also took to the streets. On the surface of these protests, students were challenging the rationale of spending huge sums on tourist hotels and athletic stadiums in Mexico City for the Olympics (scheduled for that fall) when so many in Mexico remained impoverished. But beyond this critique lay something more profound: a calling into question of the antidemocratic and corrupt system of governing behind the PRI itself. As youth discovered their solidarity in numbers, street protests turned into carnivalesque celebrations; clearly, La Onda had provided a new language for political revolt. Now adults were forced to choose between supporting a student-led movement that flouted authority in the name of democracy, or backing a wave of repression to put an end to it.

The mass media, subsidized and censored by the long reach of the PRI, unleashed a fury of negative reporting aimed at denigrating the students' cause. The students were charged not only with being "subversives" but perhaps more important as "delinquents" and "rebels without a cause." One antimovement broadsheet distributed by the government combined these elements by characterizing the movement as a "Beatlebolshevik Revolution": "The real students repudiate these [protesters] as opportunists directed by foreigners and whose members include 'pop professors' and pseudo-student 'hippies' who don't compose or represent the true student body."[4] Such attacks also appealed to many adults' own concerns about the insolence of youth—a rebelliousness already experienced by many fathers in the home and now appearing on the streets as well. As one adult summed up his view of the causes of the movement, "It's the miniskirt that's to blame."[5] Curiously, however, while the fashions, language, and sounds of La Onda were in fact an integral element characterizing youth protest (and shaping the irreverent tone that protest often took), there was no merging of Mexican rock bands and the student movement itself. This contrasted with the way rock, countercultural politics, and student protest movements engulfed the United States and western Europe at that same moment. Ironically, Mexican rock bands were tainted by association with the same conservative mass media that assaulted the students on behalf of the PRI. Moreover, although many bands had managed to deliver the inaccessible music their fans (and tourists) most wanted to hear, their own musical originality was truncated in the process. Kept from playing original music by the record companies and trapped in a cycle of performing covers in English, the bands were easily mocked by student protesters as no more than a bourgeois copy of the gringos. In the end there was little interaction, much less convergence, between the student protesters and groups like Los Dug Dug's.

The Student Movement of 1968, immortalized in yearly reenactments of principal marches and kept alive in social discourse by succeeding generations, remains an unresolved wound on the Mexican body politic despite the passage of over three decades. (The recent collapse of the PRI and opening up of government archives holds out the promise of healing some of those wounds.) The movement and subsequent repression that culminated on October 2 at the "Massacre of Tlatelolco" (when an unknown number of people were gunned down by government forces) have evolved into emblematic representations of the tensions within Mexican society then and since: the struggle for justice, representation, and accountability in the face of repression, authoritarianism, and disdain for democratic process. That summer and fall, tens of thousands of youth from the nation's capital united in protest. It was a utopian movement in that it imagined a society rid of the inequalities that plagued Mexico, but it was also a reformist movement in the sense that the students demanded not a revolutionary overthrow of the government but simply adherence to the rights and guarantees enshrined in the nation's constitution, itself already the product of a revolutionary movement.

Yet at the height of the movement, Armando and Los Dug Dug's left the ferment in Mexico City to capitalize on their fame with a triumphant return to Tijuana. By chance, an American tourist named Frank Mangano was at one of their performances and offered the band the opportunity to perform and record in the United States. For Armando this was the golden opportunity he had waited for. As he described the experience: "We had all of the hopes in the world. . . . We were looking to internationalize ourselves, that was our idea." Traveling with Mangano to the States, the band was successful at first: "[W]e had a lot of followers in New York." But legal problems and drug abuse by some of the members created frictions. "There came a point when the musicians, my *compañeros*, began to screw around a lot, they took a lot of drugs and that kind of thing. Everyone over there at that time was in the middle of being hippies and that whole scene. They got very caught up in drugs and I didn't dig that."[6] Several months later the rest of the band returned to Mexico; the opportunity had failed. Armando stayed on, however, continuing to record solo (laying down several original tunes in the process) and holding out hope of breaking into the U.S. rock scene. But several months later he, too, returned to Mexico. Not losing faith, he quickly regrouped the band and headed for Mexico City, determined this time to record his original compositions.

The Mexico City that Armando and Los Dug Dug's returned to in late 1969 had palpably changed. The street marches were over, silenced by repression, and La Onda had evolved from a fashion statement into a vehicle of direct social protest. Along with other post-Tlatelolco bands that soon emerged, Los Dug Dug's now formed the countercultural vanguard for a generation in utter disillusionment. The PRI, as Carlos Monsiváis later put it, was Mexican youth's Vietnam. In the aftermath of the crushed student movement, scores of youth "dropped out" by joining La Onda. This shift coincided with greater freedoms given to rock bands by the transnational companies, which were increasingly eager to develop the national and regional market for rock music. The days of the cultural industries' containment of rock were over (although certain limits to free expression clearly persisted). By 1970 a whole new wave of native bands had appeared, all of them recording original music and most of them aligned with one of the three transnational companies that operated in Mexico: RCA, CBS, and Polydor. With names such as La Revolución de Emiliano Zapata, Bandido, División del Norte, Peace and Love, and Three Souls in My Mind, these groups sought to distance themselves from an earlier period of emulative covers (first in Spanish, later in English) by creating a rock sound and performance style more in tune with the times. Mexican rock became unabashedly long-haired and "psychedelic," which coincided with the rapid spread of a Mexican *jipi* (sometimes written *jipiteca* and even *xipiteca*) movement and the rediscovery by youth of Mexico's indigenous heritage.

Oddly, however, these new bands embraced English as the language of rock. In part this was because of Spanish-language rock's close association with the bourgeois consumerist aspirations (the "contained rock") of an earlier period. Equally important, however, English was regarded by youth as the "authentic" language of rock; English conveyed the true "feeling" of countercultural revolt while Spanish seemed too removed from conveying rock's essence. Of course, because neither the bands nor their fans spoke English, this only limited the impact of the songs' lyrics. At any rate, most songs were not political in any explicit sense, though many did touch on themes of youth rebellion and a longing for community. The song "Let's Make It Now" from Los Dug Dug's first LP (released by RCA in 1971) displays this contradictory search for expression in another tongue:

> We're making a change, man
> The change that we want, boys
> The people refuse, God!
> And we'll make it now, now, now
> And we'll make it now, now, now
>
> I said, make it now,
> I would make it now
> Let's make it now
> Together now, now, now, now, now
>
> We just want to say, man
> They don't want a change, boy
> You don't want to hear, God
> But we'll say it loud, loud, loud
> We'll say it loud, loud, loud

Labeled La Onda Chicana by its supporters, this new phase of Mexican rock offered a fusion of identities, sounds, and aesthetics that expressed the longings of youth to redefine themselves as "Mexican" but done outside of the ideological framework imposed by a conservative government and an oppressive family structure.

La Onda Chicana climaxed at a two-day outdoor rock festival (modeled on Woodstock) in September 1971 held on the grounds of a wooded resort site called Avándaro, a few hours north of Mexico City. Estimates vary, but anywhere from 150,000 to 300,000 people attended, numbers that completely overwhelmed the logistical preparations for the event. The police and military were there in force, however, patrolling the perimeter of the festival and keeping order in the town nearby. This was the first large-scale gathering of youth since the 1968 student movement and it followed a paramilitary attack on a smaller gathering in the capital three months earlier. Both sides—youth and the government—were clearly wary of the others' potential in numbers. In the end, however, there were no bloody confrontations or acts of repression; in fact, drug use was so rampant that numerous reports circulated of police not only tolerating the use of marijuana but distributing it as well. Nearly all of Mexico's top bands performed; virtually all of the music was in English. Los Dug Dug's opened the festival and all through the night—there was no break in the music, unlike at Woodstock—the concertgoers reveled in the raw energy of their multitude. Explicit displays of any political protest were banned by the organizers at the request, no doubt, of the authorities who granted the permits, but everywhere there were signs of a generation in revolt: in the long-haired and Indian-beaded *jipitecas* whose makeshift tents littered the grounds; in the scores of national flags (some with the eagle and serpent replaced by a peace sign) that hung from tent poles, as if announcing the liberation of a once-colonized territory; in the casual nudity of those in attendance (overwhelmingly male). The festival itself was sheer *desmadre* (literally, "un-mothering"): an open flouting of a hypocritical morality (from youth's perspective) that buttressed a patriarchal ideology of repressive authoritarianism in the name of "order and progress."

The backlash following Avándaro came swiftly. While conservatives decried the collapse of *buenas costumbres*, those on the left viewed the concert as the epitome of a generation in ideological crisis, "mentally colonized" by foreign culture. Mexico's new president, Luis Echeverría, skillfully used this broad attack on Avándaro and the rock counterculture to boost his own legitimacy, attenuated by his earlier role in the repression of protesters during the previous administration. Echeverría now unleashed a new crackdown, this time against La Onda Chicana and done in the name of rescuing Mexican "national culture" from moral and ideological collapse. Rock concerts were cancelled, record contracts were severed (or left to languish), and repression set in as native rock was eliminated from the airwaves and literally pushed into the barrios on the outskirts of the city, where it remained isolated from mainstream society for more than a decade. The dream many groups had once shared of becoming international had all but ended. Most groups broke up; others hung on, at least in name, playing *cumbia* or other dance music to keep afloat. The one group to truly survive the period was Three Souls in My Mind. Later renamed the TRI (a clever play on the official party's acronym, PRI), the band thrived by exchanging the English-language songs and middle-class fans for a full embrace of the language, culture, and concerns of those on the urban margins of society. In the process they gained a national and, eventually, international reputation as the spokesgroup of the *chavos banda*—Mexico's lumpenproletariat youth, the neglected by-product of the country's quest for modernization.

The descent of Los Dug Dug's was typical. Following the backlash after Avándaro, the band suffered an internal crisis and soon dissolved. Armando was determined to keep the idea of the band alive, however, and so in 1972 he forged a new Los Dug Dug's as a power rock trio. Still under contract with RCA (though with zero promotional support), the band succeeded in recording three more albums (*Smog*, 1972; *Cambia Cambia*, 1974; and *El Loco*, 1975), mostly in Spanish though with some songs still in English. They were able to stay afloat by touring the country and playing odd gigs here and there, though without the mass fan base Armando had once enjoyed. At a certain stage, RCA provided so little support that eventually it made more sense to end the group's relationship with the transnational for good. Los Dug Dug's became a shadow of the superstar legend they once were, a living reminder of a period in Mexico's history that most others either did not know about or preferred to forget.

La Onda Chicana disappeared in the wake of Avándaro, squelched in the name of fighting "cultural imperialism," but a vibrant rock scene continued to grow and evolve in the barrios. As Mexico's middle classes turned to the more nationalist *nueva canción* and *música folklórica* movements supported by the state, youth living on the periphery of Mexico City—the *ciudades perdidas* (lost cities), as the overflowing slums came to be called—nurtured and gave meaning to a harder-edged, aggressive rock scene that survived independent of any transnational connection. In the late 1980s, as the PRI faced a series of crises that initiated the denouement of the single-party state, the rock that had been percolating in the barrios, performed in the so-called *hoyos fonquis* (literally, funky holes) and largely in isolation from mainstream youth culture, reemerged and now constituted the vanguard of a native rock revolution that swept the country. By the mid 1990s, Mexican rock culture was being embraced by middle-class youth and intellectuals alike as an active site of political discourse and struggle. There was no longer any separation between rock music and progressive politics as there had been during the 1960s. At rallies supporting the Zapatistas in the late 1990s, for example, native rock bands were a welcome and integral element of protest culture.

Ironically, however, there is little memory of La Onda Chicana and the musical revolution that culminated in the Avándaro rock festival. Unlike in the United States, where Woodstock remains a key signifier of an earlier countercultural sensibility whose images are widely disseminated through commercial culture, Mexican youth of today have little shared memory or material references to their own countercultural moment. In large part this is due to the scarcity of objects, images, and sounds from this earlier period; unlike the thorough commodification of the counterculture in the United States, Mexico's commercialization process was cut off in midstream following the backlash after Avándaro. Moreover, whereas the counterculture in the United States is a mark of pride for many on the left and Woodstock remains a utopian moment, impervious to critique, the left in Mexico feels quite differently about La Onda Chicana. Compared to the martyred victims of 1968 and police repression throughout this period, the debauchery and "colonized rock" of Avándaro is a mark of shame rather than of revolutionary pride. Although Mexico's contemporary rock scene is deeply indebted to the strides made by the earlier bands, even when they did sing in English, few seem eager (or even willing) to acknowledge that relationship.

The latest incarnation of Los Dug Dug's can still be found performing in Mexico City. At one point in the early 1990s, Armando owned his own nightclub near the National University, where his band performed a steady gig. But the clientele were mostly bureaucrats and the odd tourist, there to hear covers in English of tunes that by then were considered classic rock. A brief high point came in 1998 when Los Dug Dug's were one of the featured bands for a Twenty-seventh Anniversary concert celebrating Avándaro. Indeed, a minor revival of Avándaro memories is afoot, abetted in part by the Internet (an official Los Dug Dug's Web site, www.raybrazen.com, features a section on the festival) and efforts by an older generation of die-hard supporters to resuscitate the music and its history. No doubt as Mexicans come to terms with the meaning of national culture beyond the PRI, increasing efforts will be made to look back and revive the lost and repressed memories of earlier periods. As that happens, Los Dug Dug's might once again reclaim their rightful place as revolutionaries of a native rock counterculture that few Mexicans, much less foreigners, realize existed.

NOTES

1. "La juventud olvidó el rock'n roll y prefiere lo antiguo, *Excélsior*, 20 December 1959, B6.

2. In Spanish the lyrics are: "Ahí viene La Plaga/le gusta bailar/y cuando está rocanroleando/es la reina del lugar . . . /Vamos con el cura/que ya me quiero casar/no es que seas muy bonita/sino que sabes bailar."

3. Carlos Monsiváis, "México 1967," *La Cultura en México*, 17 January 1968, 5.

4. "Los Cerebros de la 'Revolución Bolchebeatle,' " 6 September 1968, Departamento de Investigaciones Políticas y Sociales, Archivo General de la Nación, Gallery 2, Box 2925, Folder 32, no. 3–5.

5. Quoted in Elena Poniatowska, *Massacre in Mexico*, trans. Helen Lane (New York: Viking Press, 1975), 82.

6. Interview with Armando Nava, June 5, 1993, Mexico City.

SUGGESTED READINGS

Agustín, José. "Cuál es La Onda." *Diálogos* 10, no. 1 (1974): 11–13.

_____. *Tragicomédia mexicana 1: La vida en México de 1940 a 1970*. Mexico City: Planeta, 1990.

_____. *Tragicomédia mexicana 2: La vida en México de 1970 a 1982*. Mexico City: Planeta, 1992.

Arana, Federico. *Guaraches de ante azul: Historia del rock mexicano*, vols. 1–4. Mexico City: Posada, 1985.

Bellinghausen, Hermann, ed. *Pensar el 68*. Mexico City: Cal y Arena, 1988.

Chimal, Carlos, ed. *Crines: Lecturas de rock*. Mexico City: Penélope, 1984.

Gilbert, Joseph, Anne Rubenstein, and Eric Zolov, eds. *Fragments of a Golden Age: The Politics of Culture in Mexico Since 1940*. Durham: Duke University Press, 2001.

Marroquín, Enrique. *La contracultura como protesta: Análisis de un fenómeno juvenil*. Mexico City: Joaquín Mortiz, 1975.

Monsiváis, Carlos. *Amor Perdido*. Mexico City: Biblioteca Era, 1977.

_____. *Días de Guardar*. Mexico City: Biblioteca Era, 1970 [1988].

Poniatowska, Elena. *Massacre in Mexico*. Translated by Helen Lane. New York: Viking Press, 1975.

Stigberg, David K. "Foreign Currents during the 60s and 70s in Mexican Popular Music: Rock and Roll, the Romantic Ballad, and the Cumbia." *Studies in Latin American Popular Culture* 4 (1985): 170–84.

Zolov, Eric. *Refried Elvis: The Rise of the Mexican Counterculture*. Berkeley: University of California Press, 1999.

USEFUL WEB SITES ON MEXICAN ROCK

"El Mundo Loco de Los Dug Dug's," www.raybrazen.com
"Rockeras/Culturales/ContraCulturales," www.rockeros.com/links.htm
"El Tianguis del Chopo," www.reforma.com.mx/flashes/cultura/chopo/

CHAPTER FIFTEEN

Gabriel Espíndola Martínez

Tequila Master

JOSÉ OROZCO

 *Garibaldi, the endpoint of the new green line (number 8), is a lively center of working-class sociability, where mariachis still serenade families each night with the romantic songs of Jorge Negrete, the singing cowboy* (charro). *The folkloric musicians naturally attract tourists as well, and the bars surrounding the plaza are often filled with visitors from the United States who still associate Mexico with the Prohibition-era vice of border towns like Tijuana or their modern-day counterparts, spring break in Cancún. This tourist Mexico is a land of bean burritos and cheap tequila, consumed in great quantities and the cause of untold cases of indigestion and hangover. But Gabriel Espíndola Martínez wants to change that image of Mexico. Having dedicated his life to modernizing the tequila industry, he hopes to win international recognition for the rising quality of the Mexican national drink. Like fine French cognac or single-malt Scotch whiskey, tequila should be savored, not gulped down with salt and lime.*

Foreigners are not the only ones changing their views of tequila, which was once considered an essential element of working-class masculinity in Mexico. This stereotype dates back to the 1940s, to the films of Jorge Negrete and the advertising campaigns of Javier Sauza, who built the first national brand. Negrete's image combined nostalgic scenes of an idyllic rural Mexico with a retrograde masculinity of drunken brawls and abandoned women. Yet as Espíndola Martínez illustrates, modern Mexicans are reformulating this masculine ideal by combining the nostalgic memories of an imagined past with the more equal gender roles of Mexico's emerging future. One of the most popular contemporary interpreters of ranchero music, Juan Gabriel, provides a perfect example of this transformation. Old-style machos who buy tickets to his concerts just to taunt him for homosexuality break down in tears and begin to sing along with his romantic melodies. *

*Alma Guillermoprieto, *The Heart That Bleeds* (New York: Knopf, 1994), 257–58.

José Orozco completed his doctorate at Harvard University with a dissertation entitled "¡Esos altos de Jalisco! Emigration and the Idea of Alteño Exceptionalism, 1926–1952." He is assistant professor of history at Whittier College in California.

$\mathcal{D}$rinking tequila is an exercise in nostalgia for a Mexico that never was: a social and racial landscape filled with white-skinned *rancheros* living in a rural idyll where most people owned their own, yeoman-sized plots of land and spent their days riding around on beautiful horses, drinking tequila, and singing melancholy songs for the love of handsome, equally light-skinned women. This Mexico, conjured up by Jorge Negrete and Pedro Infante movies, Sauza Tequila ads, and José Alfredo Jiménez songs, never existed. In fact, it stood in stark contrast to the urban, industrial, cosmopolitan, and hierarchical Mexico that most Mexicans lived in during the latter half of the twentieth century. Still, the power of this imagery is such that many Mexicans (and foreigners) believe that somewhere (in the not-so-distant past? in our hearts?), somehow (by watching enough old movies, listening to enough old songs, or drinking enough shots of tequila), this Mexico could be conjured into existence. Through an alchemy of desire, nostalgia, and alcohol, homes could be made into places one can return to, even when those homes never actually existed.

I am a historian; I have read Barthes; I should know how myths work; still, it came as a surprise when, in my attempts to interview a tequila *catador* (tequila taster)—the person I assumed was the individual whose highly trained senses defined what the Mexican national drink tasted like—I met up with Gabriel Espíndola Martínez. I cannot say I was consciously waiting for Jorge Negrete to walk into the seafood restaurant in Tepatitlán, Jalisco, where Sr. Espíndola had agreed to meet me; but I did experience a momentary sense of dissonance when I finally met him. Urbane, sharply dressed, with cell phone at hip, he stood five feet six inches tall and had cinnamon-brown skin—the very antithesis of the rural, mariachi-costumed, gun-toting, light-skinned and rosy-cheeked *ranchero* usually associated with the tequila industry.

Having recovered from this initial shock, I was once again surprised when Mr. Espíndola informed me that he was technically not a *catador*, but a university-trained chemical engineer. I should not have been surprised by this, either, because I knew that most tequila factories had been transformed during the 1940s and 1950s from small, artisan-like producers to large industrialized and highly capitalized industries whose employees were not simple artisans carrying on the family craft in traditional ways, but rather educated specialists with modern sensibilities. Very few factories could afford to allow the rural nostalgia they used in their advertising to enter the production process. Still, I had come to Mexico to interview a tequila taster, and what I found was a chemist. Sensing my disappointment, he began by stating: "Before I tell you about me, or what I do, I have to explain to you how it is that we produce tequila. When you understand that, you will see why there is not one, single person whose job it is to taste tequila and say whether it is good or not. But before I begin, let's order a tequila so I can show you how to drink our national drink."

ESPÍNDOLA TEQUILA-DRINKING
LESSON NUMBER ONE

"Never drink tequila out of the small shot glasses we call *caballitos*. These glasses almost force the drinker to slurp the tequila, or swallow it whole. When you do that, all you taste is the alcohol. Tequila comes from Jalisco and when you slurp it out of the *caballito* you not only miss the range of subtle flavors that distinguish tequila from other drinks, and one tequila brand from another, you also miss tasting the culture of the people who grow the agave and produce the tequila. The best type of glass to sip tequila out of is the wide-mouth cognac glass. Let me show you the difference with this Centinela *añejo*."

To begin with, as Espíndola explained, tequila is only as good as the raw materials from which it is extracted. In this case, the raw material is the blue agave plant whose scientific name, *tequilana weber azul*, was given to it by a German botanist named Weber in 1905. The plant is not a cactus, but a succulent that is best grown in regions at least 1,500 meters above sea level, with semiarid climates, and red or black oxide-rich soil. While the law limits the regions where the agave used in the production of tequila must come from—anywhere in Jalisco, six municipalities in Guanajuato, seven from Nayarit, eleven from Tamaulipas, and twenty-eight from Michoacán—it is generally agreed that the best agave is grown in the Los Altos region of Jalisco, especially in the municipality of Arandas. The agave takes between seven and ten years to mature to the point that it can be harvested for tequila production. When it reaches maturity, the long pointy leaves are pruned by a worker called a *jimador*, and the naked agave (it is called a *piña*, because it resembles a pineapple) is left in the groves to allow the natural sugars it contains to mature. After a period that varies from region to region, the *piña*, weighing anywhere between 80 and 400 pounds, is removed and taken to the factory where it is converted into tequila.

ESPÍNDOLA TEQUILA-DRINKING
LESSON NUMBER TWO

"Always drink tequila straight. I know Americans have been taught to drink it with lime and salt, or, as is popular now, to mix it with citrus-flavored drinks; but the best way to consume it is with a glass of natural, not carbonated, water. This allows you to taste the more than 175 chemical components or attributes that the agave has; it also helps keep you hydrated and lessens the chance of getting a hangover. This may sound romantic to you, but I really believe you violate the agave by mixing anything with the tequila. You know it takes about ten years for the plant to mature. In all those years, the agave absorbs the natural world around it: the rain, the sun, the dawns, the sunsets, the shadows, and the wind. The agave also retains and reflects the culture of its human ambient: tequila is, and should be, from Jalisco. After all that, the last thing you want to do with good tequila is suck a lime after you drink it. Try this Pueblo Viejo *reposado*, and see if I am lying."

In the factory the first thing that is done to the *piña* is to remove some of the impurities that the agave comes with. The washed *piñas* are then cooked in steam-injected, stainless steel autoclaves (for eight to fourteen hours), or in the more traditional brick ovens (fifty to seventy-two hours at 140 to 185 degrees). Espíndola prefers the autoclaves because they are more efficient and do not add any flavors to the agave it did not originally come with; but either way, the baking or steam cooking breaks down the complex carbohydrates into fermentable sugars. Next, the cooked *piñas* are taken to a mechanical shredder or a rustic *tahona* (a giant stone wheel pulled by a horse or an ox) that grinds the cooked *piña* and extracts its juices. Once the juices are extracted and strained, they are taken to huge vats where they are mixed with water and yeast to initiate fermentation. The fermentation process takes between two days (in modern plants) and twelve days (in the more traditional factories). After the fermented juice has settled, it is distilled twice in *alambiques* (stills) made out of either copper (the traditional material) or stainless steel.

ESPÍNDOLA TEQUILA-DRINKING
LESSON NUMBER THREE

"Always drink tequila that is made from 100 percent blue agave. By law any tequila containing at least 51 percent blue agave can be called tequila. The rest of the drink can be made up of any type of sugar [the law doesn't specify]. Traditionally, it is mixed with sugar alcohol or beet sugar. This *mixto* (mixed) tequila is what is usually sold in the United States. It gives people headaches and upset stomachs, and gives good, 100 percent blue agave, like this Campanario tequila that I was involved in producing, a bad reputation. This *mixto* tequila is cheap and does not taste good but it is produced because it is a way of extending the production of a product that is dependent on a raw material that has the longest growth cycle of any raw material used for alcoholic drinks. Waiting seven to ten years to harvest the agave is an eternity compared to the maturation period of grapes [one year] and sugar cane [twice a year]. Still, it is worth it. Here, taste this Campanario *añejo*."

Once the tequila has been distilled twice it is taken to large oak *barrias* (barrels) to age. Usually, *blanco* or *plata* (silver) tequila is bottled immediately after distillation; *reposado* (rested) tequila is aged from two to twelve months; *añejo* (aged) is kept in wooden barrels from twelve months to five years; *oro* (gold) is bottled immediately after distillation but is colored with one of several ingredients (usually caramel or oak essence). *Mixto* does not have to be bottled in Mexico, and is usually shipped abroad for packaging and bottling.

ESPÍNDOLA TEQUILA-DRINKING LESSON NUMBER FOUR

"When drinking tequila, listen to, or sing, mariachi music. You should also eat so the tequila doesn't go straight to your head. I like to eat plain white bread when I drink, but let's order some food. Here, just try this Cazadores *reposado* and see how it compares to the last one.

"It's funny," Espíndola begins as he finally starts to recount his life story to me, "but prior to beginning my work in the tequila industry, I neither liked tequila, nor *ranchero* mariachi music. Now I love them both. . . .

"I was born September 3, 1947, in a small village in Michoacán named Angangueo. It is located about thirty-five miles north of Zitácauro, Michoacán, near a monarch butterfly sanctuary. My father was a metallurgical engineer who worked for American Smelting and Refining Co. [which eventually became Industrias Mineras Mexicanas]. He was also born in Angangueo, and in his youth began working for American Smelting as a laborer. Even though he had very little formal education, my father was always very smart and curious about the inner workings of whatever he did. While working with American Smelting he slowly started to learn about the chemical properties of the minerals he was extracting and became a practical chemist whose knowledge was very valuable to the company. He worked himself up and ended up being an *asesor* for the company; he traveled around Mexico and Central America setting up and maintaining the equipment for the on-site labs.

"Because my father moved around so much, our family lived in many places. When I was about eight, in 1956, we left Angangueo and moved to Sinaloa. In Sinaloa we lived for nine years. There I completed *la primaria* [elementary school]. After *la primaria*, we went to live in Guadalajara, [Jalisco], where I finished my first two years of *la secundaria* [secondary school]. I ended up finishing *la secundaria* in Chihuahua. There I started *la preparatoria* [high school], but finished in Guadalajara, where my family had again moved to because of my father's work.

"After *la prepa*, I entered the Universidad de Guadalajara to study chemical engineering. Initially, I never thought of following my dad into the mining business; but, eventually I decided to go into chemical engineering because I was good at math and science and because it was a career that offered many possibilities.

"I finished my career and received my degree in 1975. It was quite by accident that I even started to work in the tequila industry, which, when I began in 1976, was considered lower class [the drink as well as the industry]. I was debating whether to continue school and get a master's in chemical engineering or get a job, when one of the secretaries at the school received a phone call asking if there was anyone in the program interested in working for a tequila company. She looked at my friend and me and asked us if either one of us was interested. My friend didn't want to work because he wanted to finish his thesis. I was initially reluctant; but I figured I'd give it a chance and work there for two years until I could get something better.

"I started to work in Tequila Viuda de Romero, which at the time was a *maquila* [export factory] for Tequila Virreyes. This was 1976 and wouldn't you know it, I didn't leave until eight and a half years later in 1984. *Dios castiga* [literally, the phrase is translated as, God punishes; but it is often used to highlight the ironies of life when one's best-laid plans are foiled by the vagaries that come with being human], I ended up being very good at what I did, and ended up liking my job. I was initially a worker at the factory's lab. Our job, [there were two more chemists in the lab] was to make sure that the factory was running efficiently, and that at every step of the production process the product was within the norms set by the government and by our own standards. We checked the sugar level of the cooked agave and *aguamiel* [the sap of the *piña*] once they were extracted, we oversaw the fermentation process, we checked the alcohol level of the fermented juice and made sure that the *mixto* tequila had at least 51 percent blue agave and that the finished product was all 40 percent alcohol.

"The work was laborious, but not difficult. After six months in the lab, and after I had acquired a taste for tequila (curiosity killed the cat), I was allowed to wander from the lab and involve myself, more hands-on, in the production process. I tasted the product at each step and learned how each step of the process was done, or should be done. I have never considered what I do as work. I like it. I love it; and I got so good that after a while I became a supervisor in the plant.

"After eight years working for Tequila Virreyes in their Viuda de Romero plant, Viuda de Romero established itself as its own independent factory and hired me. I worked for them for thirteen years and ended up being the plant manager [*jerente de planta*]. In the end, I was overseeing all production and quality control. Since 1997, I have worked as a consultant to tequila companies all over Jalisco. I am hired to go to the factories and make sure that their production is at optimal levels and that the quality of their product is within the norms that they have set for themselves. In this way I help in determining the taste of their product. Even though I do not set the norms that determine the taste of their tequila—those are set a long time before I arrive—I am hired to make sure that their tequila tastes like what it should.

"The raw material and its elaboration are what determine the flavor of any tequila. You always try to abide by the norms and parameters that the company has set up for making the tequila; you always try to make sure that your product is uniform in its quality. There are physical norms and chemical norms to consider, measure, and adjust. But over time, details are forgotten, norms are softened. Making tequila isn't like making nails or pens, where you can pretty much insure a uniform product. There is great variety in the agave that changes the taste and quality of the tequila: Where was it grown: Arandas or Tamaulipas? At what density was it grown: about 2,500 [plants] per hectare in the region of Tequila, sometimes up to 6,000 in Los Altos. When were its *pencas* [the spiky leaves of the agave] removed? How much rain, sunshine, or cold did it receive over its decade of maturation? Were the mature plants the product of good mature *hijuelos* [the young agave shoots that grow around mature (mother) agaves and are transplanted] or young *hijuelos* that are more susceptible to disease?

"There is also contamination to consider. Environmental contamination is a big problem; but so is the contamination of oils, greases, and chemicals that accumulate in the machinery if one is not very careful. I am hired to make sure that everything is well in the production process. I am an outsider with no vested interest in the product. I am also a person whose taste buds are not too familiar with the particular tequila the company produces. I make judgments about the quality of their product, suggest ways to remedy the problems, and get paid—whether they implement my suggestions or not is not my business.

"Traditionally, tequila factories had a person, a mayordomo, or someone who had worked for the company for a long time, who was the individual who would taste the tequila and suggest, 'Put this in it or take this out.' With the modernization of the process, these people have all but disappeared, though there still are some old-timers who run their tequila companies like the haciendas of old. Now we have chemists and other professionals who have their labs and machines to insure quality and taste. But don't get me wrong. What I do is an art form. Tequila isn't only an alcoholic drink: it is tradition, custom, and music. There is a mystique in the process and in the product that I take seriously. That is why you have to smell and taste the client's product. You have to experience what it is to drink the tequila: What does it feel like going down your throat? How does it affect you the next morning? Because if you drink a product, and the next day your head hurts, your stomach bothers you, or bright lights bother you, that's a sign that the product leaves much to be desired.

"Currently I am working for the [*tequilería*] San Matías that produces an excellent tequila, Pueblo Viejo. I am the *director de fábrica*; I oversee production and involve myself with everything but the actual lifting of the *piñas* into the autoclaves. I am responsible for the quality of the tequila from the moment the *piñas* arrive at the factory to the point [in the production process] when the distilled tequila comes out of the *alambiques* [distillers]. From that point the tequila leaves our factory to be aged and bottled. In this second phase, someone else is responsible for the quality of the tequila. But we periodically have reunions when we taste our product and compare it to other products. At these meetings everyone from the owner of the company to the field workers are involved. We put out several tequilas and blind-taste them. We ask that no one wear deodorants or perfumes because that interferes with our job. Once everyone has tasted the tequilas we talk about what we liked and what we didn't. Even the workers, especially the workers, because they have been here the longest and they represent the perspective of the consuming public. We take what they say seriously. Even though I think that I am very good at my job, I still have to listen to what others say so that I don't fall into the belief that because I have been doing this for many years, I don't have anything to learn. Not all companies are this careful, '*unos meten agave y sacan tequila*' [some put in agave and ship out tequila]. But we don't.

"Recently, I was involved in producing my own brand of tequila. With the twenty-four years of experience I have in the business, and the twenty-six my friend and partner, Leopoldo Solís, has, we figured we could produce a tequila that was of the highest quality. We produced Tequila Campanario to penetrate a very crowded high-end market. It comes in a bottle shaped like the huge bell that is the icon of Arandas [the center of tequila production in the Los Altos region]. We intend to compete not with other tequilas, but with other high-end alcoholic beverages: cognac, vodka, gin. What some people in our industry do not understand is that our competition isn't with ourselves but with others. When we sell bad tequila abroad, as people used to do, it reflects badly on the industry and we get a reputation as an *albañil* [worker's] drink. We need to insure that this does not happen, '*porque hablar de tequila, es hablar de México* [because to speak of tequila is to speak of Mexico].' "

SUGGESTED READINGS

Barthes, Roland. *Mythologies*. Paris: Seuil, 1957.

Emmons, Bob. *The Book of Tequila: A Complete Guide*. Chicago: Open Court Press, 1997.

Gutmann, Matthew C. *The Meanings of Macho: Being a Man in Mexico City*. Berkeley: University of California Press, 1996.

Luna Zamora, Rogelio. *La historia del tequila, de sus regiones y sus hombres*. Mexico City: Dirección General de Publicaciones del Consejo Nacional para la Cultura y las Artes, 1991.

Martínez Limón, Enrique. *Tequila: The Spirit of Mexico*. Prologue by Carlos Monsiváis. Mexico City: Revimundo, 1998.

Murià, José María. *El tequila: boceto histórico de una industria*. Guadalajara, Jalisco: Universidad de Guadalajara, 1990.

"Tequila: In Search of the Blue Agave," http://www.ianchadwick.com/tequila/

Index

Iglesias, José María, 52
Independence 1, 2, 23, 32, 41, 42, 43,
  50, 83, 109, 152, 155, 191
Indians, 1, 25–26; Aztec, 26, 33, 91,
  152, 204, 211; Caxcan, 114; Maya,
  140–41; Mixteca, 175; Tarahumara,
  178; Triqui, 78; Yaqui, 139; Zapotec,
  75–86
Indigenismo, 121, 149, 155–57, 174–75,
  203–4
Infante, Pedro, 226
Inquisition, 1, 5, 11–13, 27–28
Instituto Nacional de Antropología e
  Historia (INAH, National Institute
  of Anthropology and History), 54
Instituto Nacional de Nutrición (INN,
  National Institute of Nutrition), 208
International Harvester Corporation,
  139–40
Isabel la Católica, 199
Iturbide, Agustín de, 2, 33, 43, 206
Iturribarria, Luis, 30
Iturrigaray, José de, 2, 28
Ixtlán, 78–85
Izamal, 144

Jalapa, 189
Jalisco, 105, 226–31
Jazz, 187–89
Jiménez, Angela, 142
Jiménez, José Alfredo, 226
Jiménez y Muro, Dolores, 111–12, 114
Johnson, Andrew, 64, 68
Joseph, Gilbert, 140
Jovellanos, Gaspar Melchor de, 29
Juárez, Benito: French intervention,
  58, 61, 63, 83–84; as governor of
  Oaxaca, 77–78; presidency, 112;
  Reform, 57, 103–5; renown, 42, 75–
  76, 85–86, 109, 113, 206, 213; trial
  of Maximilian, 67–70; youth, 76
Juárez, Diego, 14

Kahlo, Frida, 162
Katz, Friedrich, 141
Keynes, John Maynard, 169
Knight, Alan, 166

La Corregidora. *See* Ortiz de
  Domínguez, Josefa
Lake Texcoco, 91

Lara, Agustín: celebrity image, 181,
  185–87, 190, 193–94, 211; jealousy,
  195–96; marriages, 188, 194–96; as
  radio personality, 189–90; as
  songwriter, 189–90, 194–95; stage
  career, 188–89, 195
Las Casas, Bartolomé de, 30–31
León, Antonio, 51
Leopold II, 64
Lerdo de Tejada, Miguel, 57
Lerdo de Tejada, Sebastián, 112
Lerdo Law, 53, 57–58
Ley del caso, 47
Lezama, Juan Cayetano, 7
Liberalism: European, 75; folk, 58, 75;
  government, 47, 76; *moderados*, 48–
  53; *puros*, 2, 47–50; radical, 58, 103–
  4, 109–13. *See also* Constitution of
  1857; Lerdo Law; *Reforma*
Little Richard, 212, 214
Lizardi, José Joaquín Fernández de,
  30
Locke, John, 30
London, 23, 28–31
López, Nicolás, 100
López Méndez, Luis, 29
Loredo, José Inés, 207
Los Angeles, 191, 196
Loyo, Gilberto, 168

Madero, Francisco I.: anti-reelection
  campaign, 112–13, 141, 146; death,
  114; revolutionary movement, 59,
  119, 138, 141, 165, 212
Magnus, Anton von, 63–64
Mainero, Guadalupe, 94
Maldonado, Joseph Vicente, 15
Mangano, Frank, 219
Maraboto, José María, 97–98
Mariachis, 211, 225–26, 229
Marín, Gloria, 192
Márquez, María Elena, 192
Martínez, Lauro, 100
Masonic lodges, 43–47
Mata, Filomeno, 58, 107
Maternalism, 138–39, 142, 146
Maximilian, Emperor, 57–58, 61–71,
  83, 149, 200, 206
Meixueiro, Guillermo, 81
Meixueiro Pérez, Francisco, 81
Mejía, Tomás, 68, 70